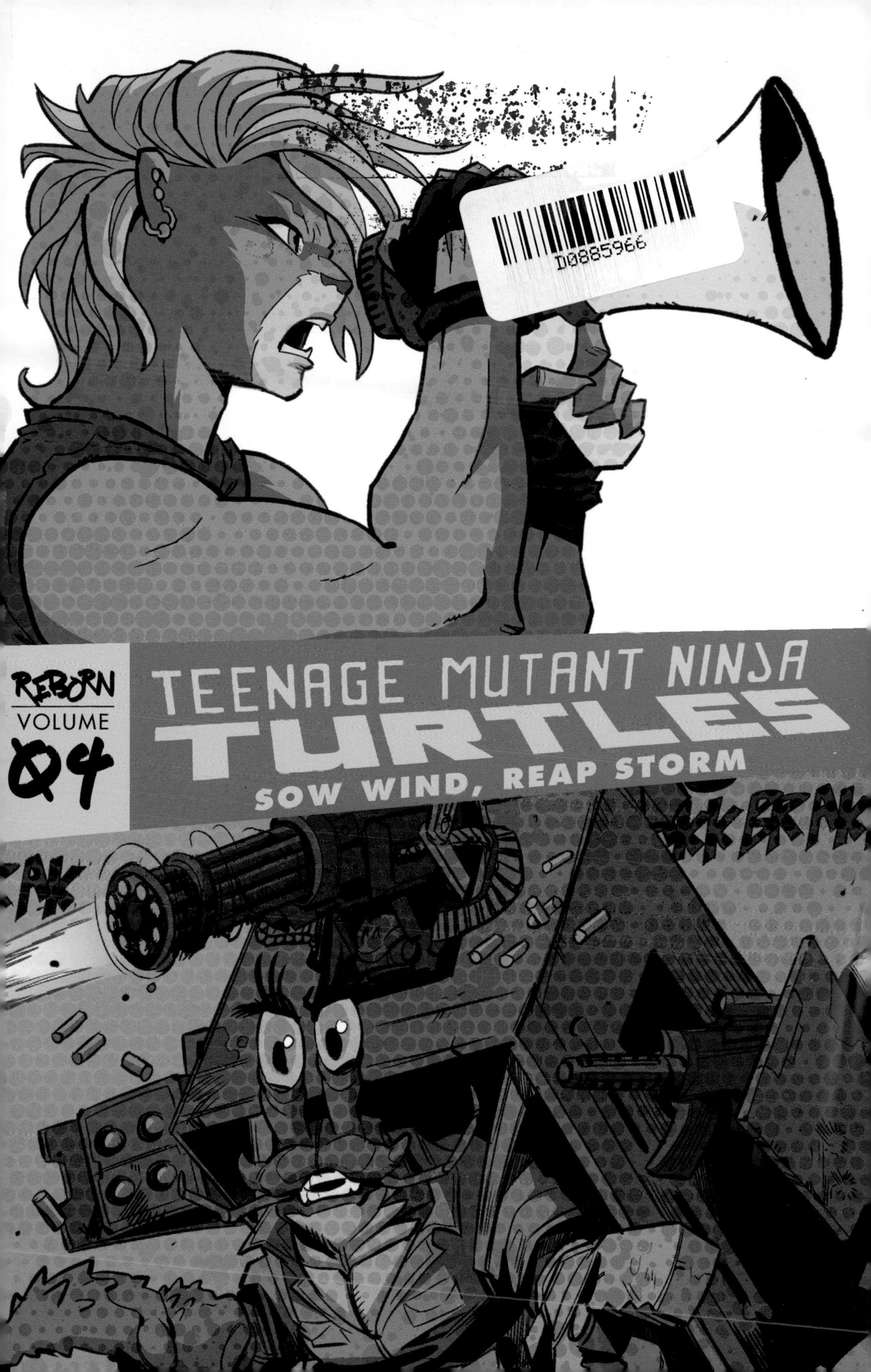
REBORN
VOLUME
04
TEENAGE MUTANT NINJA
TURTLES
SOW WIND, REAP STORM

25 24 23 22   1 2 3 4

ISBN: 978-1-68405-880-8

TEENAGE MUTANT NINJA TURTLES: REBORN, VOLUME 4 – SOW WIND, REAP STORM. APRIL 2022. FIRST
PRINTING. © 2022 Viacom International Inc. All Rights Reserved. Nickelodeon, TEENAGE MUTANT NINJA TURTLES,
and all related titles, logos and characters are trademarks of Viacom International Inc. © 2022 Viacom Overseas
Holdings C.V. All Rights Reserved. Nickelodeon, TEENAGE MUTANT NINJA TURTLES, and all related titles, logos
and characters are trademarks of Viacom Overseas Holdings C.V. Based on characters created by Peter Laird and
Kevin Eastman. © 2022 Idea and Design Works, LLC. The IDW Logo is registered in the U.S. Patent and Trademark
Office. IDW Publishing, a division of Idea and Design Works, LLC. Editorial offices: 2765 Truxtun Road, San Diego, CA
92106. Any similarities to persons living or dead are purely coincidental. With the exception of artwork used for review
purposes, none of the contents of this publication may be reprinted without permission of Idea and Design Works,
LLC. IDW Publishing does not read or accept unsolicited submissions of ideas, stories, or artwork. Printed in Korea.

Originally published as TEENAGE MUTANT NINJA TURTLES issues #118–123.

Nachie Marsham, Publisher • Blake Kobashigawa, VP of Sales • Tara McCrillis, VP Publishing Operations • John Barber, Editor-in-Chief • Mark Doyle, Editorial Director,
Originals • Scott Dunbier, Director, Special Projects • Lauren LePera, Managing Editor • Joe Hughes, Director, Talent Relations • Anna Morrow, Sr. Marketing Director •
Alexandra Hargett, Book & Mass Market Sales Director • Keith Davidsen, Director, Marketing & PR • Topher Alford, Sr. Digital Marketing Manager • Shauna Monteforte,
Sr. Director of Manufacturing Operations • Jamie Miller, Sr. Operations Manager • Nathan Widick, Sr. Art Director, Head of Design • Neil Uyetake, Sr. Art Director, Design
& Production • Shawn Lee, Art Director, Design & Production • Jack Rivera, Art Director, Marketing

Ted Adams and Robbie Robbins, IDW Founders

Special thanks to Joan Hilty & Linda Lee for their invaluable assistance.

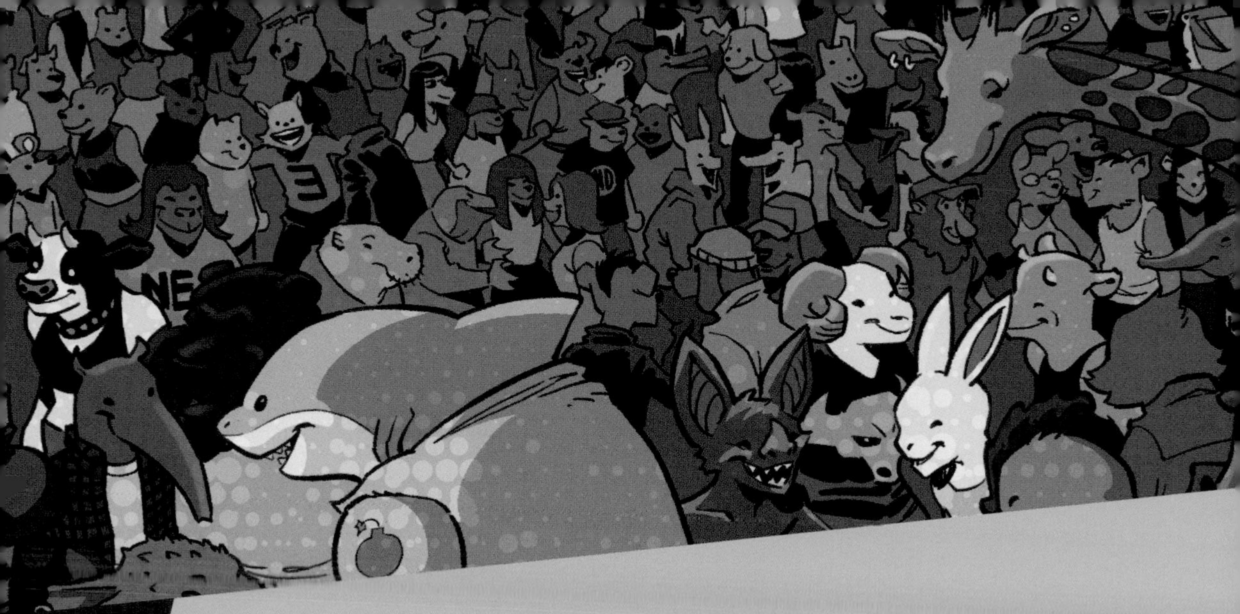

STORY
SOPHIE CAMPBELL

ART
NELSON DÁNIEL
PARTS 1–2

JODI NISHIJIMA
PARTS 3–6

COLORS
RONDA PATTISON

LETTERS
SHAWN LEE

STORY CONSULTING
KEVIN EASTMAN & TOM WALTZ

COVER BY NELSON DÁNIEL | SERIES EDITS BY BOBBY CURNOW
COLLECTION EDITS BY ALONZO SIMON AND ZAC BOONE
COLLECTION DESIGN BY SHAWN LEE

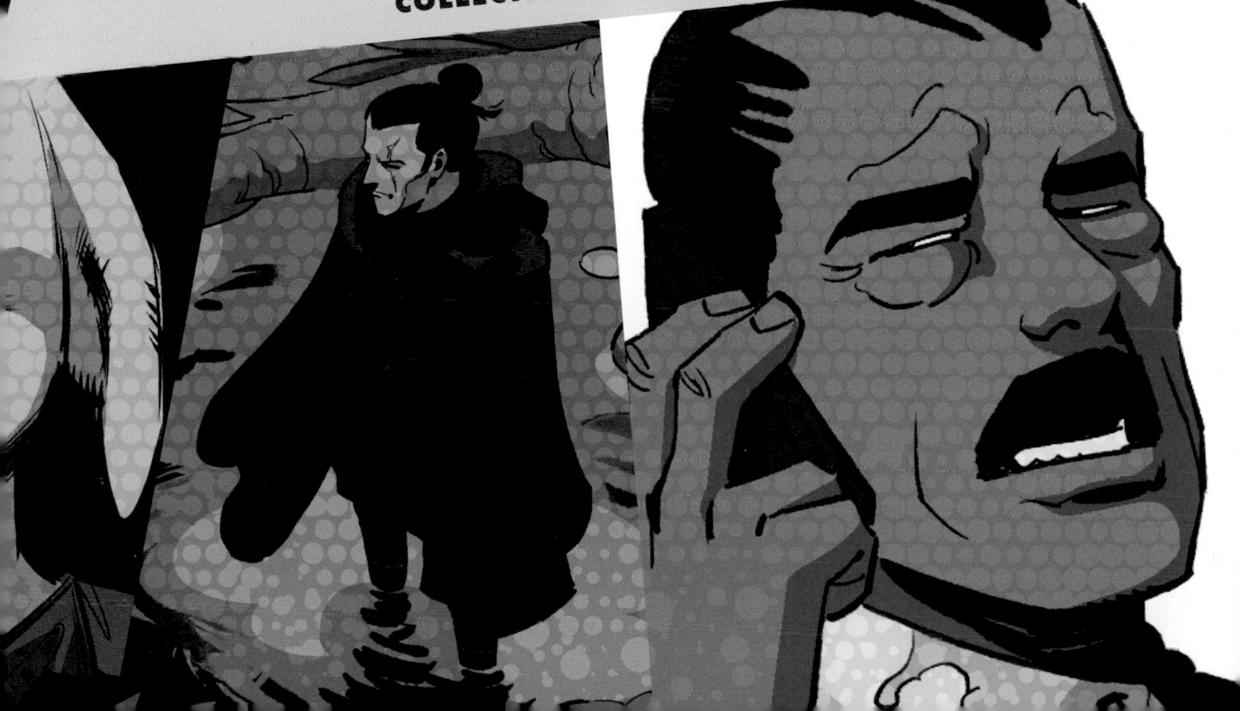

ART BY
NELSON DÁNIEL

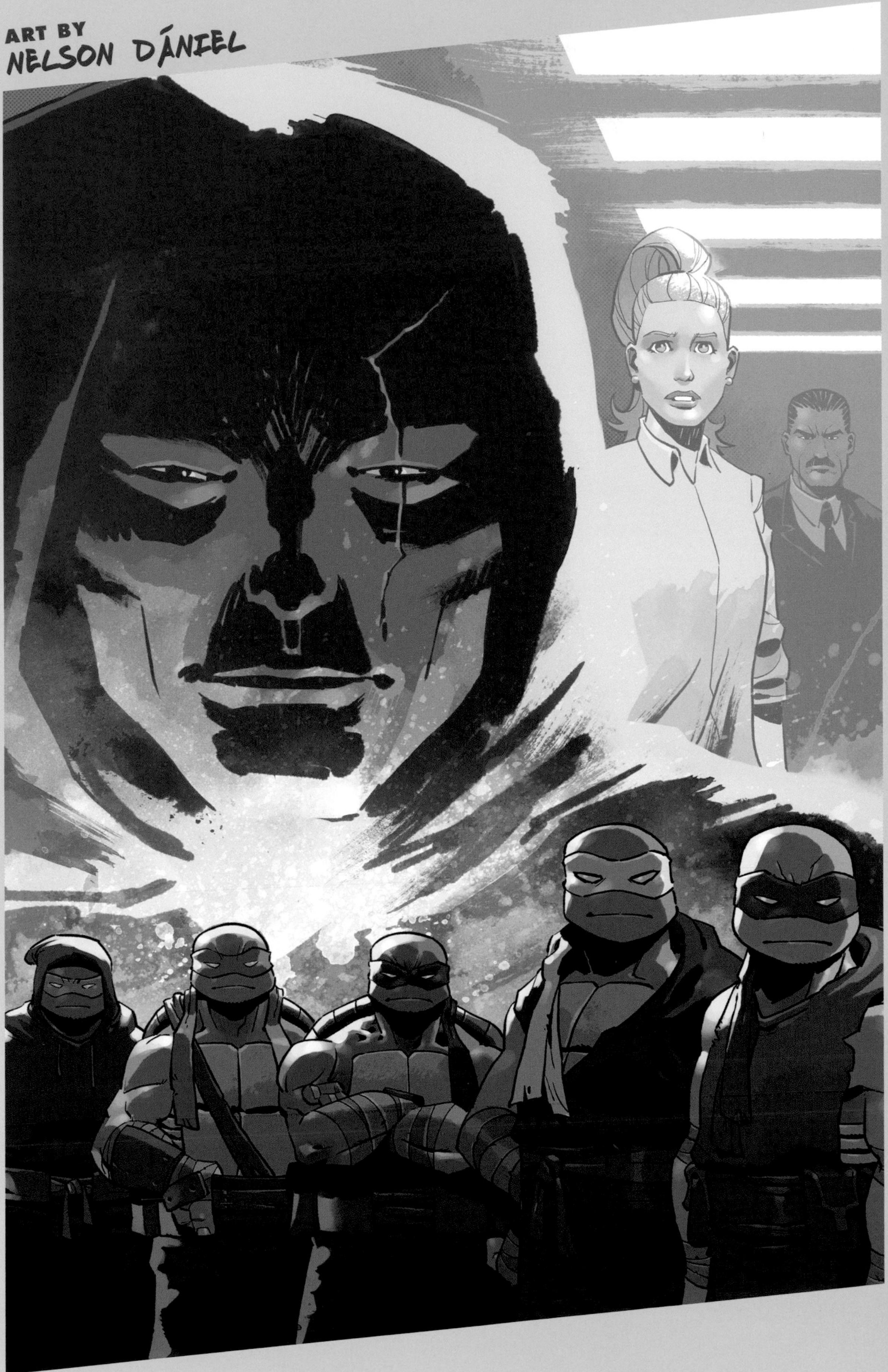

ONE MONTH AGO.

TIME TO LEAVE, I SUPPOSE.

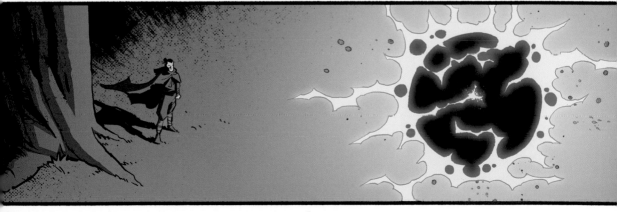

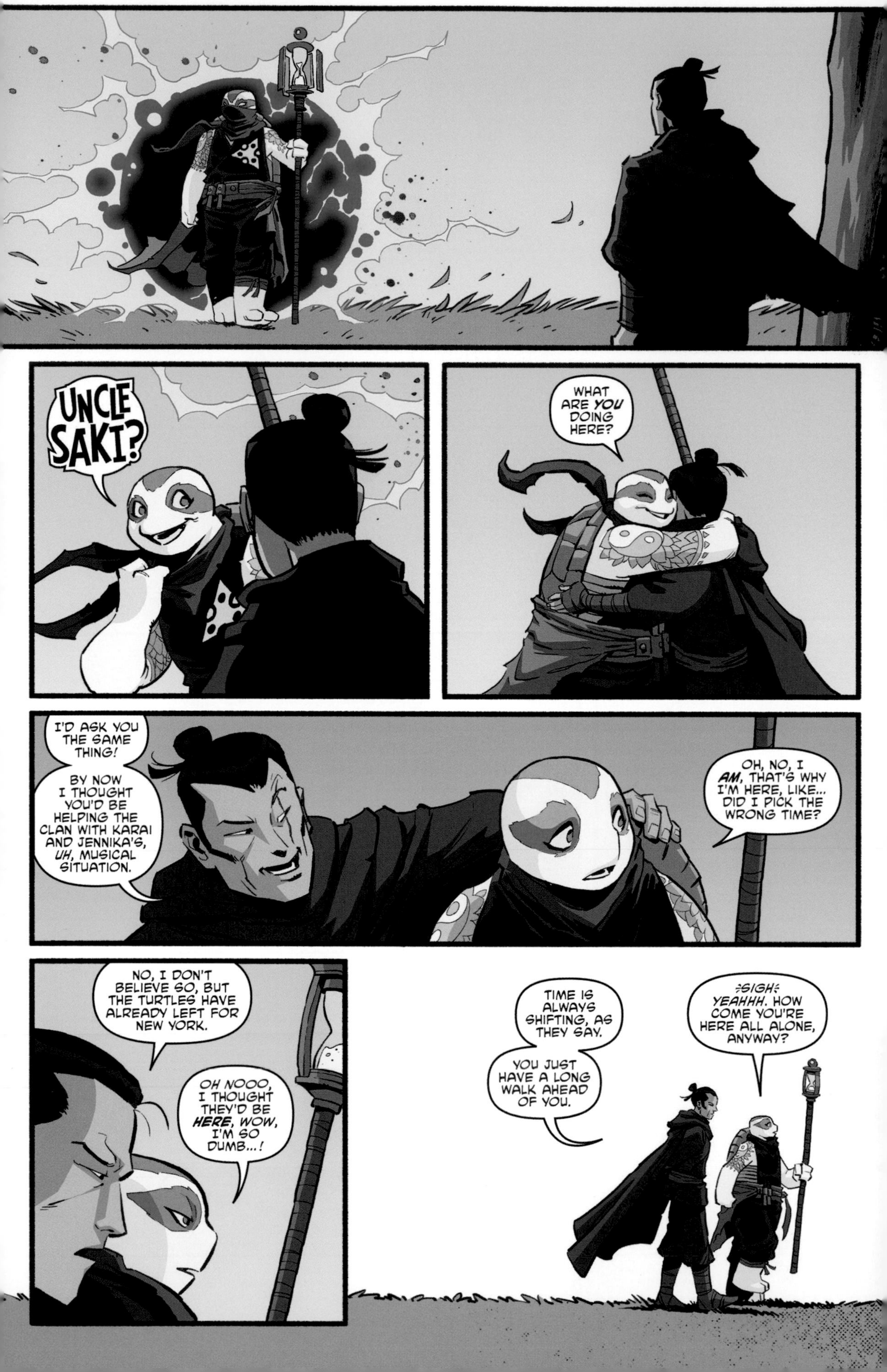
UNCLE SAKI?
WHAT ARE *YOU* DOING HERE?
I'D ASK YOU THE SAME THING!
BY NOW I THOUGHT YOU'D BE HELPING THE CLAN WITH KARAI AND JENNIKA'S, *UH*, MUSICAL SITUATION.
OH, NO, I ***AM***, THAT'S WHY I'M HERE, LIKE... DID I PICK THE WRONG TIME?
NO, I DON'T BELIEVE SO, BUT THE TURTLES HAVE ALREADY LEFT FOR NEW YORK.
OH NOOO, I THOUGHT THEY'D BE ***HERE***, WOW, I'M SO DUMB...!
TIME IS ALWAYS SHIFTING, AS THEY SAY.
YOU JUST HAVE A LONG WALK AHEAD OF YOU.
SIGH *YEAHHH*. HOW COME YOU'RE HERE ALL ALONE, ANYWAY?

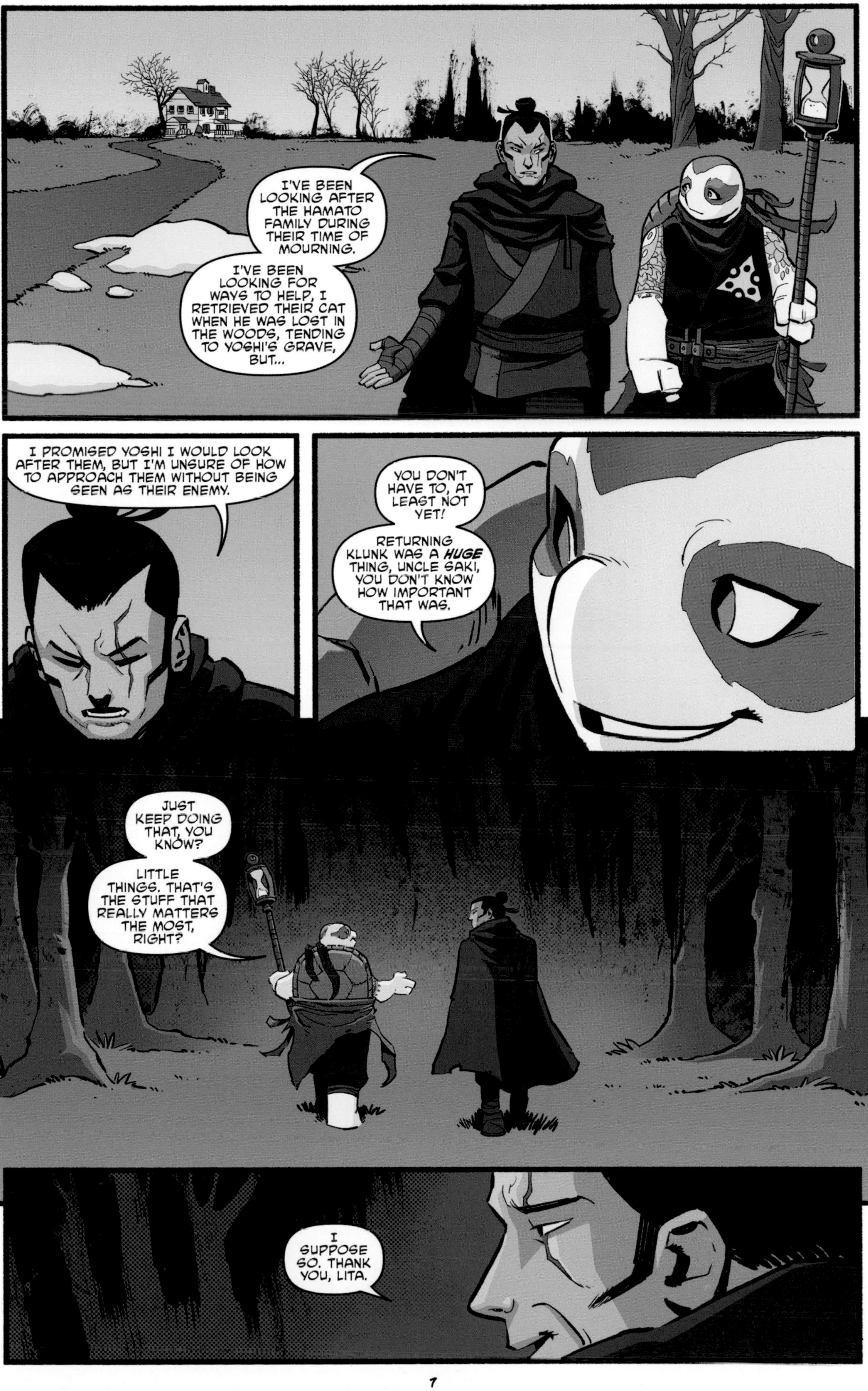
I'VE BEEN LOOKING AFTER THE HAMATO FAMILY DURING THEIR TIME OF MOURNING.
I'VE BEEN LOOKING FOR WAYS TO HELP, I RETRIEVED THEIR CAT WHEN HE WAS LOST IN THE WOODS, TENDING TO YOSHI'S GRAVE, BUT...
I PROMISED YOSHI I WOULD LOOK AFTER THEM, BUT I'M UNSURE OF HOW TO APPROACH THEM WITHOUT BEING SEEN AS THEIR ENEMY.
YOU DON'T HAVE TO, AT LEAST NOT YET!
RETURNING KLUNK WAS A HUGE THING, UNCLE SAKI, YOU DON'T KNOW HOW IMPORTANT THAT WAS.
JUST KEEP DOING THAT, YOU KNOW?
LITTLE THINGS. THAT'S THE STUFF THAT REALLY MATTERS THE MOST, RIGHT?
I SUPPOSE SO. THANK YOU, LITA.

TODAY.

JUST LET ME FINISH WRITING THIS CHAPTER, OKAY? I'M REALLY MAKING PROGRESS.

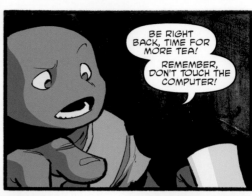

BE RIGHT BACK, TIME FOR MORE TEA! REMEMBER, DON'T TOUCH THE COMPUTER!

I REALLY GOTTA MAKE A BACK-UP OF MY BOOK...

UH OH!

8

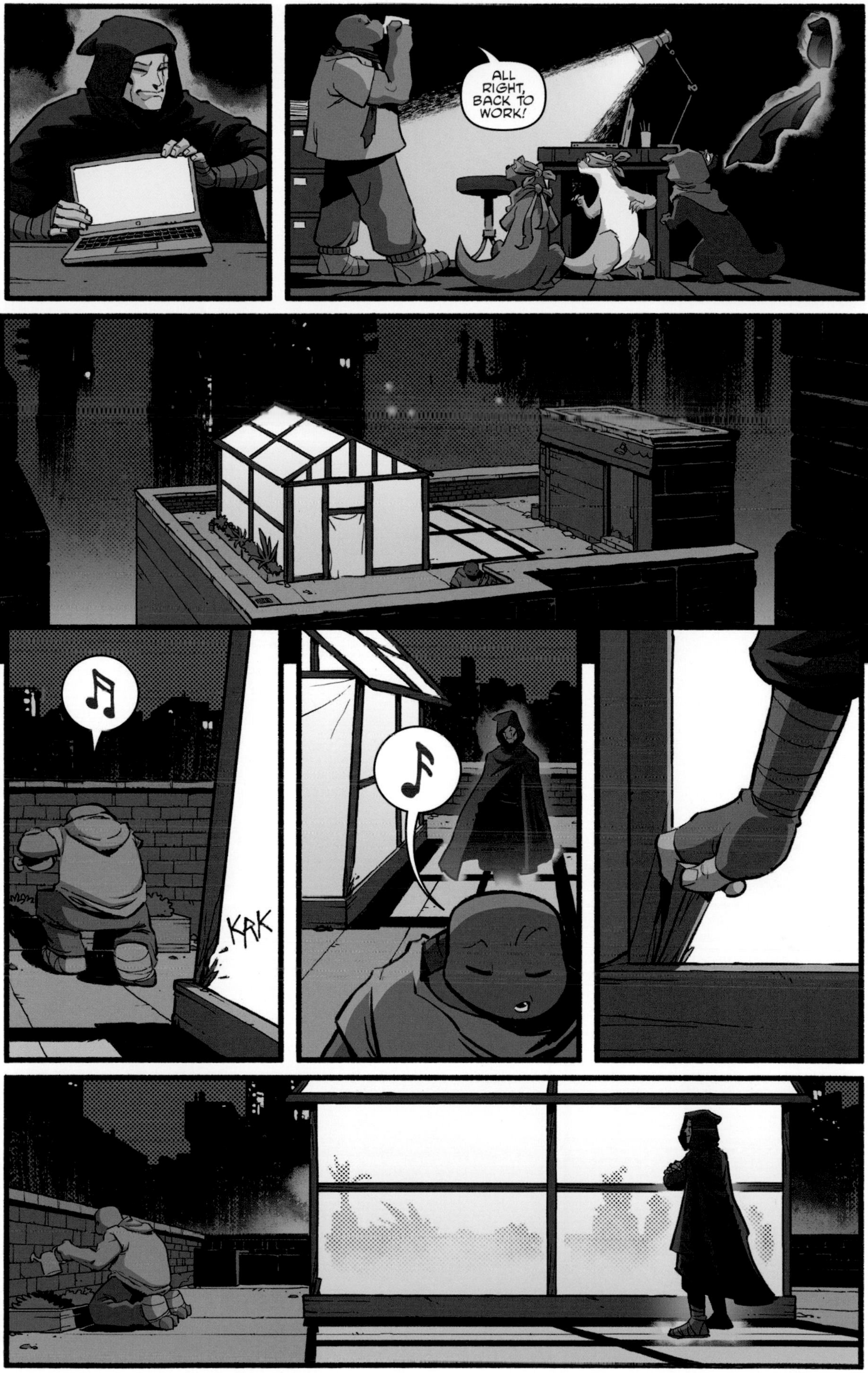
ALL RIGHT, BACK TO WORK!
KRK

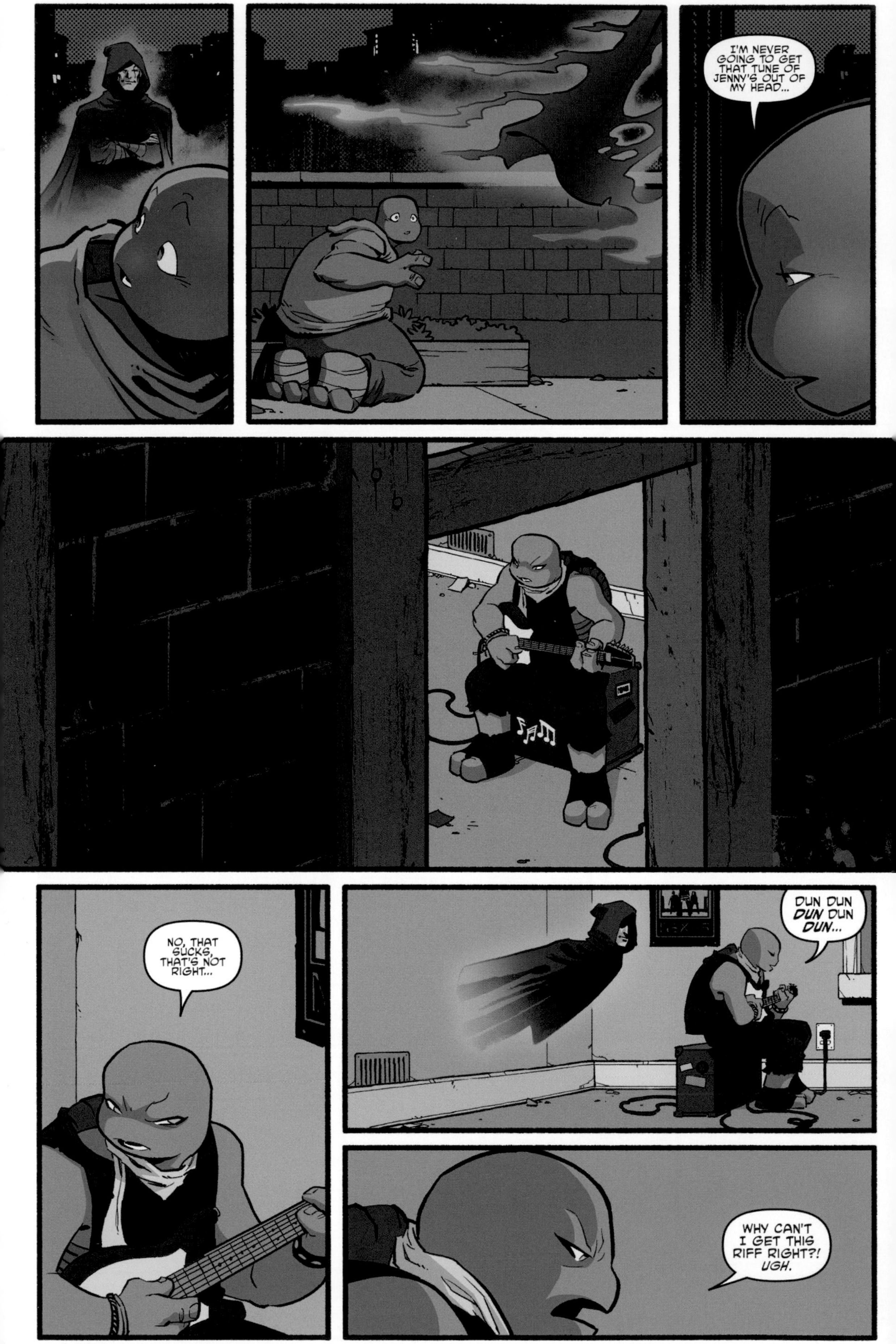
I'M NEVER GOING TO GET THAT TUNE OF JENNY'S OUT OF MY HEAD...
NO, THAT SUCKS, THAT'S NOT RIGHT...
DUN DUN *DUN* DUN DUN *DUN*...
WHY CAN'T I GET THIS RIFF RIGHT?! *UGH.*

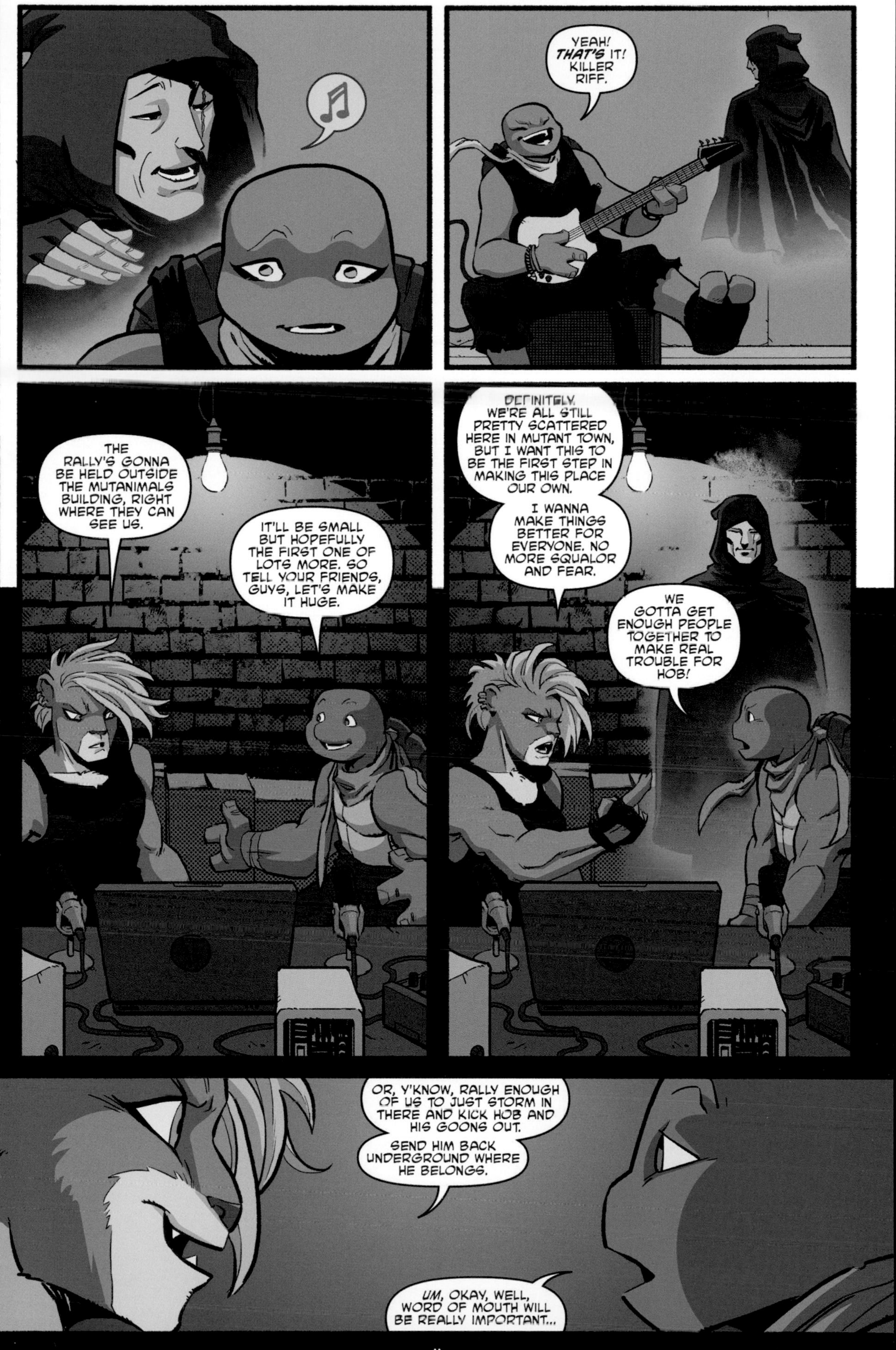
YEAH! *THAT'S* IT! KILLER RIFF.
THE RALLY'S GONNA BE HELD OUTSIDE THE MUTANIMALS BUILDING, RIGHT WHERE THEY CAN SEE US.
IT'LL BE SMALL BUT HOPEFULLY THE FIRST ONE OF LOTS MORE. SO TELL YOUR FRIENDS, GUYS, LET'S MAKE IT HUGE.
DEFINITELY. WE'RE ALL STILL PRETTY SCATTERED HERE IN MUTANT TOWN, BUT I WANT THIS TO BE THE FIRST STEP IN MAKING THIS PLACE OUR OWN.
I WANNA MAKE THINGS BETTER FOR EVERYONE. NO MORE SQUALOR AND FEAR.
WE GOTTA GET ENOUGH PEOPLE TOGETHER TO MAKE REAL TROUBLE FOR HOB!
OR, Y'KNOW, RALLY ENOUGH OF US TO JUST STORM IN THERE AND KICK HOB AND HIS GOONS OUT.
SEND HIM BACK UNDERGROUND WHERE HE BELONGS.
UM, OKAY, WELL, WORD OF MOUTH WILL BE REALLY IMPORTANT...

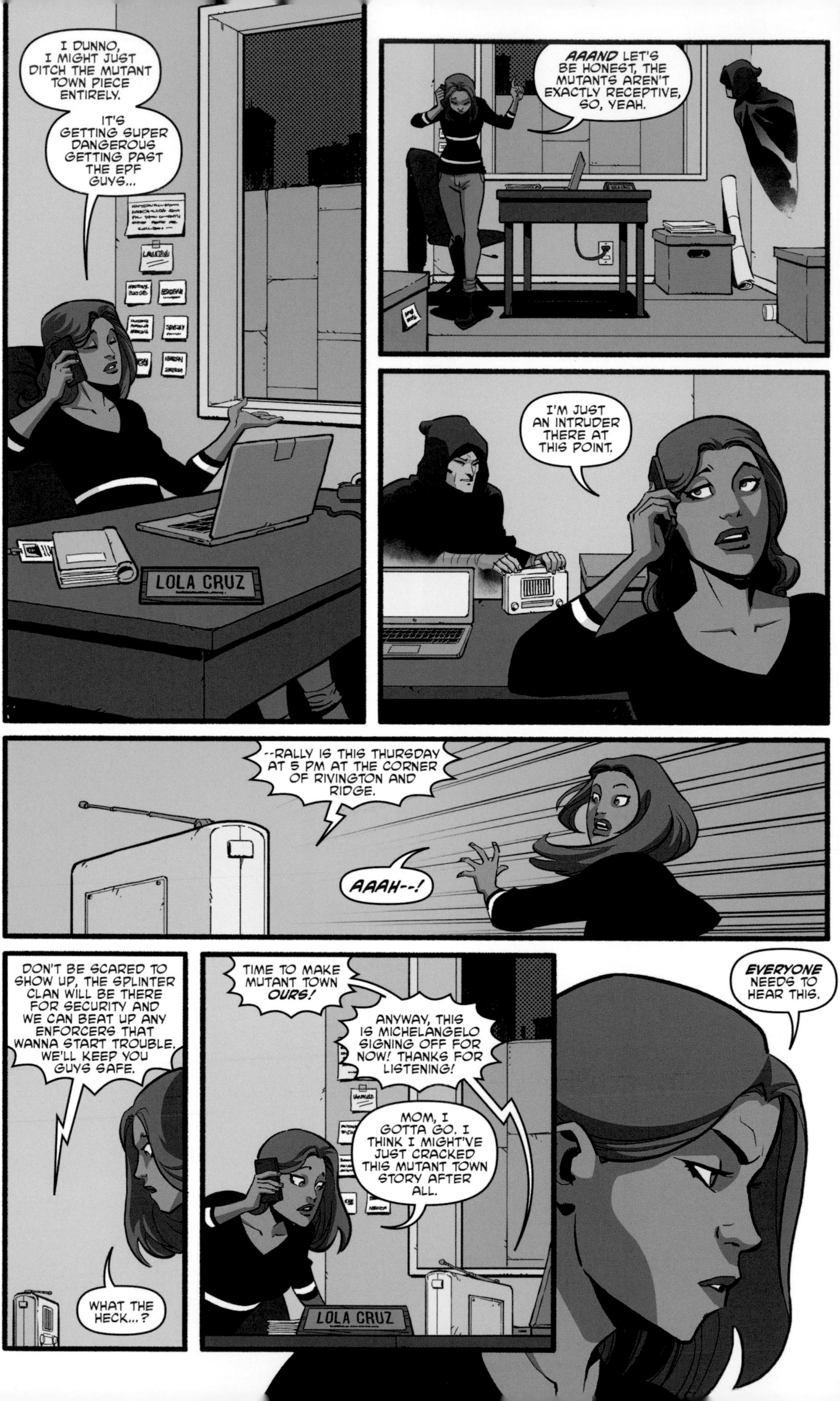
I DUNNO, I MIGHT JUST DITCH THE MUTANT TOWN PIECE ENTIRELY.
IT'S GETTING SUPER DANGEROUS GETTING PAST THE EPF GUYS...
LOLA CRUZ
AAAND LET'S BE HONEST, THE MUTANTS AREN'T EXACTLY RECEPTIVE, SO, YEAH.
I'M JUST AN INTRUDER THERE AT THIS POINT.
--RALLY IS THIS THURSDAY AT 5 PM AT THE CORNER OF RIVINGTON AND RIDGE.
AAAH--!
DON'T BE SCARED TO SHOW UP, THE SPLINTER CLAN WILL BE THERE FOR SECURITY AND WE CAN BEAT UP ANY ENFORCERS THAT WANNA START TROUBLE. WE'LL KEEP YOU GUYS SAFE.
WHAT THE HECK...?
TIME TO MAKE MUTANT TOWN OURS!
ANYWAY, THIS IS MICHELANGELO SIGNING OFF FOR NOW! THANKS FOR LISTENING!
MOM, I GOTTA GO. I THINK I MIGHT'VE JUST CRACKED THIS MUTANT TOWN STORY AFTER ALL.
LOLA CRUZ
EVERYONE NEEDS TO HEAR THIS.

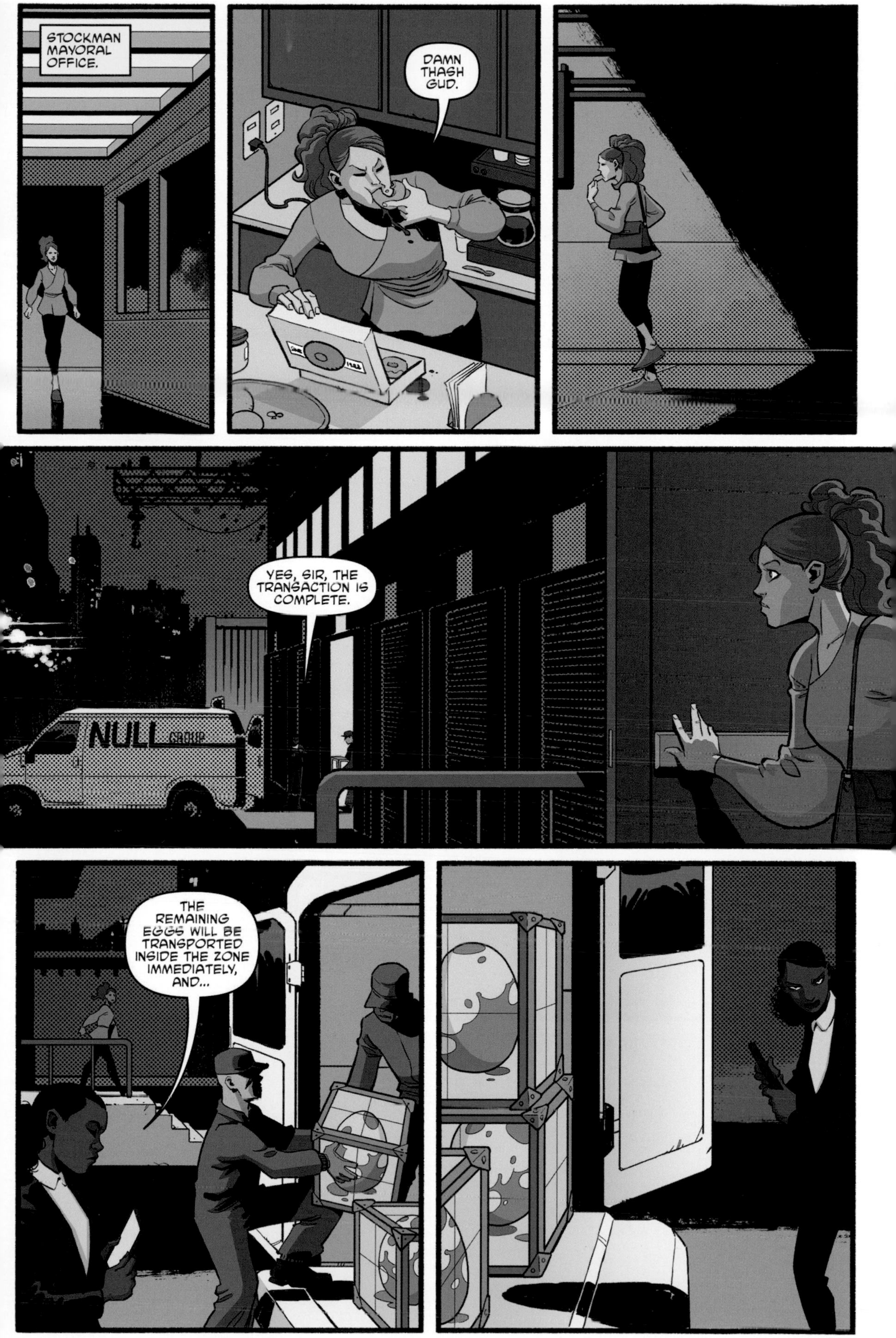
STOCKMAN MAYORAL OFFICE.
DAMN THASH GUD.
YES, SIR, THE TRANSACTION IS COMPLETE.
NULL GROUP
THE REMAINING EGGS WILL BE TRANSPORTED INSIDE THE ZONE IMMEDIATELY, AND...

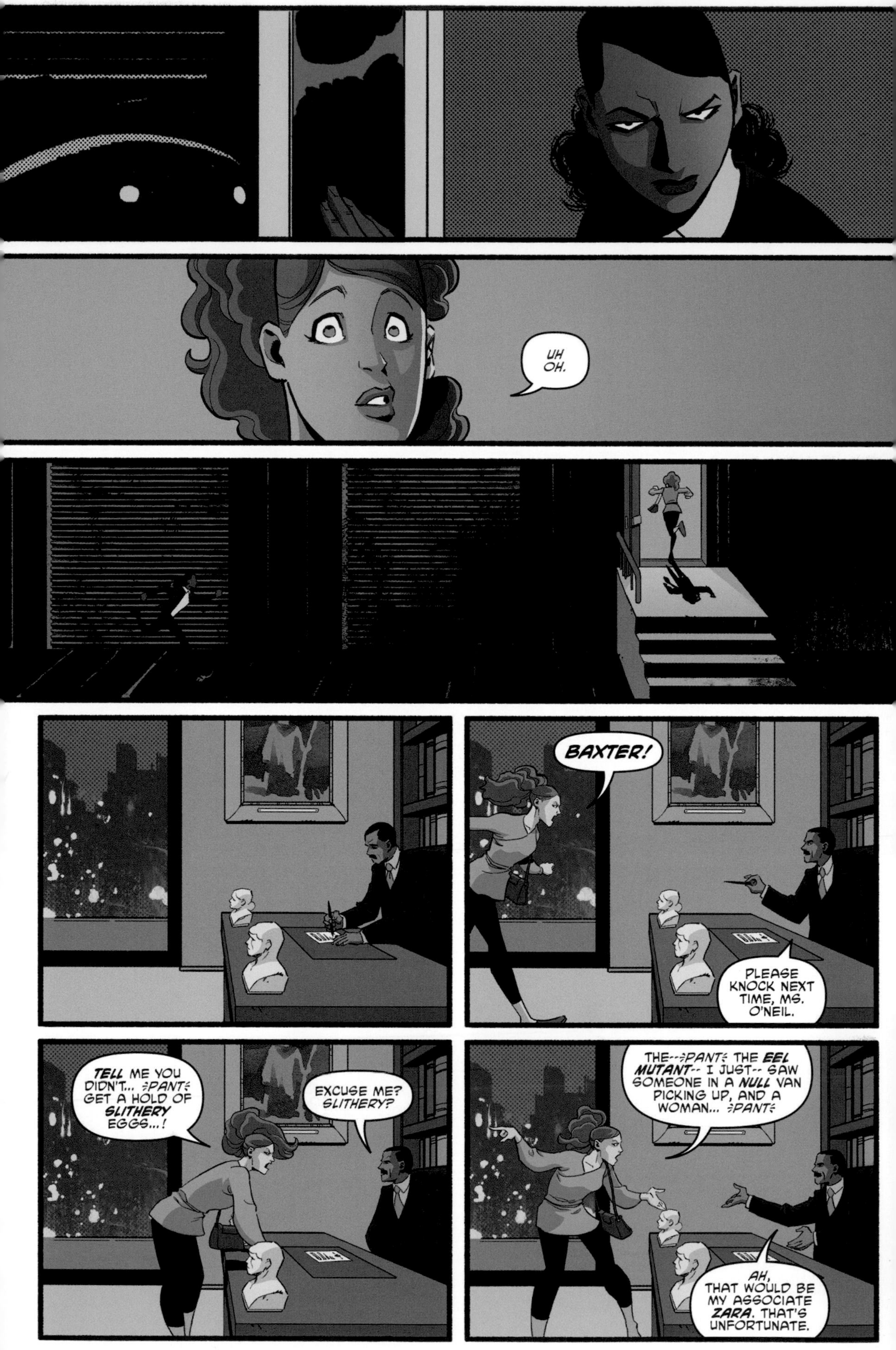
UH OH.
BAXTER!
PLEASE KNOCK NEXT TIME, MS. O'NEIL.
TELL ME YOU DIDN'T... ≠PANT≠ GET A HOLD OF SLITHERY EGGS...!
EXCUSE ME? SLITHERY?
THE-- ≠PANT≠ THE EEL MUTANT-- I JUST-- SAW SOMEONE IN A NULL VAN PICKING UP, AND A WOMAN... ≠PANT≠
AH, THAT WOULD BE MY ASSOCIATE ZARA. THAT'S UNFORTUNATE.

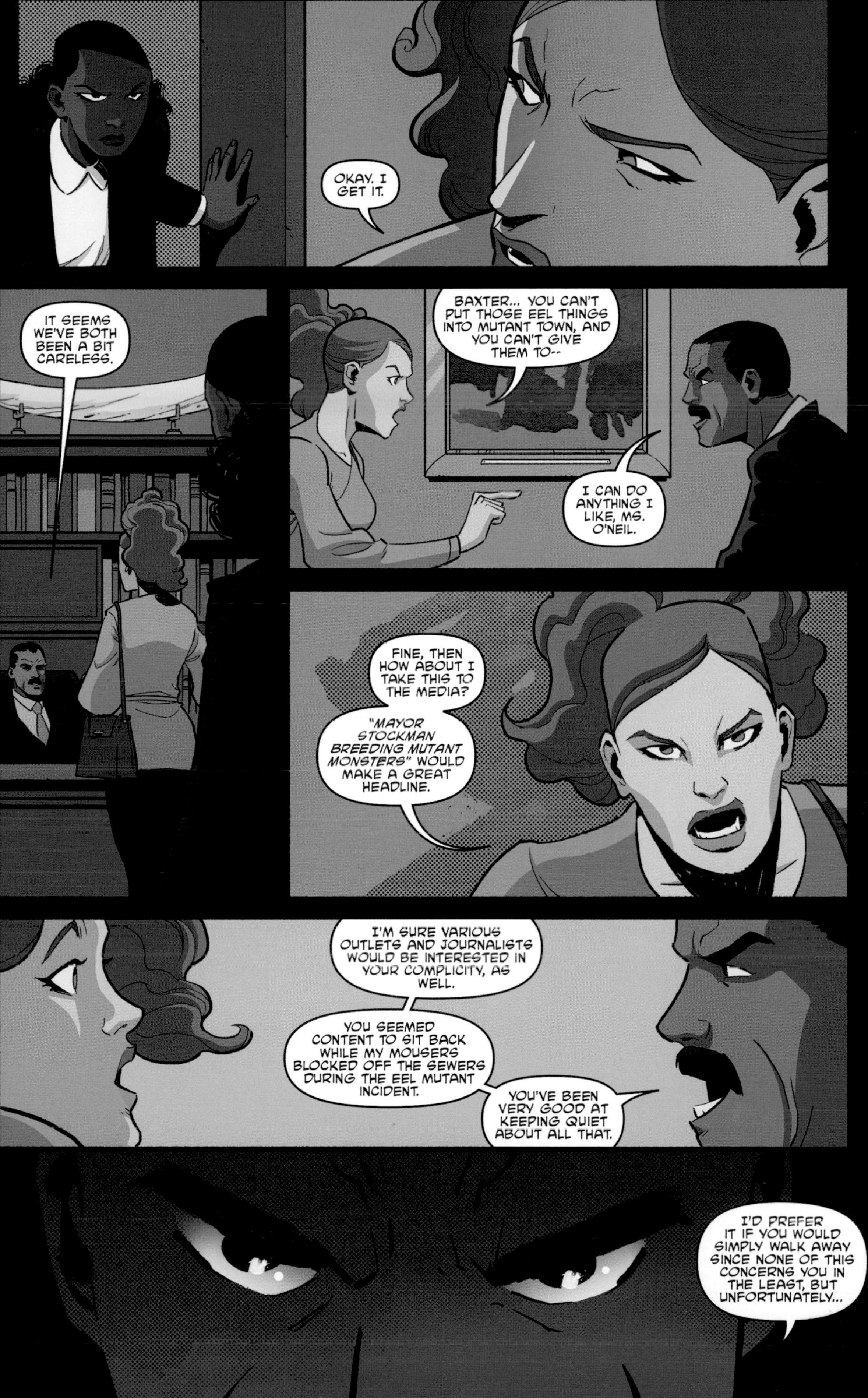
OKAY. I GET IT.
IT SEEMS WE'VE BOTH BEEN A BIT CARELESS.
BAXTER... YOU CAN'T PUT THOSE EEL THINGS INTO MUTANT TOWN, AND YOU CAN'T GIVE THEM TO--
I CAN DO ANYTHING I LIKE, MS. O'NEIL.
FINE, THEN HOW ABOUT I TAKE THIS TO THE MEDIA?
"MAYOR STOCKMAN BREEDING MUTANT MONSTERS" WOULD MAKE A GREAT HEADLINE.
I'M SURE VARIOUS OUTLETS AND JOURNALISTS WOULD BE INTERESTED IN YOUR COMPLICITY, AS WELL.
YOU SEEMED CONTENT TO SIT BACK WHILE MY MOUSERS BLOCKED OFF THE SEWERS DURING THE EEL MUTANT INCIDENT.
YOU'VE BEEN VERY GOOD AT KEEPING QUIET ABOUT ALL THAT.
I'D PREFER IT IF YOU WOULD SIMPLY WALK AWAY SINCE NONE OF THIS CONCERNS YOU IN THE LEAST, BUT UNFORTUNATELY...

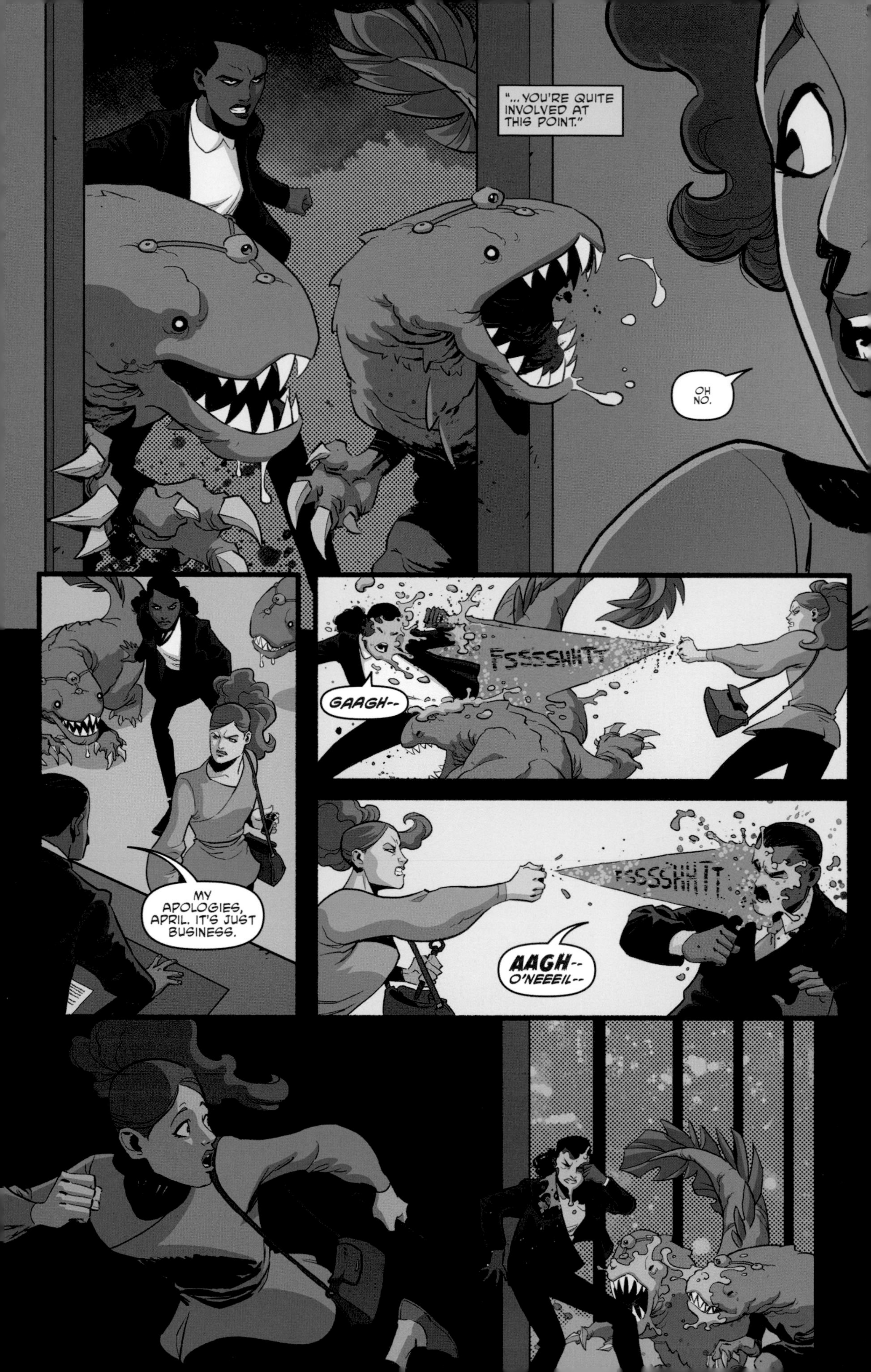
"...YOU'RE QUITE INVOLVED AT THIS POINT."
OH NO.
MY APOLOGIES, APRIL. IT'S JUST BUSINESS.
FSSSSHHTT
GAAGH--
FSSSSHHTT
AAGH-- O'NEEEIL--

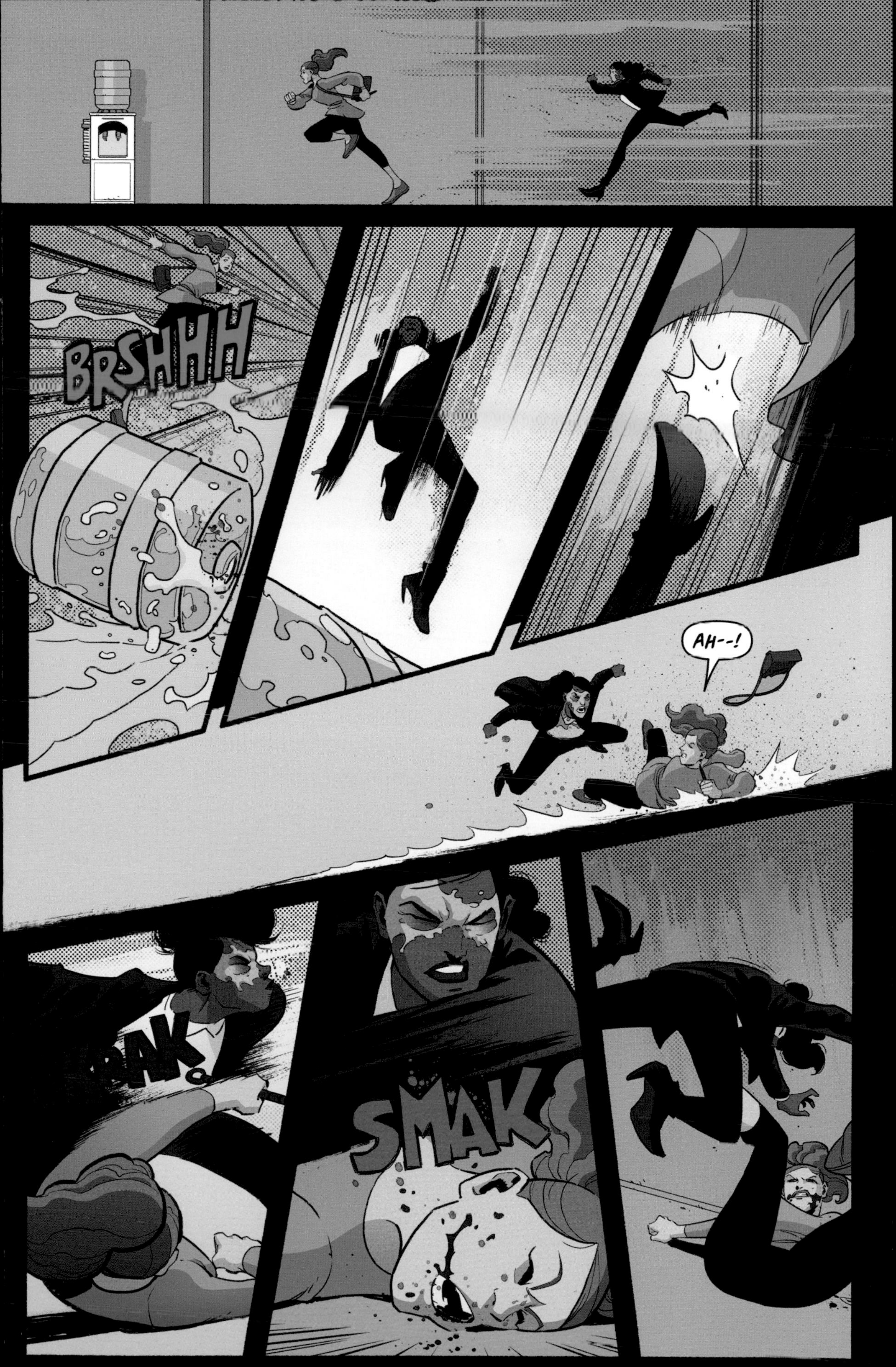
BRSHHH
AH--!
SMAK

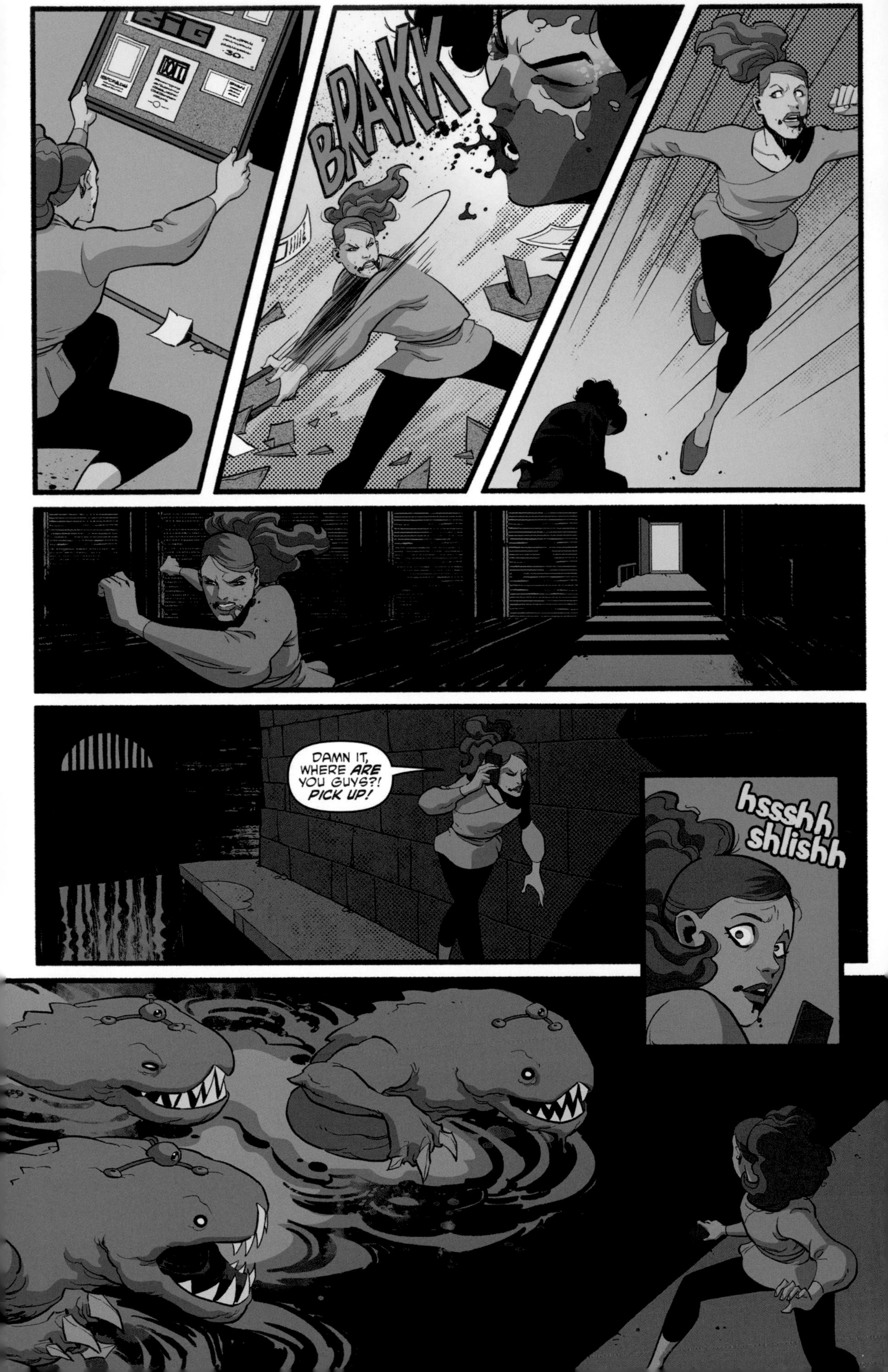
BRAKK
DAMN IT, WHERE ARE YOU GUYS?! PICK UP!
hssshh shlishh

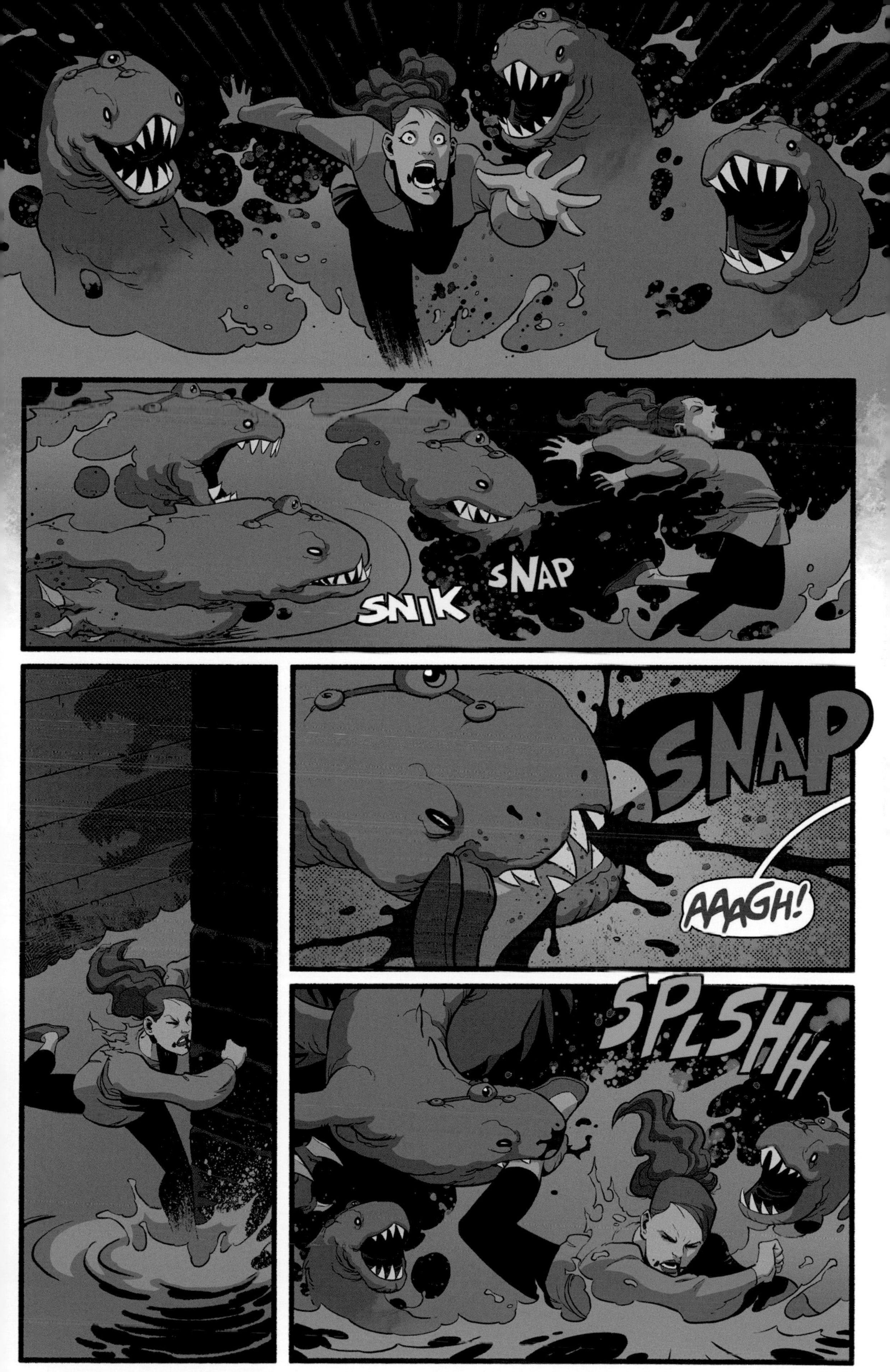
SNAP
SNIK
SNAP
AAAGH!
SPLSHH

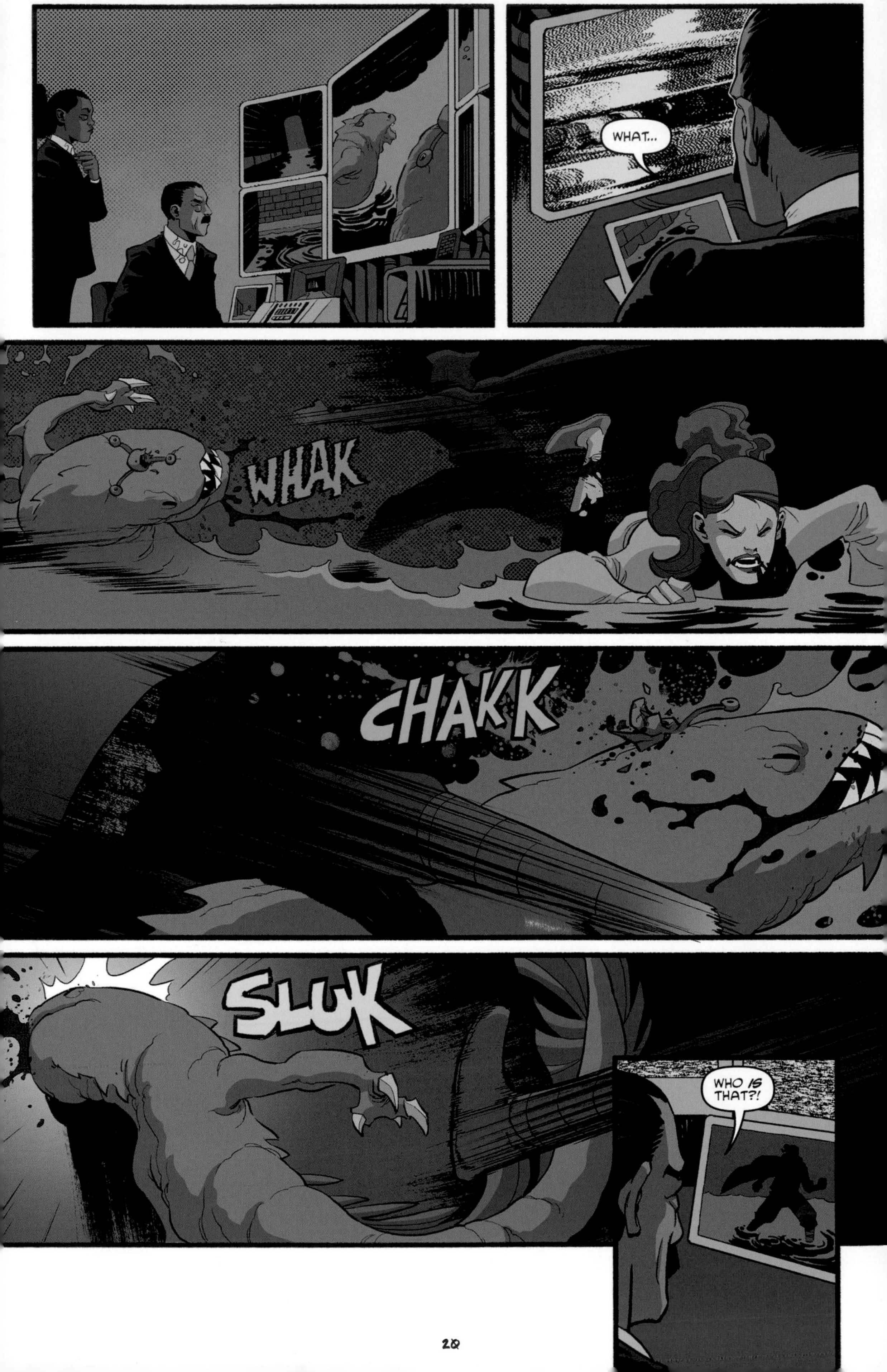
WHAT...
WHAK
CHAKK
SLUK
WHO IS THAT?!

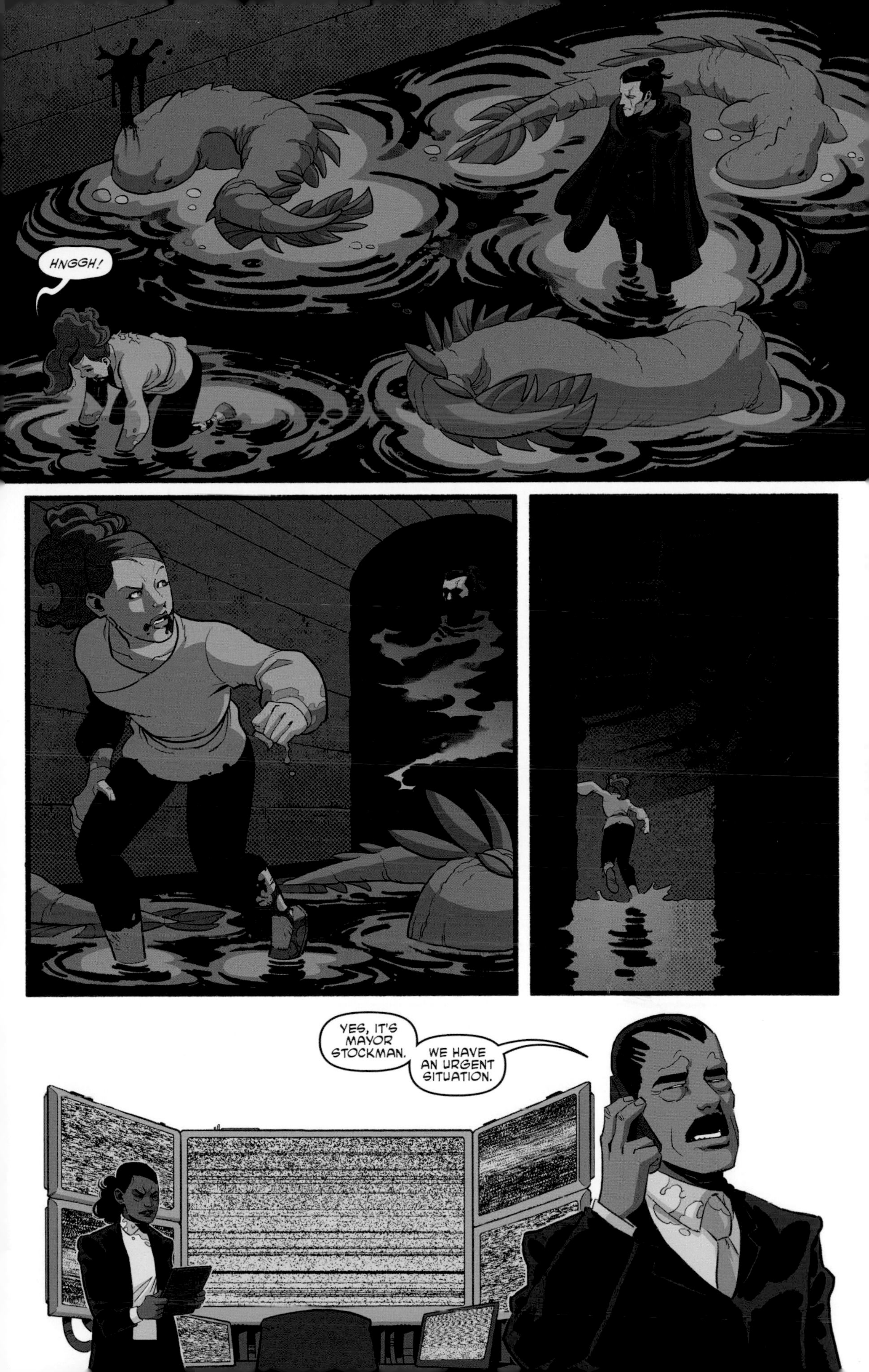
HNGGH!
YES, IT'S MAYOR STOCKMAN.
WE HAVE AN URGENT SITUATION.

ARE YOU BUMMED ABOUT BABYSITTING INSTEAD OF DOING SECURITY DUTY AT THE RALLY?

NAH.

BZZZ

YOU'RE GOOD AT THIS STUFF. YOU'RE GOOD WITH KIDS.

I AM?

YEAH! YOU'RE PRACTICALLY A *DAD* NOW.

WHAT?!

UGH, DON'T SAY THAT. I AM *NOT*.

YOU'RE SO *DOMESTIC* NOW.

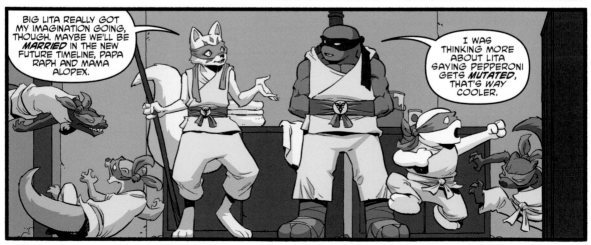

BIG LITA REALLY GOT MY IMAGINATION GOING, THOUGH. MAYBE WE'LL BE *MARRIED* IN THE NEW FUTURE TIMELINE, PAPA RAPH AND MAMA ALOPEX.

I WAS THINKING MORE ABOUT LITA SAYING PEPPERONI GETS *MUTATED*, THAT'S WAY COOLER.

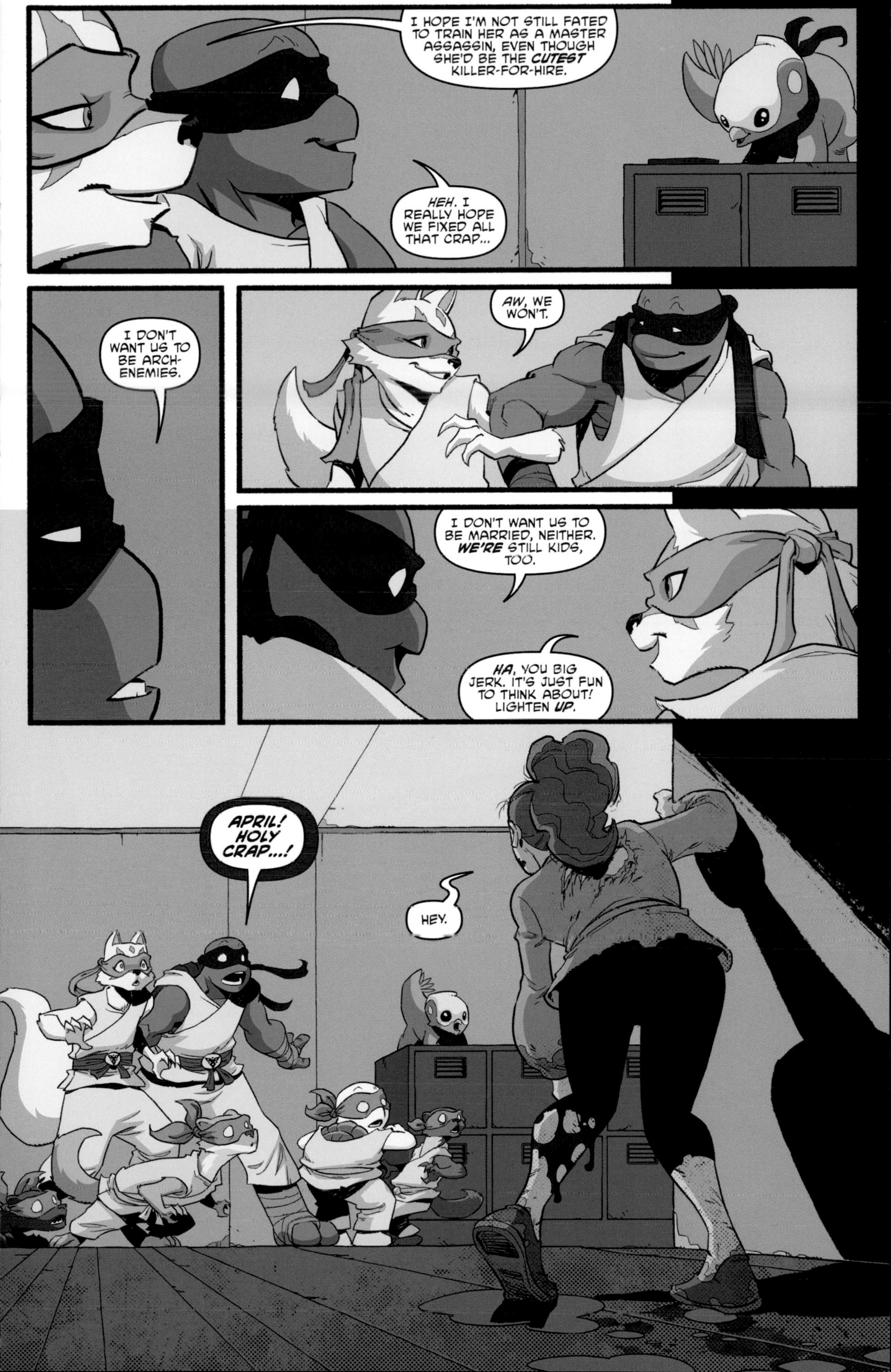
I HOPE I'M NOT STILL FATED TO TRAIN HER AS A MASTER ASSASSIN, EVEN THOUGH SHE'D BE THE CUTEST KILLER-FOR-HIRE.
HEH. I REALLY HOPE WE FIXED ALL THAT CRAP...
I DON'T WANT US TO BE ARCH-ENEMIES.
AW, WE WON'T.
I DON'T WANT US TO BE MARRIED, NEITHER. WE'RE STILL KIDS, TOO.
HA, YOU BIG JERK. IT'S JUST FUN TO THINK ABOUT! LIGHTEN UP.
APRIL! HOLY CRAP...!
HEY.

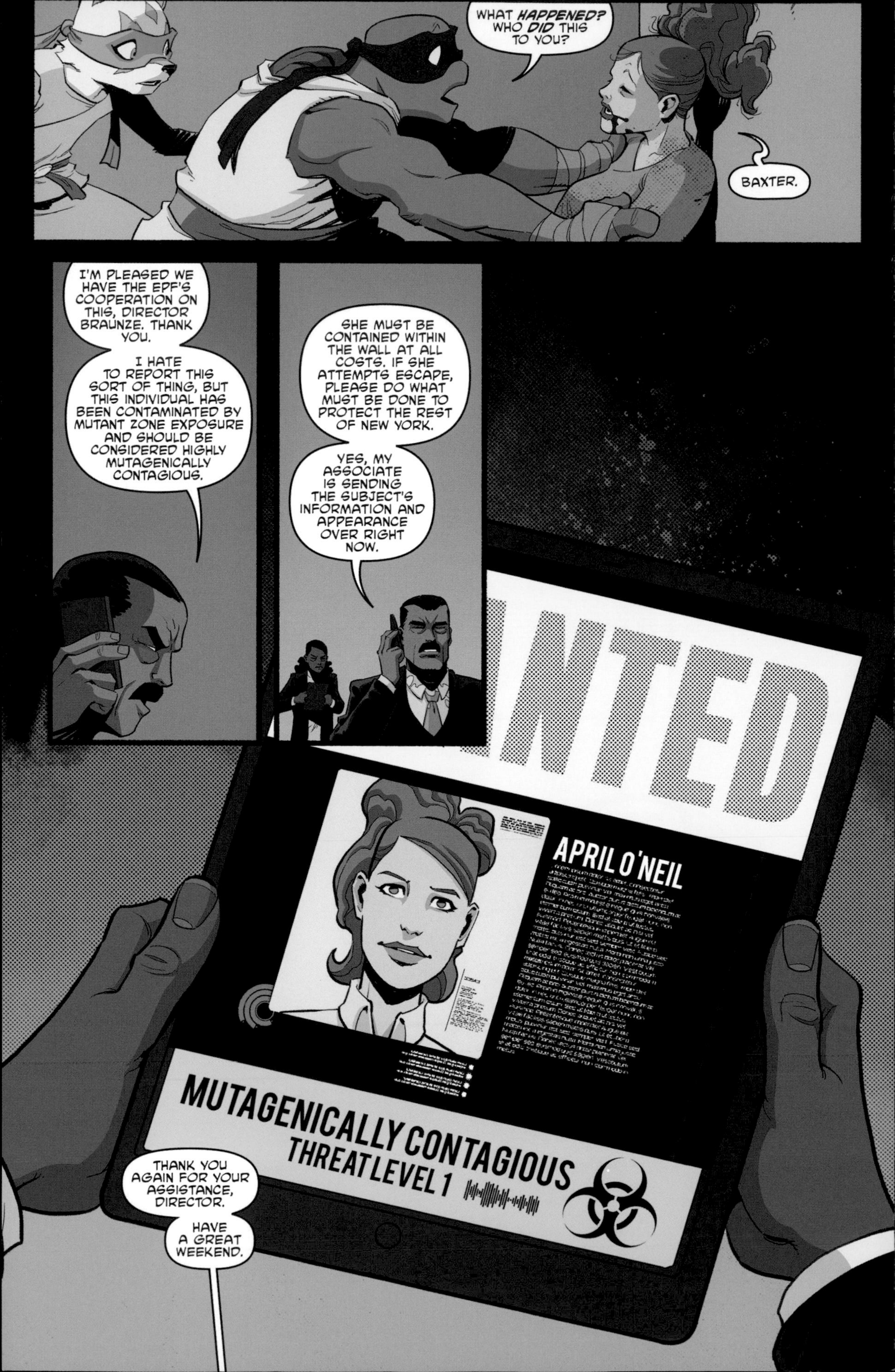
WHAT HAPPENED? WHO DID THIS TO YOU?
BAXTER.
I'M PLEASED WE HAVE THE EPF'S COOPERATION ON THIS, DIRECTOR BRAUNZE. THANK YOU.
I HATE TO REPORT THIS SORT OF THING, BUT THIS INDIVIDUAL HAS BEEN CONTAMINATED BY MUTANT ZONE EXPOSURE AND SHOULD BE CONSIDERED HIGHLY MUTAGENICALLY CONTAGIOUS.
SHE MUST BE CONTAINED WITHIN THE WALL AT ALL COSTS. IF SHE ATTEMPTS ESCAPE, PLEASE DO WHAT MUST BE DONE TO PROTECT THE REST OF NEW YORK.
YES, MY ASSOCIATE IS SENDING THE SUBJECT'S INFORMATION AND APPEARANCE OVER RIGHT NOW.
NTED
APRIL O'NEIL
MUTAGENICALLY CONTAGIOUS
THREAT LEVEL 1
THANK YOU AGAIN FOR YOUR ASSISTANCE, DIRECTOR.
HAVE A GREAT WEEKEND.

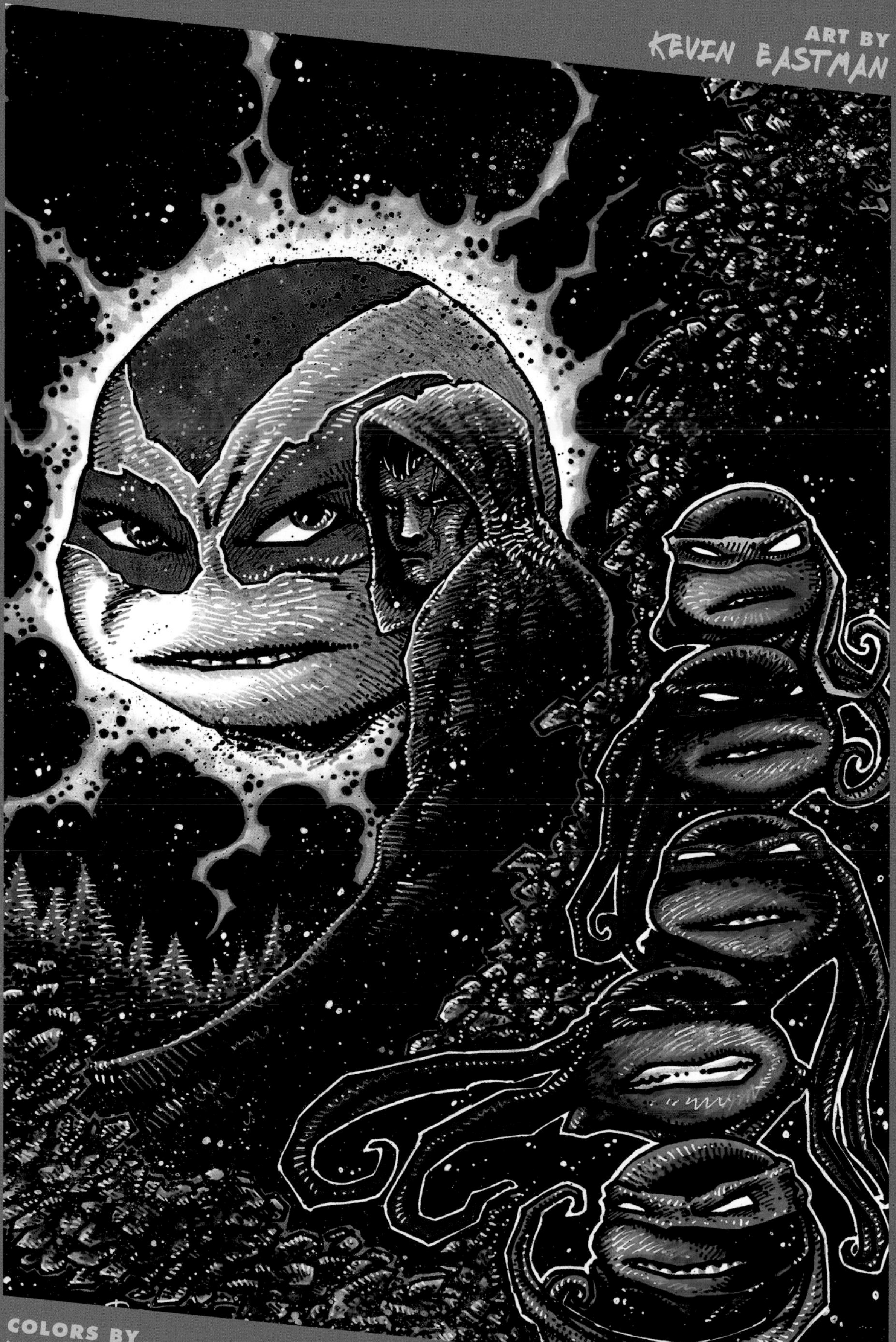

ART BY
KEVIN EASTMAN

COLORS BY
FAHRIZA KAMAPUTRA

ART BY
NELSON D'ANIEL

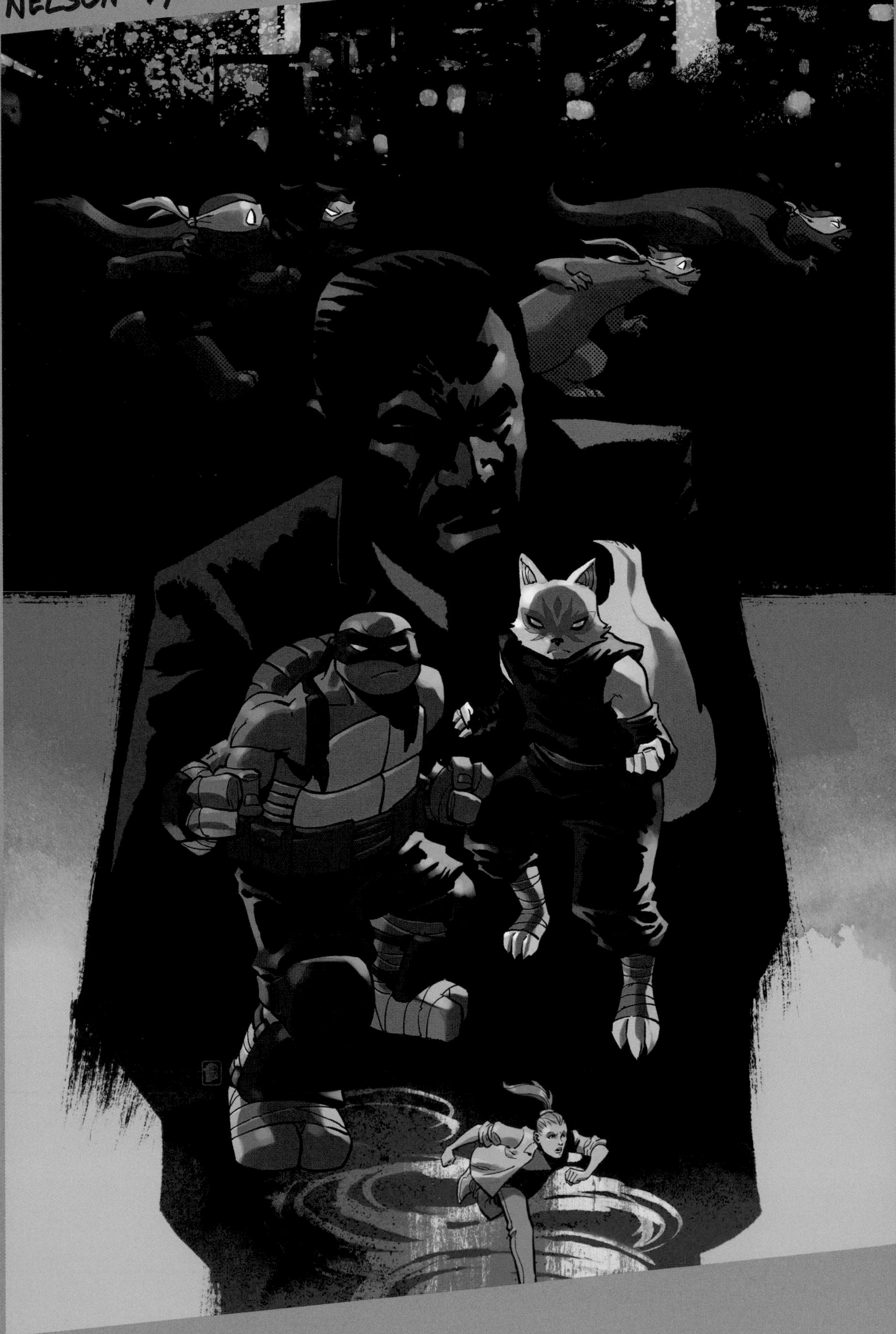

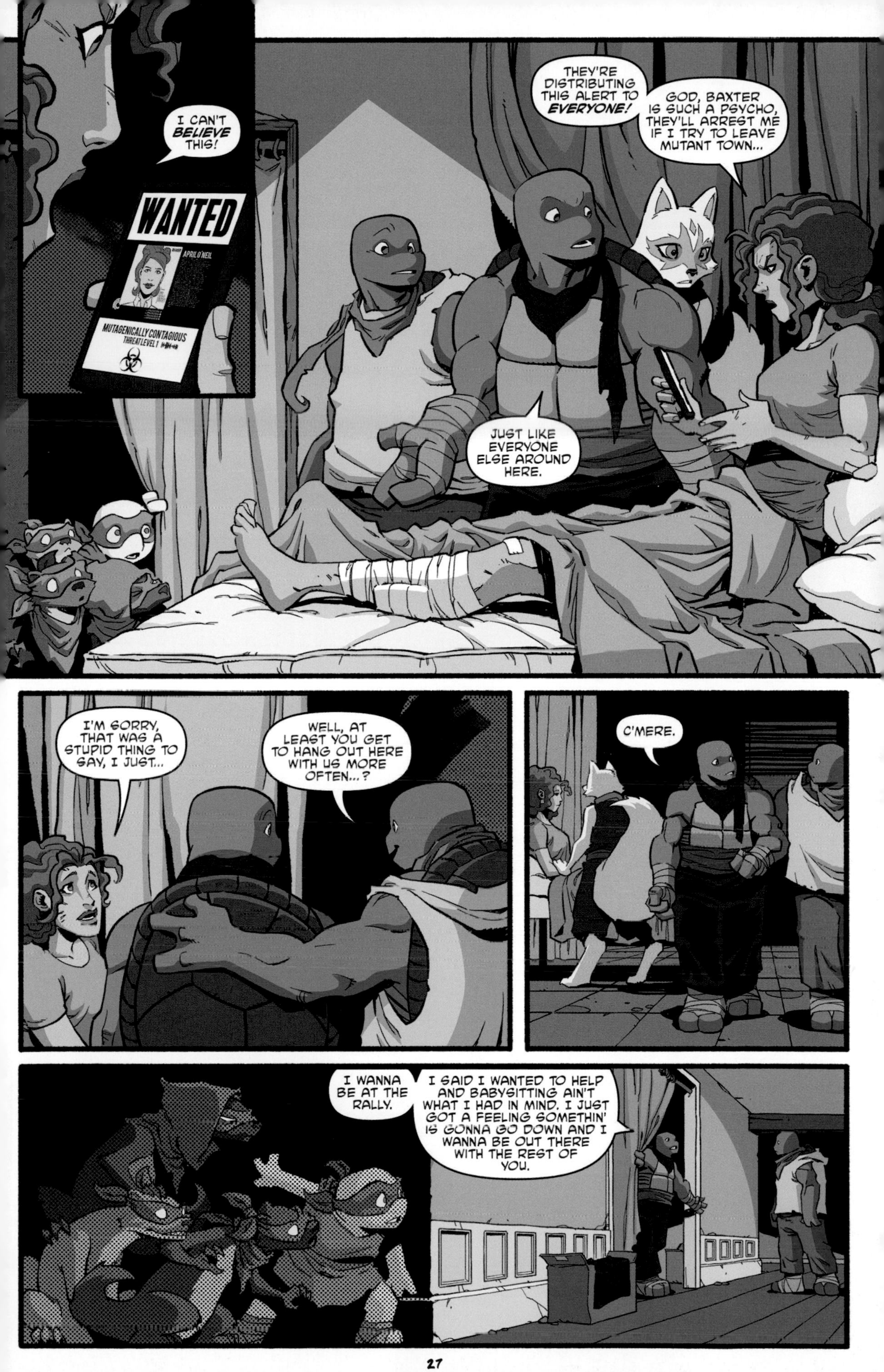
I CAN'T *BELIEVE* THIS!
WANTED
APRIL O'NEIL
MUTAGENICALLY CONTAGIOUS
THREAT LEVEL 1
THEY'RE DISTRIBUTING THIS ALERT TO *EVERYONE!*
GOD, BAXTER IS SUCH A PSYCHO, THEY'LL ARREST ME IF I TRY TO LEAVE MUTANT TOWN...
JUST LIKE EVERYONE ELSE AROUND HERE.
I'M SORRY, THAT WAS A STUPID THING TO SAY, I JUST...
WELL, AT LEAST YOU GET TO HANG OUT HERE WITH US MORE OFTEN...?
C'MERE.
I WANNA BE AT THE RALLY.
I SAID I WANTED TO HELP AND BABYSITTING AIN'T WHAT I HAD IN MIND. I JUST GOT A FEELING SOMETHIN' IS GONNA GO DOWN AND I WANNA BE OUT THERE WITH THE REST OF YOU.

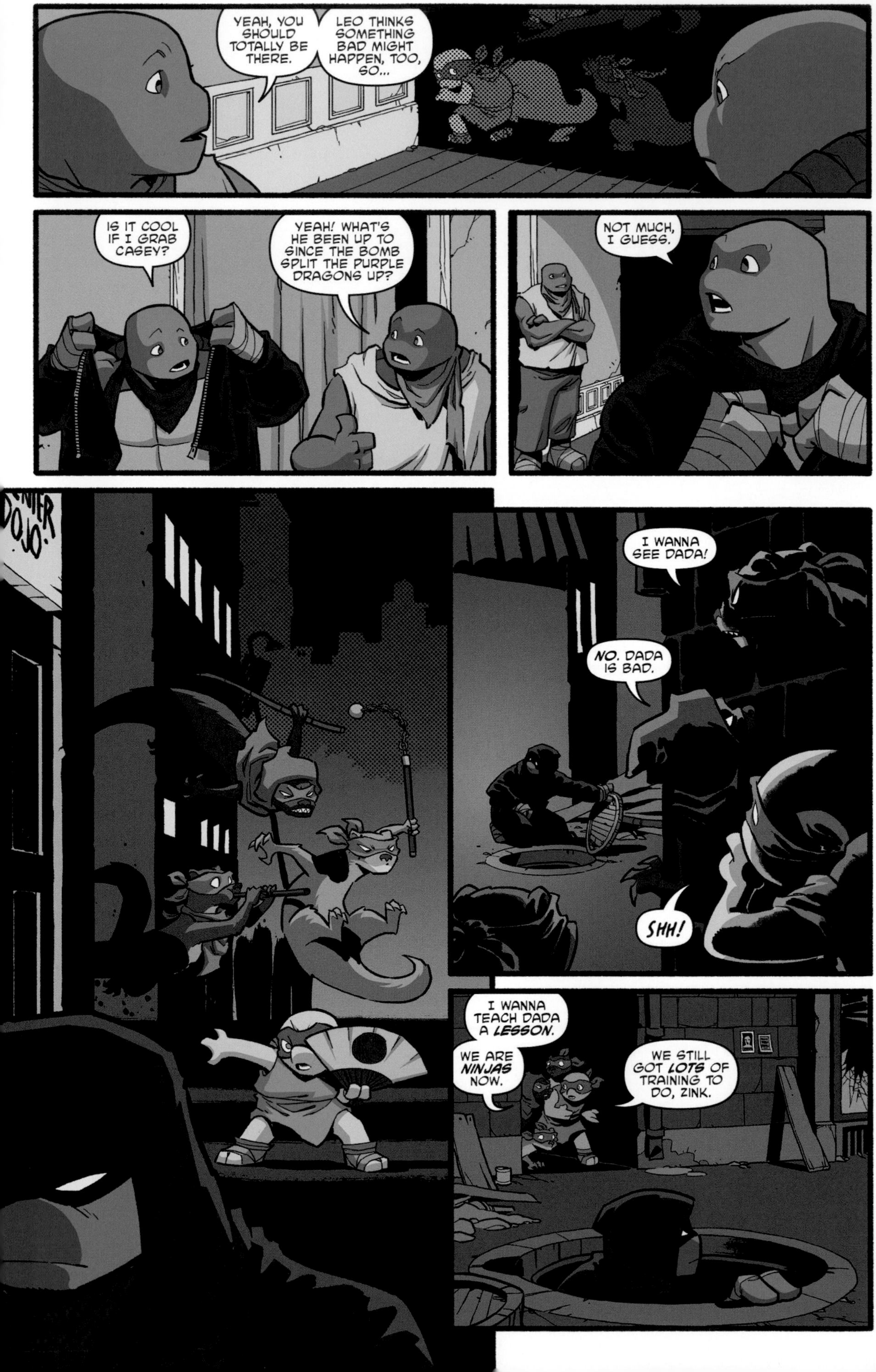
YEAH, YOU SHOULD TOTALLY BE THERE.
LEO THINKS SOMETHING BAD MIGHT HAPPEN, TOO, SO...
IS IT COOL IF I GRAB CASEY?
YEAH! WHAT'S HE BEEN UP TO SINCE THE BOMB SPLIT THE PURPLE DRAGONS UP?
NOT MUCH, I GUESS.
DOJO
I WANNA SEE DADA!
NO. DADA IS BAD.
SHH!
I WANNA TEACH DADA A LESSON.
WE ARE NINJAS NOW.
WE STILL GOT LOTS OF TRAINING TO DO, ZINK.

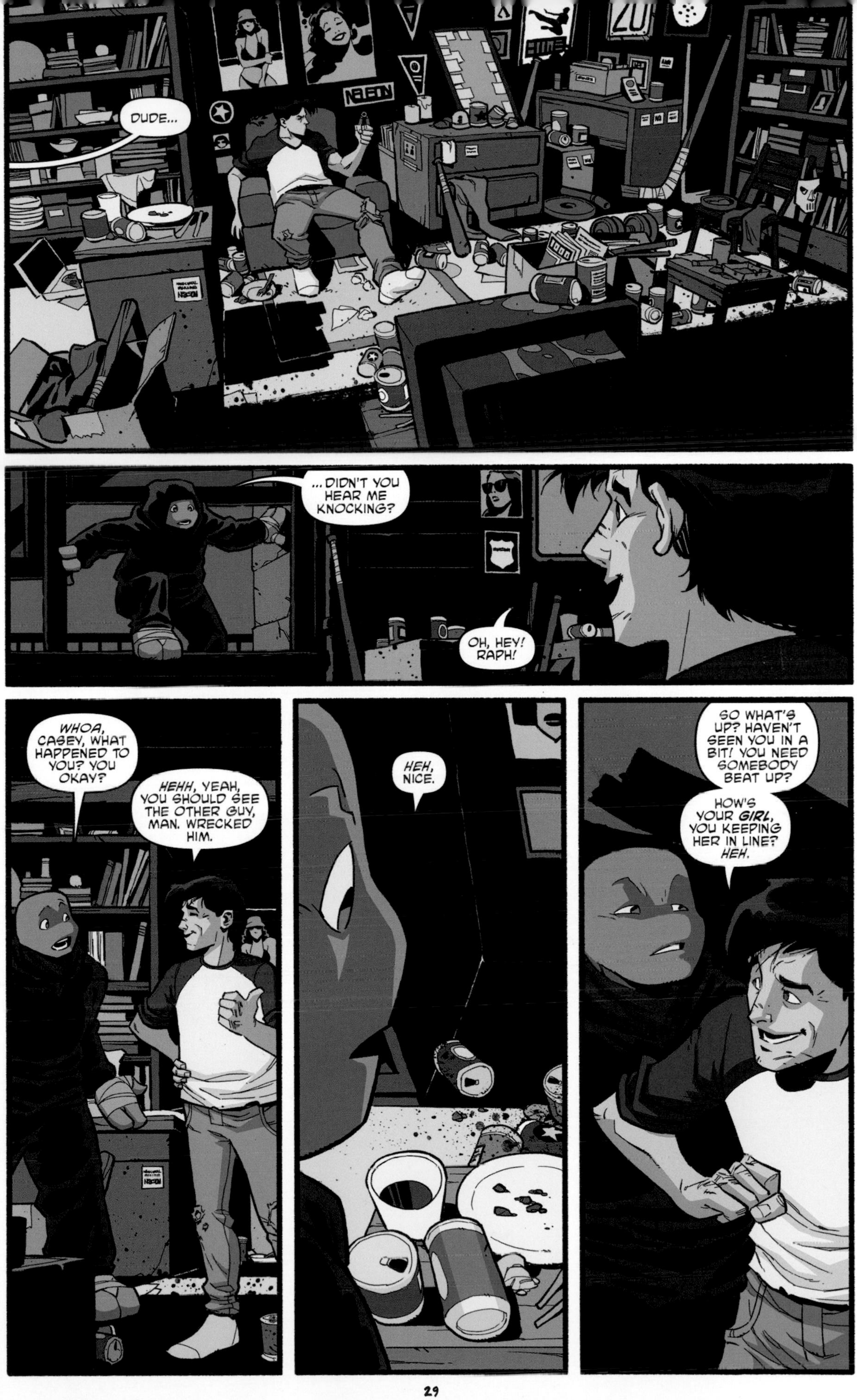
DUDE...
...DIDN'T YOU HEAR ME KNOCKING?
OH, HEY! RAPH!
WHOA, CASEY, WHAT HAPPENED TO YOU? YOU OKAY?
HEHH, YEAH, YOU SHOULD SEE THE OTHER GUY, MAN. WRECKED HIM.
HEH, NICE.
SO WHAT'S UP? HAVEN'T SEEN YOU IN A BIT! YOU NEED SOMEBODY BEAT UP?
HOW'S YOUR ***GIRL***, YOU KEEPING HER IN LINE? *HEH*.

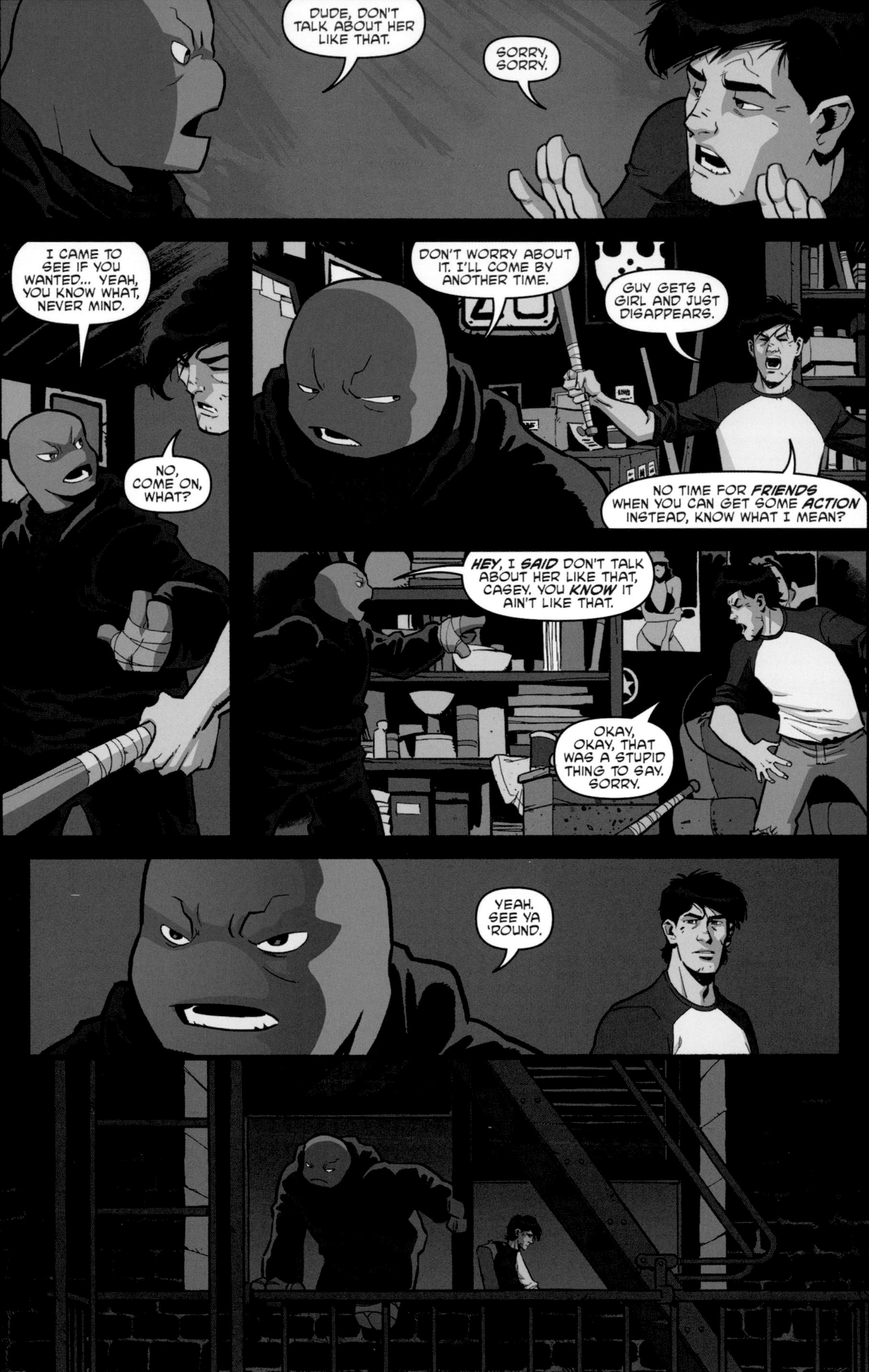
DUDE, DON'T TALK ABOUT HER LIKE THAT.
SORRY, SORRY.
I CAME TO SEE IF YOU WANTED... YEAH, YOU KNOW WHAT, NEVER MIND.
NO, COME ON, WHAT?
DON'T WORRY ABOUT IT. I'LL COME BY ANOTHER TIME.
GUY GETS A GIRL AND JUST DISAPPEARS.
NO TIME FOR FRIENDS WHEN YOU CAN GET SOME ACTION INSTEAD, KNOW WHAT I MEAN?
HEY, I SAID DON'T TALK ABOUT HER LIKE THAT, CASEY. YOU KNOW IT AIN'T LIKE THAT.
OKAY, OKAY, THAT WAS A STUPID THING TO SAY. SORRY.
YEAH. SEE YA 'ROUND.

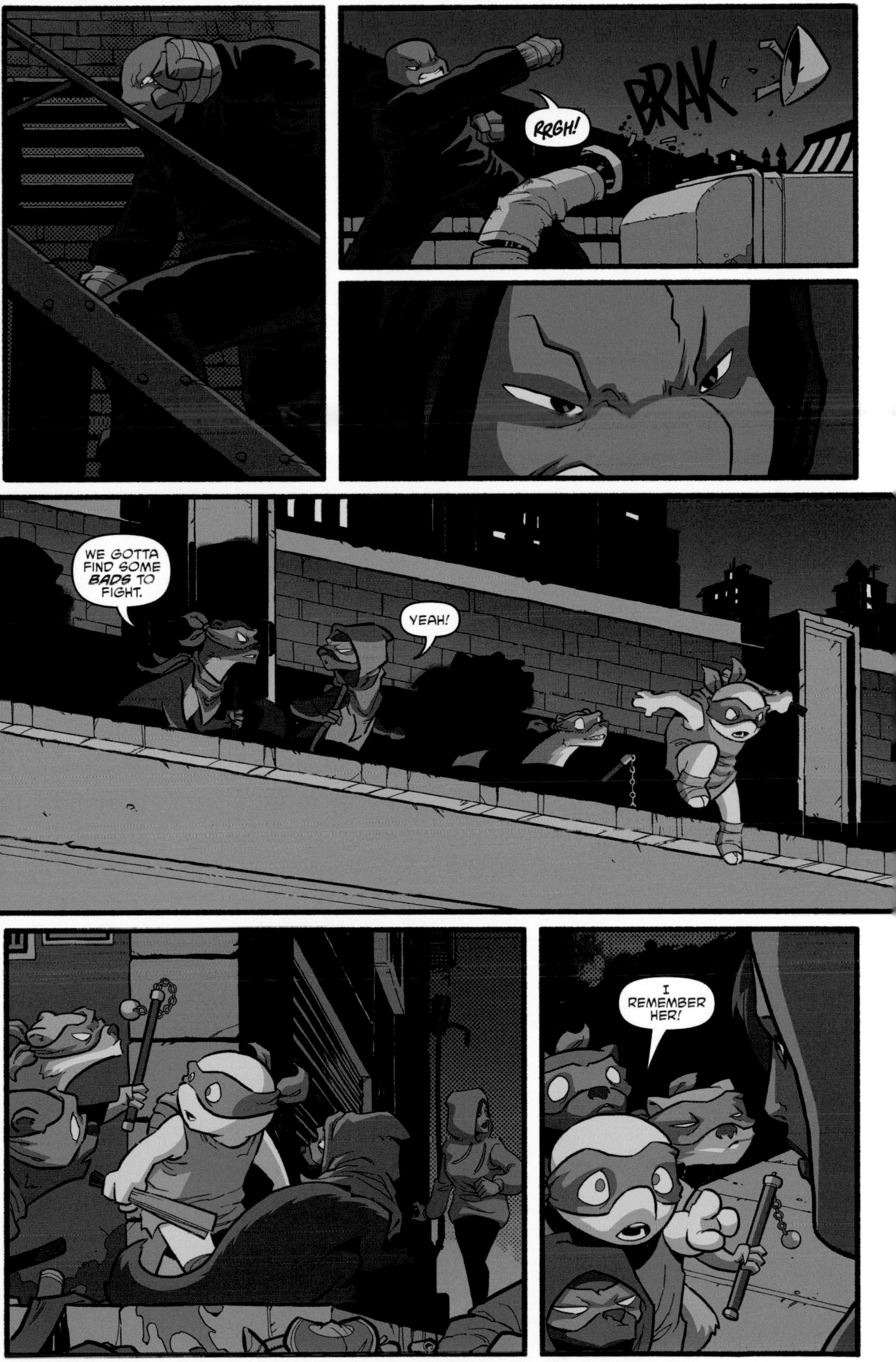
RRGH!
BRAK
WE GOTTA FIND SOME BADS TO FIGHT.
YEAH!
I REMEMBER HER!

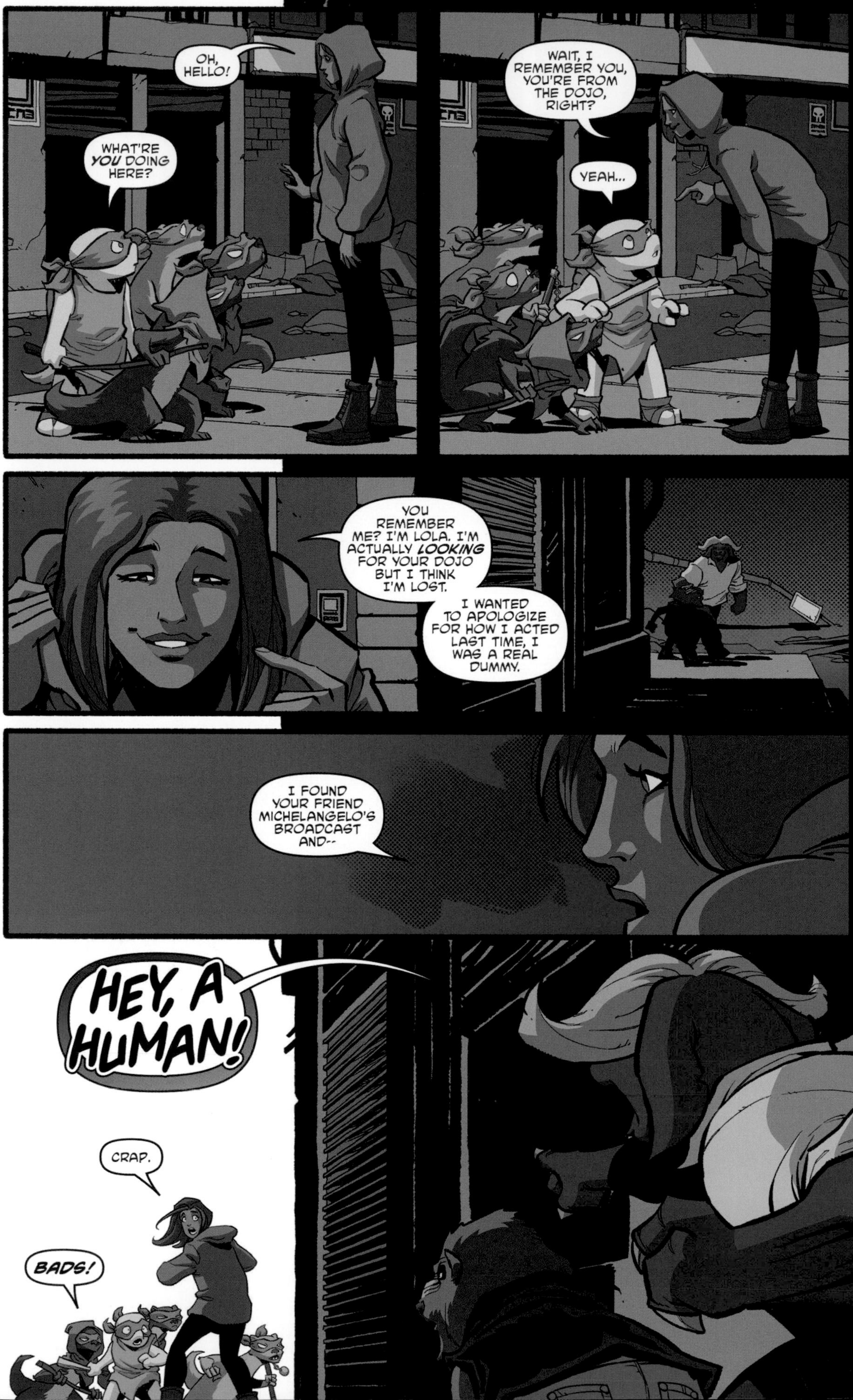
OH, HELLO!
WHAT'RE YOU DOING HERE?
WAIT, I REMEMBER YOU, YOU'RE FROM THE DOJO, RIGHT?
YEAH...
YOU REMEMBER ME? I'M LOLA. I'M ACTUALLY LOOKING FOR YOUR DOJO BUT I THINK I'M LOST.
I WANTED TO APOLOGIZE FOR HOW I ACTED LAST TIME, I WAS A REAL DUMMY.
I FOUND YOUR FRIEND MICHELANGELO'S BROADCAST AND--
HEY, A HUMAN!
CRAP.
BADS!

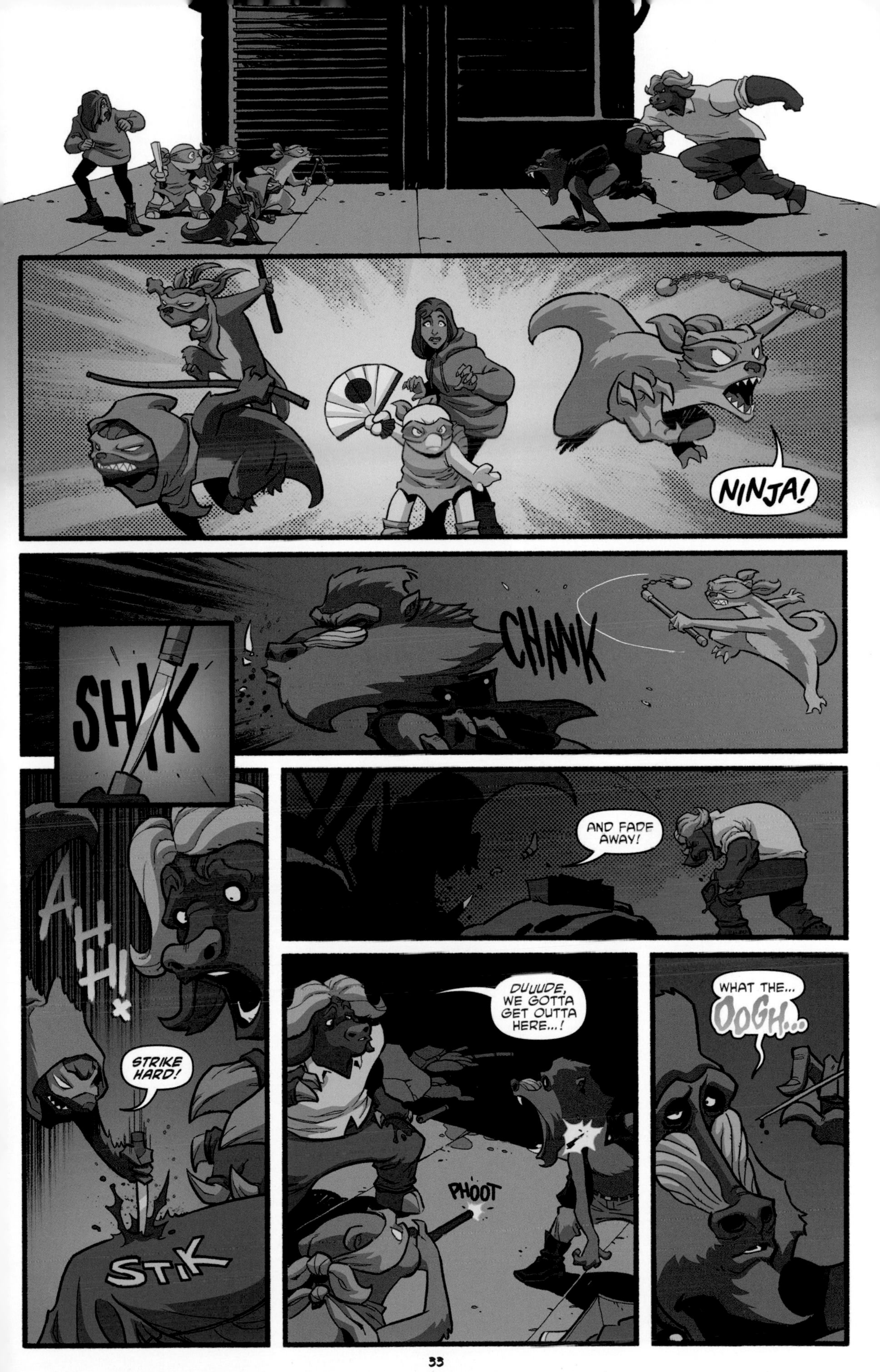
NINJA!
SHIK
CHANK
AHH!
STRIKE HARD!
STIK
AND FADE AWAY!
DUUUDE, WE GOTTA GET OUTTA HERE...!
PHOOT
WHAT THE...
OOGH...

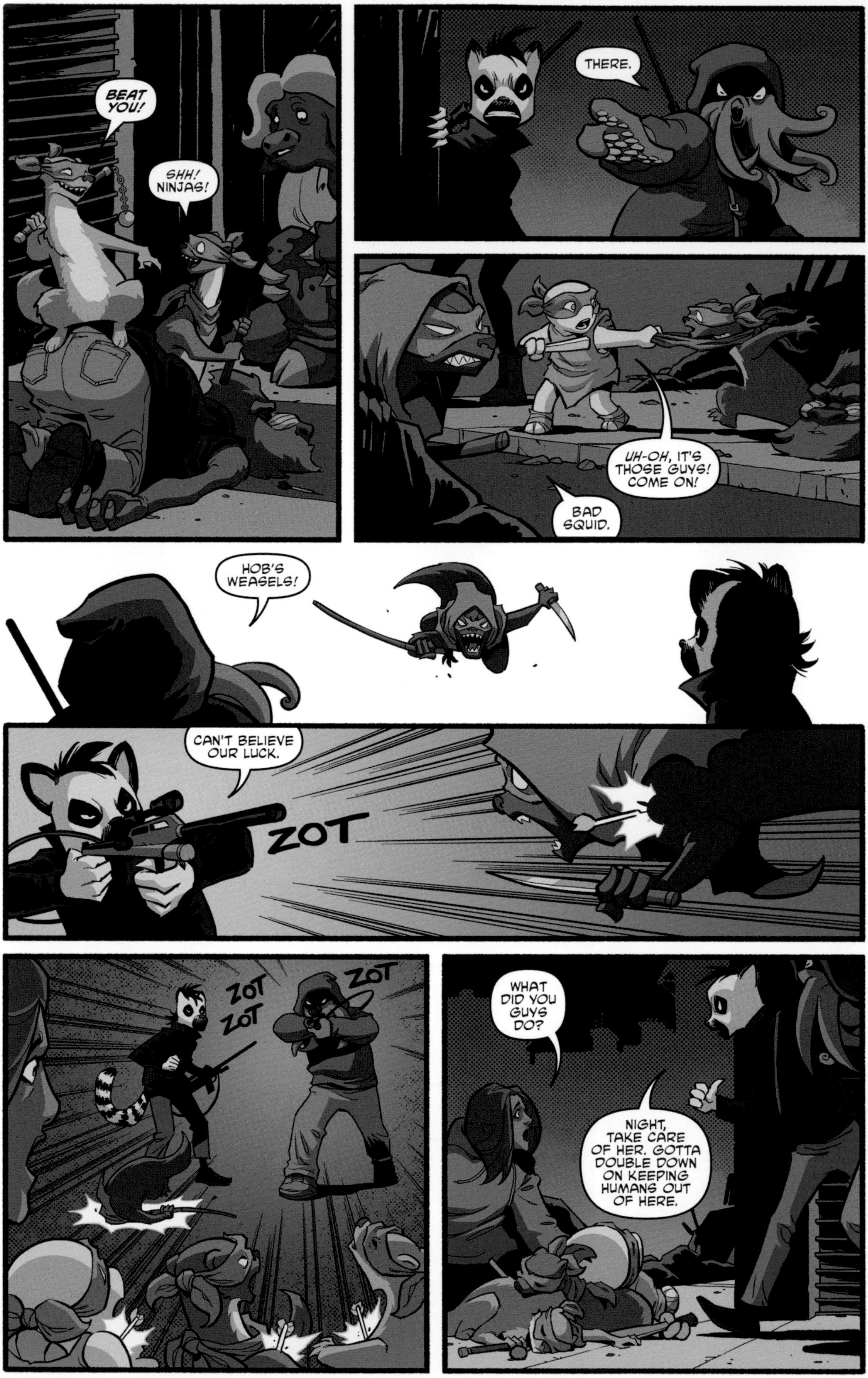

BEAT YOU!
SHH! NINJAS!
THERE.
UH-OH, IT'S THOSE GUYS! COME ON!
BAD SQUID.
HOB'S WEASELS!
CAN'T BELIEVE OUR LUCK.
ZOT
ZOT
ZOT
ZOT
WHAT DID YOU GUYS DO?
NIGHT, TAKE CARE OF HER. GOTTA DOUBLE DOWN ON KEEPING HUMANS OUT OF HERE.

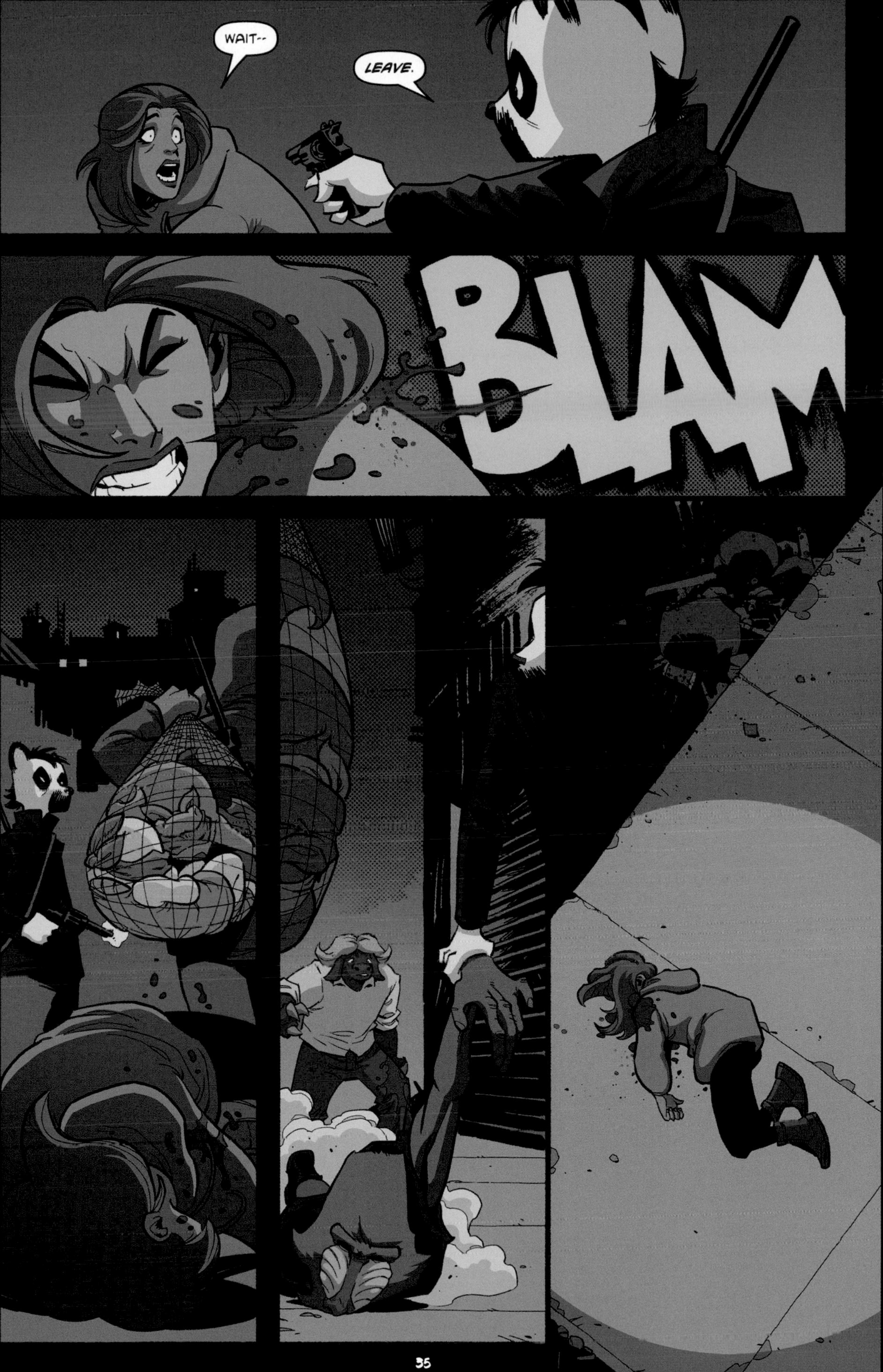
WAIT--
LEAVE.
BLAM

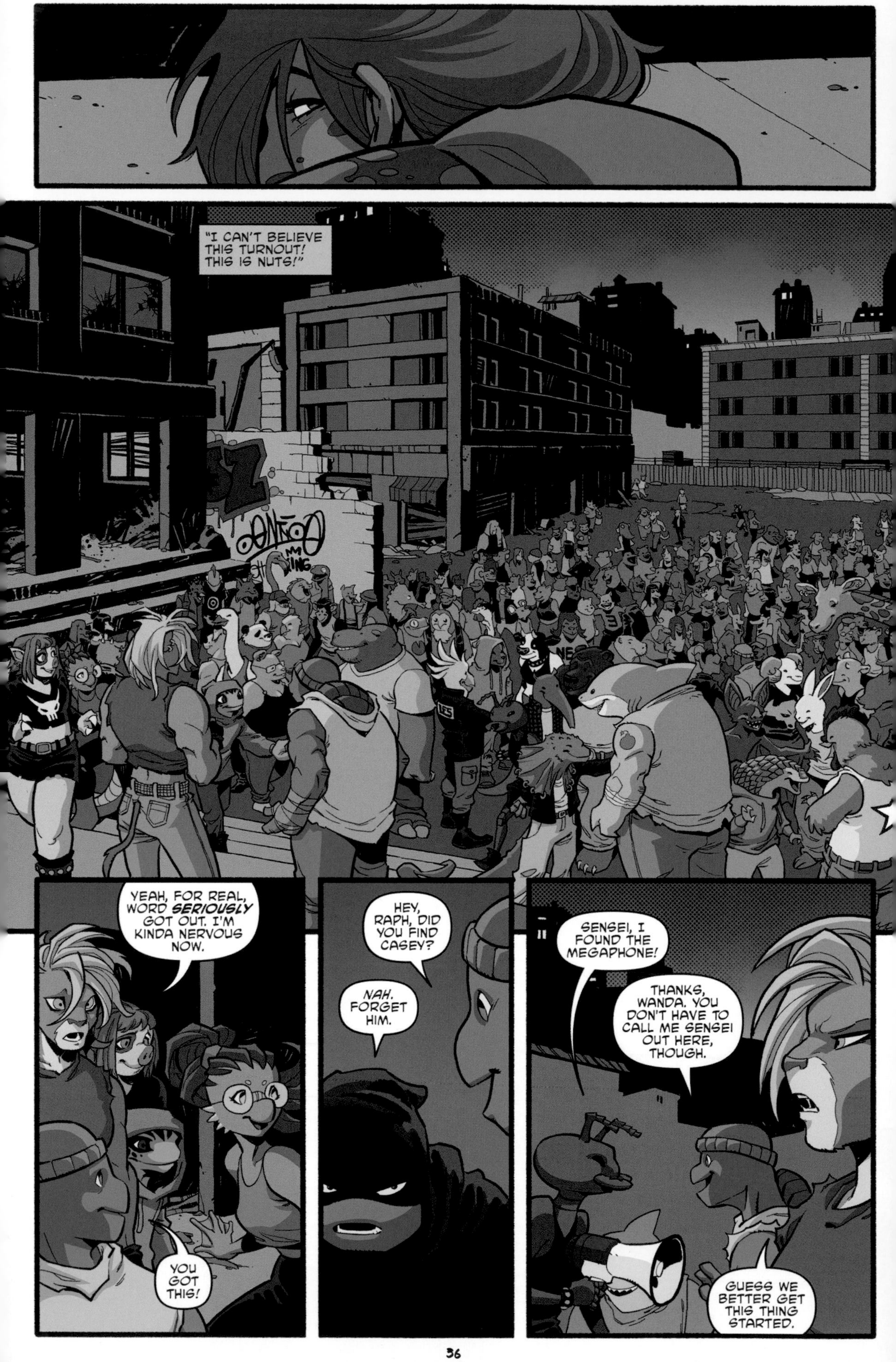
"I CAN'T BELIEVE THIS TURNOUT! THIS IS NUTS!"
YEAH, FOR REAL, WORD **SERIOUSLY** GOT OUT. I'M KINDA NERVOUS NOW.
YOU GOT THIS!
HEY, RAPH, DID YOU FIND CASEY?
NAH. FORGET HIM.
SENSEI, I FOUND THE MEGAPHONE!
THANKS, WANDA. YOU DON'T HAVE TO CALL ME SENSEI OUT HERE, THOUGH.
GUESS WE BETTER GET THIS THING STARTED.

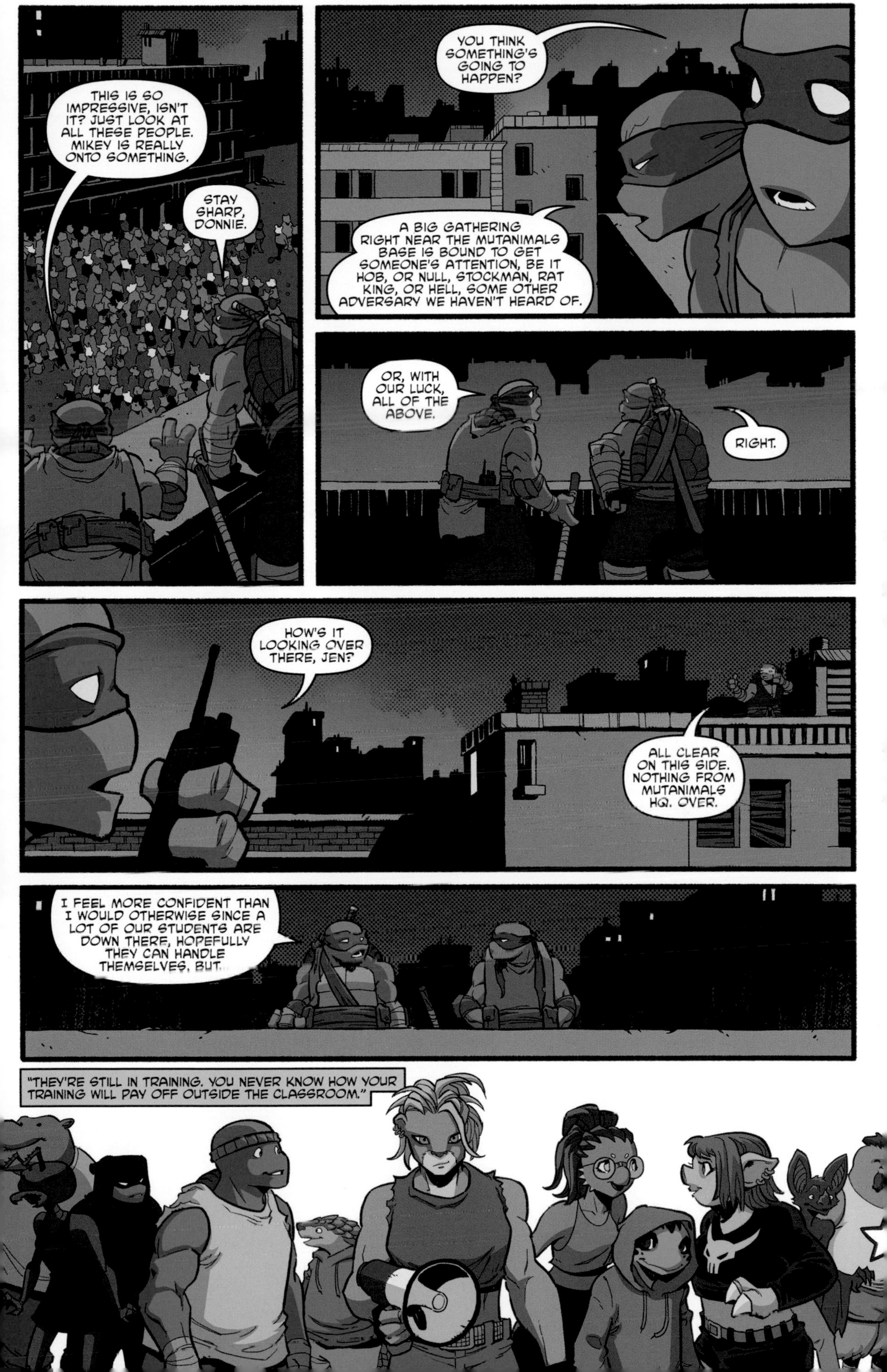
THIS IS SO IMPRESSIVE, ISN'T IT? JUST LOOK AT ALL THESE PEOPLE. MIKEY IS REALLY ONTO SOMETHING.
STAY SHARP, DONNIE.
YOU THINK SOMETHING'S GOING TO HAPPEN?
A BIG GATHERING RIGHT NEAR THE MUTANIMALS BASE IS BOUND TO GET SOMEONE'S ATTENTION, BE IT HOB, OR NULL, STOCKMAN, RAT KING, OR HELL, SOME OTHER ADVERSARY WE HAVEN'T HEARD OF.
OR, WITH OUR LUCK, ALL OF THE ABOVE.
RIGHT.
HOW'S IT LOOKING OVER THERE, JEN?
ALL CLEAR ON THIS SIDE. NOTHING FROM MUTANIMALS HQ. OVER.
I FEEL MORE CONFIDENT THAN I WOULD OTHERWISE SINCE A LOT OF OUR STUDENTS ARE DOWN THERE, HOPEFULLY THEY CAN HANDLE THEMSELVES, BUT...
"THEY'RE STILL IN TRAINING. YOU NEVER KNOW HOW YOUR TRAINING WILL PAY OFF OUTSIDE THE CLASSROOM."

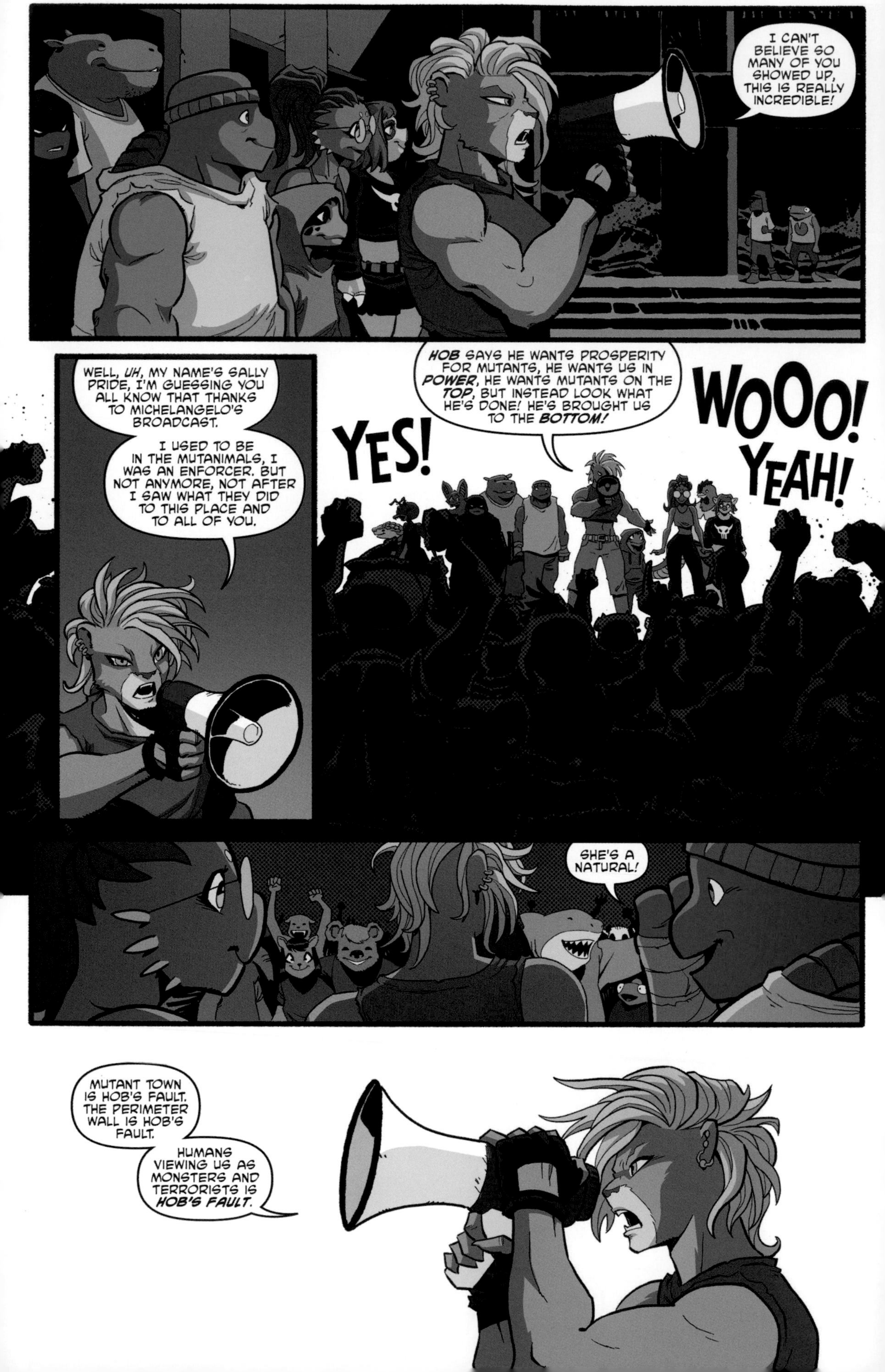

I CAN'T BELIEVE SO MANY OF YOU SHOWED UP, THIS IS REALLY INCREDIBLE!
WELL, *UH*, MY NAME'S SALLY PRIDE, I'M GUESSING YOU ALL KNOW THAT THANKS TO MICHELANGELO'S BROADCAST.
I USED TO BE IN THE MUTANIMALS, I WAS AN ENFORCER. BUT NOT ANYMORE, NOT AFTER I SAW WHAT THEY DID TO THIS PLACE AND TO ALL OF YOU.
HOB SAYS HE WANTS PROSPERITY FOR MUTANTS, HE WANTS US IN *POWER*, HE WANTS MUTANTS ON THE *TOP*, BUT INSTEAD LOOK WHAT HE'S DONE! HE'S BROUGHT US TO THE *BOTTOM!*
YES!
WOOO! YEAH!
SHE'S A NATURAL!
MUTANT TOWN IS HOB'S FAULT. THE PERIMETER WALL IS HOB'S FAULT.
HUMANS VIEWING US AS MONSTERS AND TERRORISTS IS *HOB'S FAULT*.

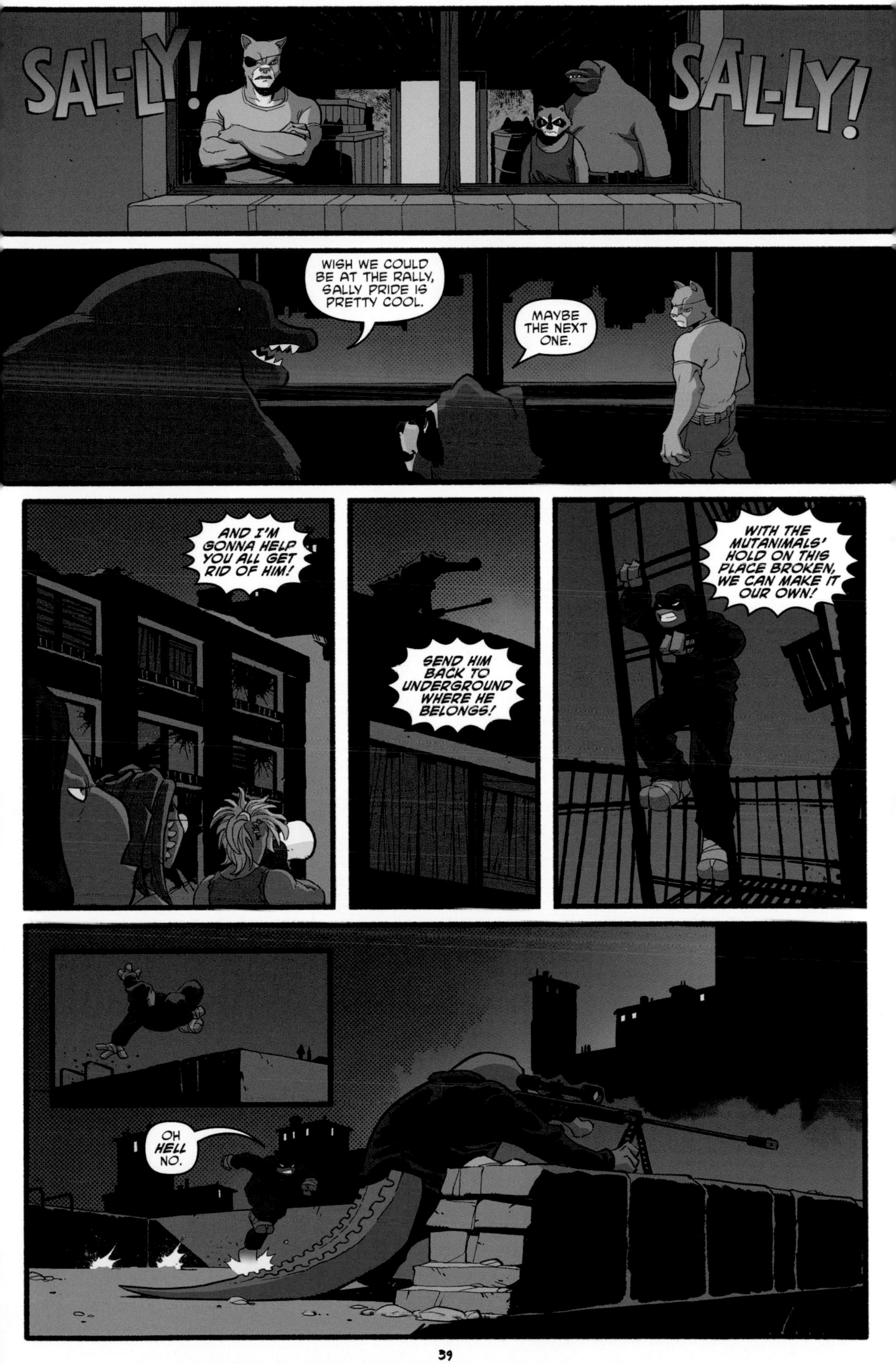
SAL-LY!
SAL-LY!
WISH WE COULD BE AT THE RALLY, SALLY PRIDE IS PRETTY COOL.
MAYBE THE NEXT ONE.
AND I'M GONNA HELP YOU ALL GET RID OF HIM!
SEND HIM BACK TO UNDERGROUND WHERE HE BELONGS!
WITH THE MUTANIMALS' HOLD ON THIS PLACE BROKEN, WE CAN MAKE IT OUR OWN!
OH HELL NO.

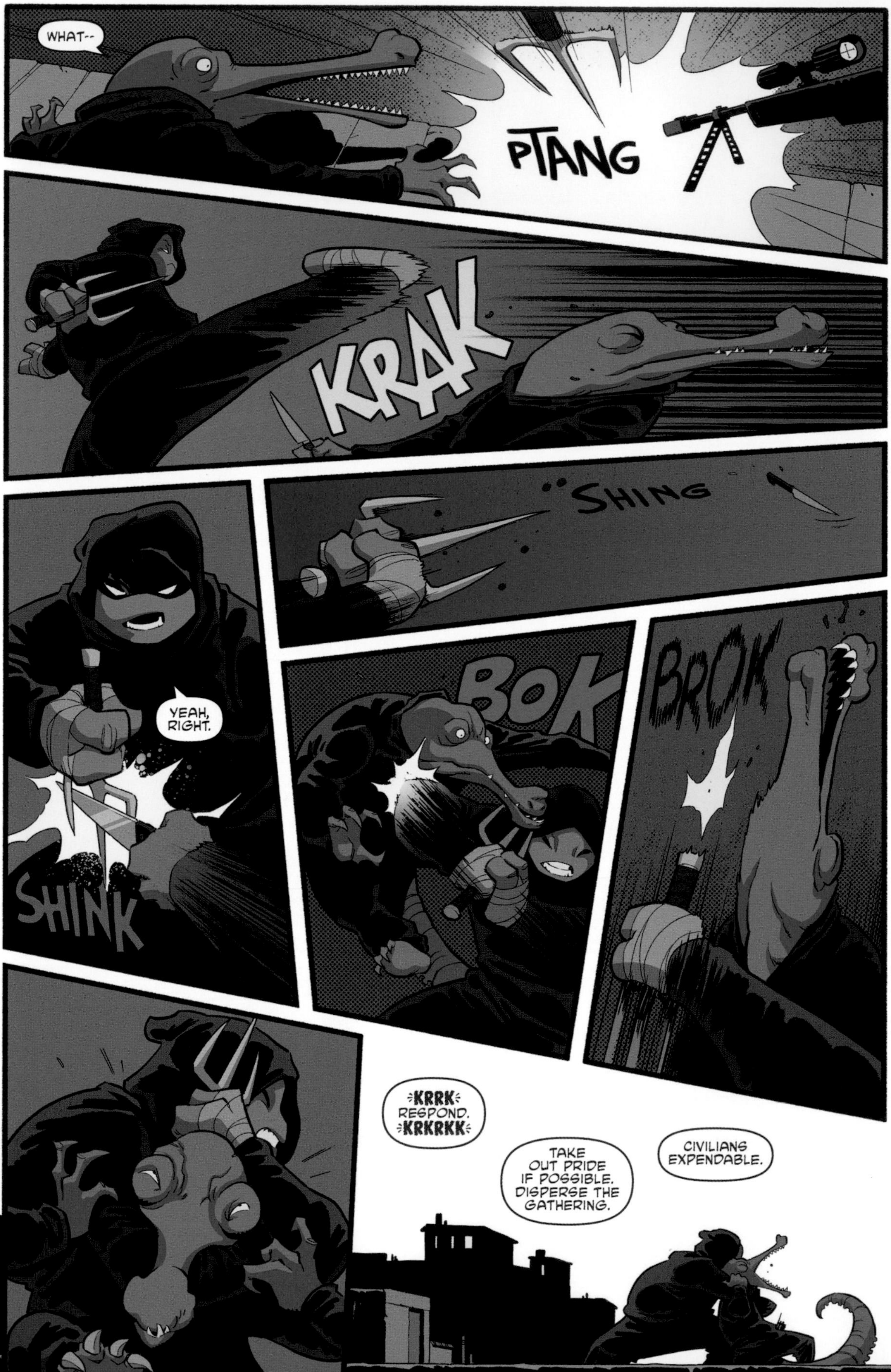
WHAT--
PTANG
KRAK
SHING
YEAH, RIGHT.
SHINK
BOK
BROK
KRRK RESPOND. KRKRKK
TAKE OUT PRIDE IF POSSIBLE. DISPERSE THE GATHERING.
CIVILIANS EXPENDABLE.

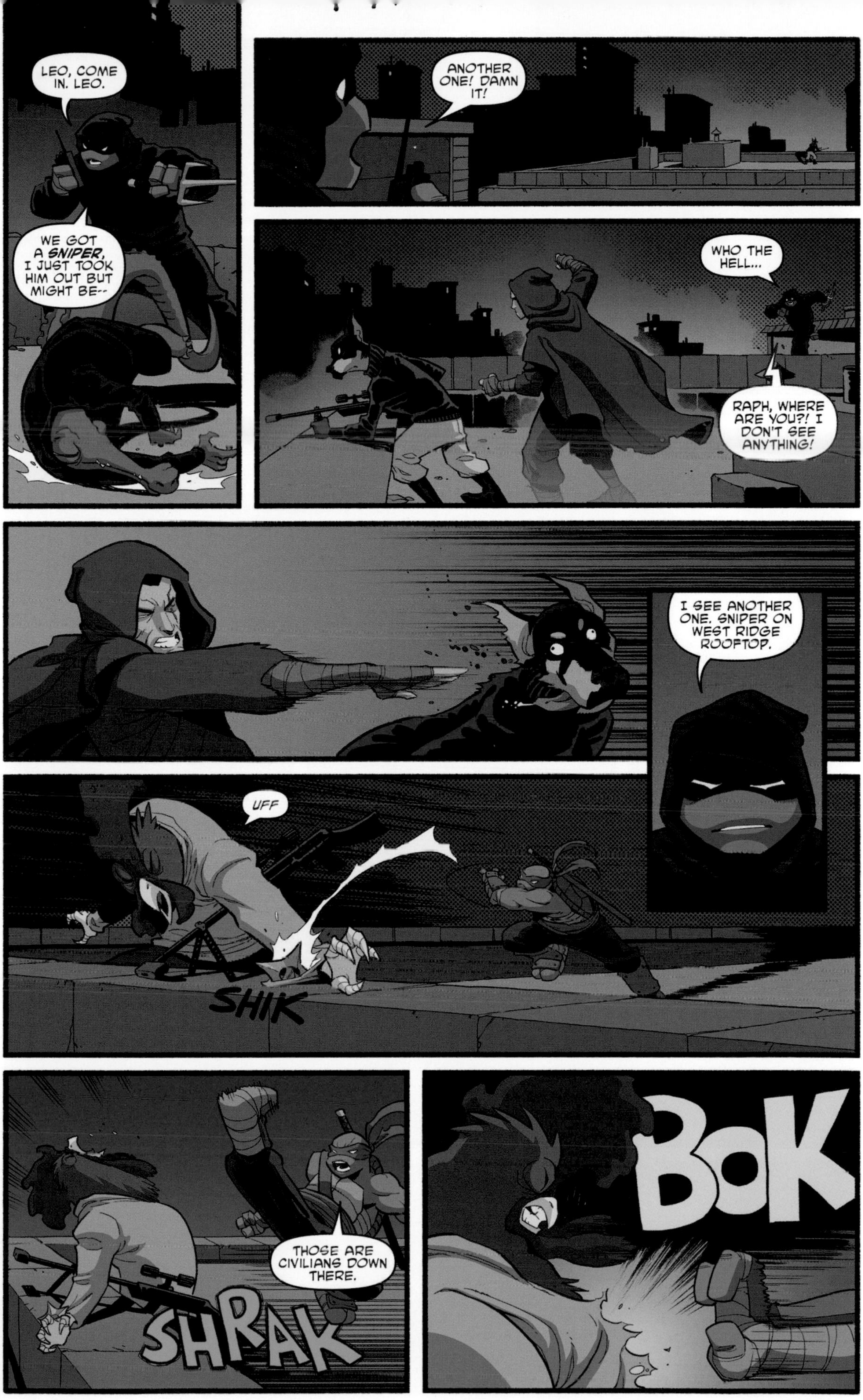
LEO, COME IN. LEO.
WE GOT A SNIPER, I JUST TOOK HIM OUT BUT MIGHT BE--
ANOTHER ONE! DAMN IT!
WHO THE HELL...
RAPH, WHERE ARE YOU?! I DON'T SEE ANYTHING!
I SEE ANOTHER ONE. SNIPER ON WEST RIDGE ROOFTOP.
UFF
SHIK
THOSE ARE CIVILIANS DOWN THERE.
SHRAK
BOK

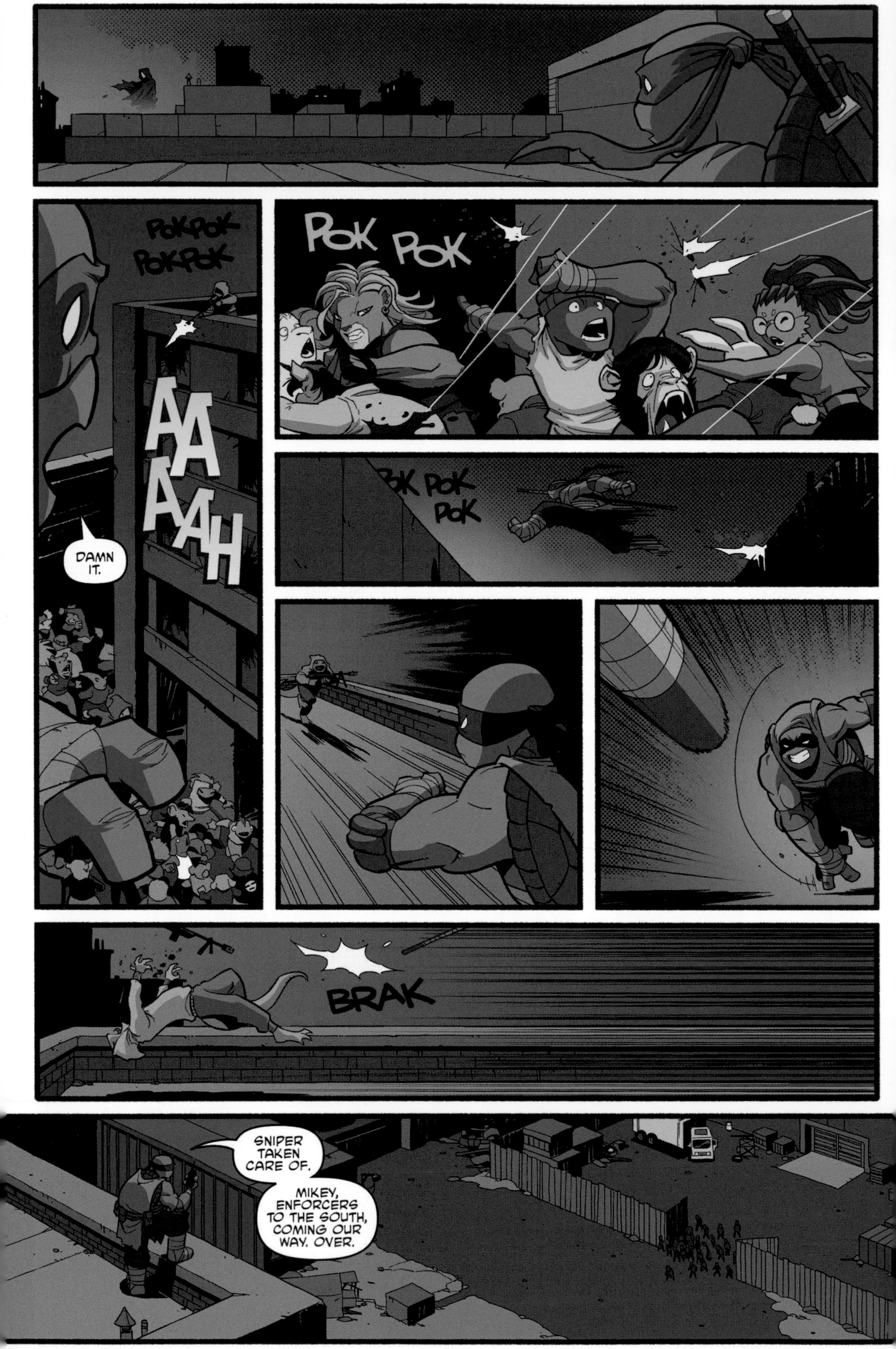
POKPOK
POKPOK
AAAAAH
DAMN IT.
POK POK
POK POK
POK
BRAK
SNIPER TAKEN CARE OF.
MIKEY, ENFORCERS TO THE SOUTH, COMING OUR WAY. OVER.

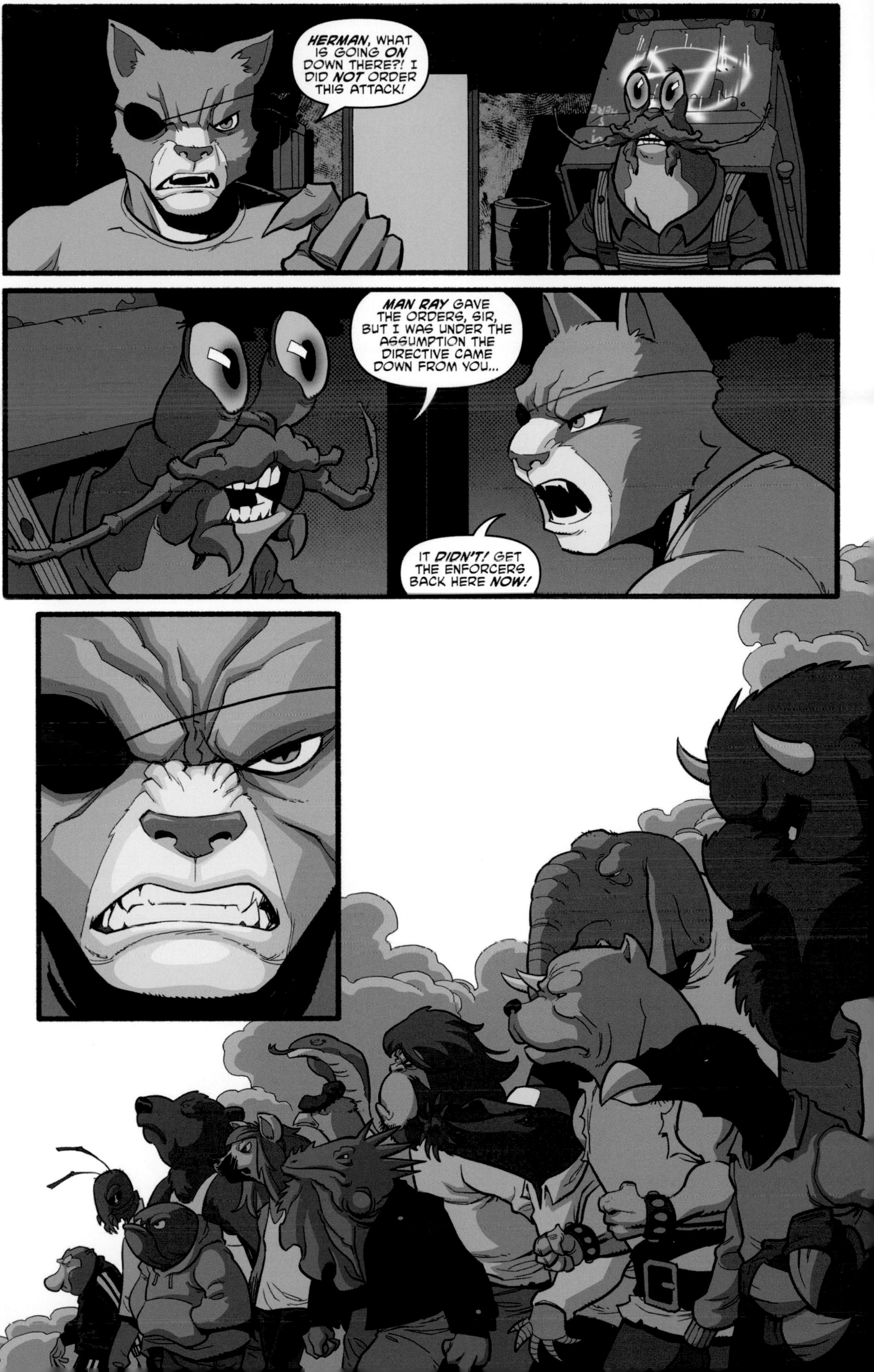
HERMAN, WHAT IS GOING ON DOWN THERE?! I DID NOT ORDER THIS ATTACK!
MAN RAY GAVE THE ORDERS, SIR, BUT I WAS UNDER THE ASSUMPTION THE DIRECTIVE CAME DOWN FROM YOU...
IT DIDN'T! GET THE ENFORCERS BACK HERE NOW!

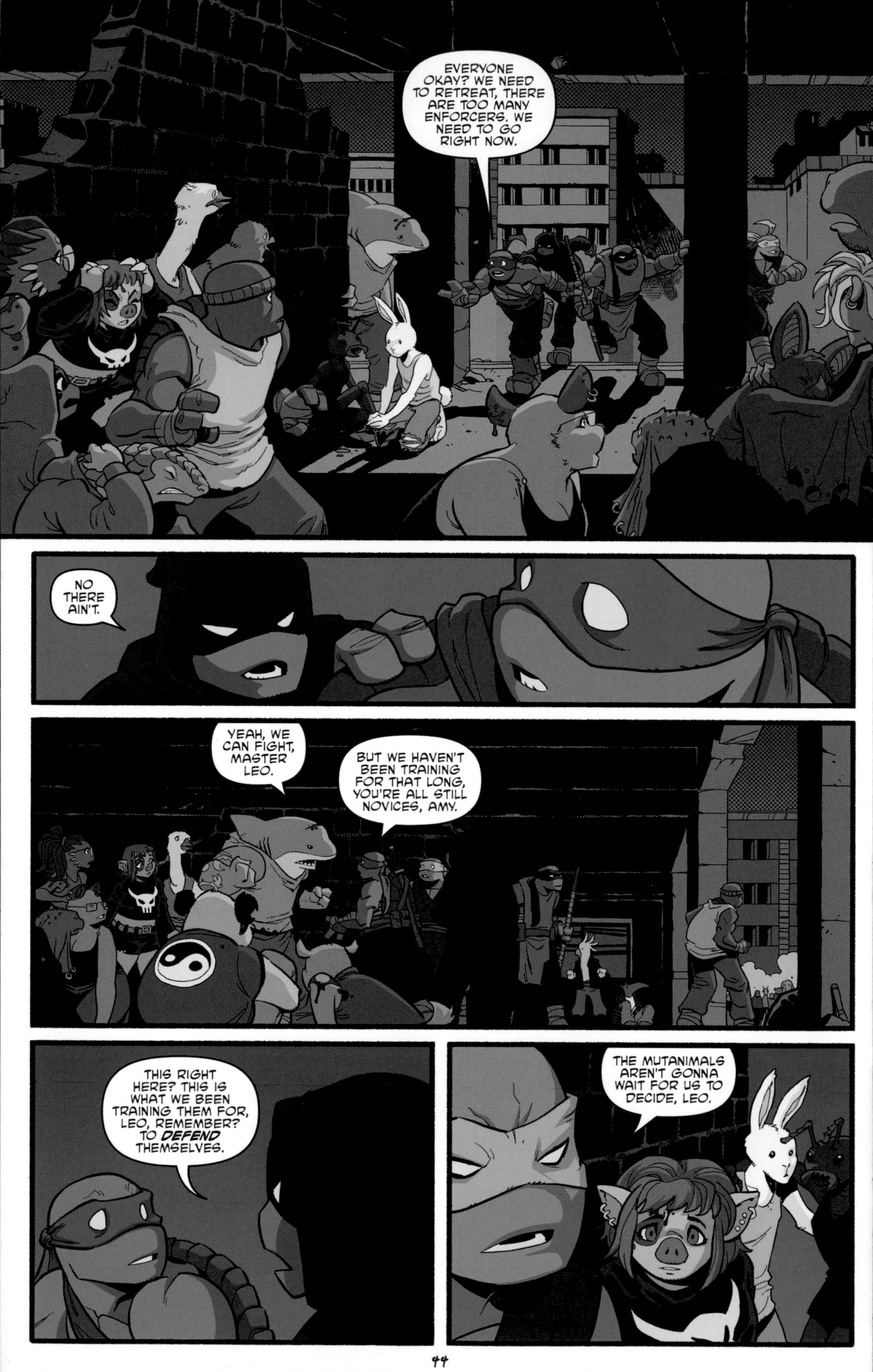
EVERYONE OKAY? WE NEED TO RETREAT, THERE ARE TOO MANY ENFORCERS. WE NEED TO GO RIGHT NOW.
NO THERE AIN'T.
YEAH, WE CAN FIGHT, MASTER LEO.
BUT WE HAVEN'T BEEN TRAINING FOR THAT LONG, YOU'RE ALL STILL NOVICES, AMY.
THIS RIGHT HERE? THIS IS WHAT WE BEEN TRAINING THEM FOR, LEO, REMEMBER? TO *DEFEND* THEMSELVES.
THE MUTANIMALS AREN'T GONNA WAIT FOR US TO DECIDE, LEO.

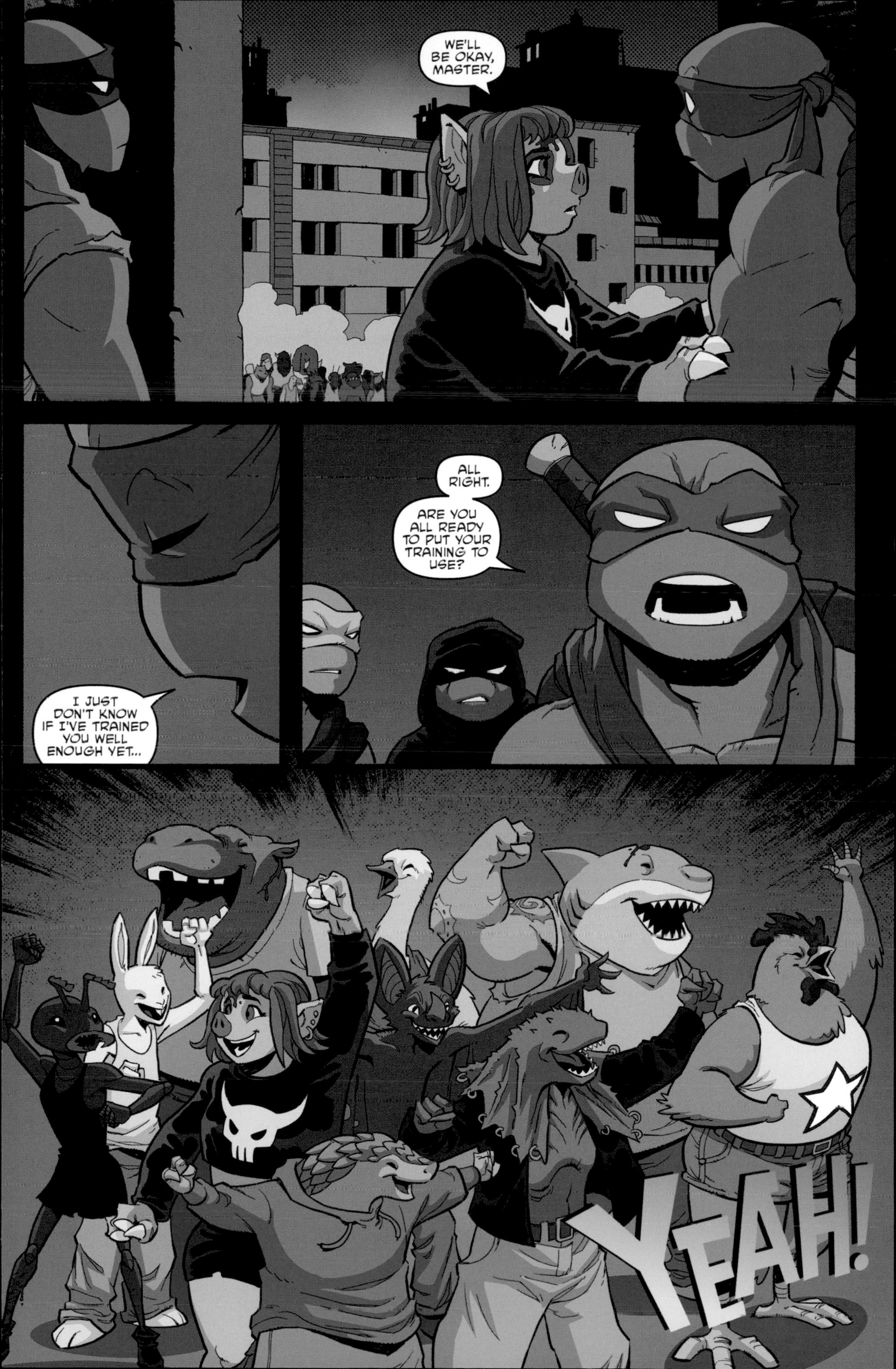
WE'LL BE OKAY, MASTER.
I JUST DON'T KNOW IF I'VE TRAINED YOU WELL ENOUGH YET...
ALL RIGHT.
ARE YOU ALL READY TO PUT YOUR TRAINING TO USE?
YEAH!

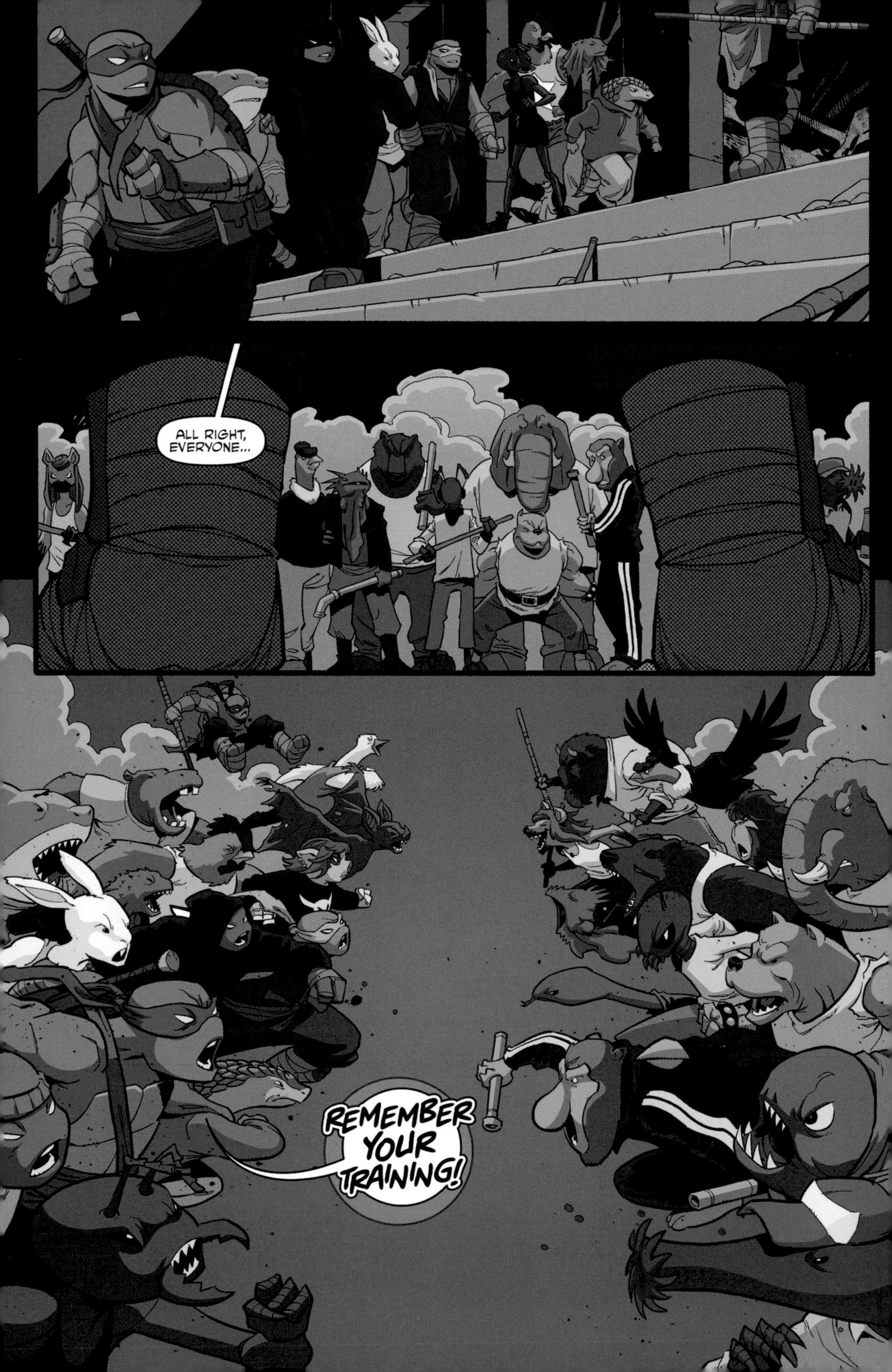
ALL RIGHT, EVERYONE...
REMEMBER YOUR TRAINING!

ART BY
KEVIN EASTMAN

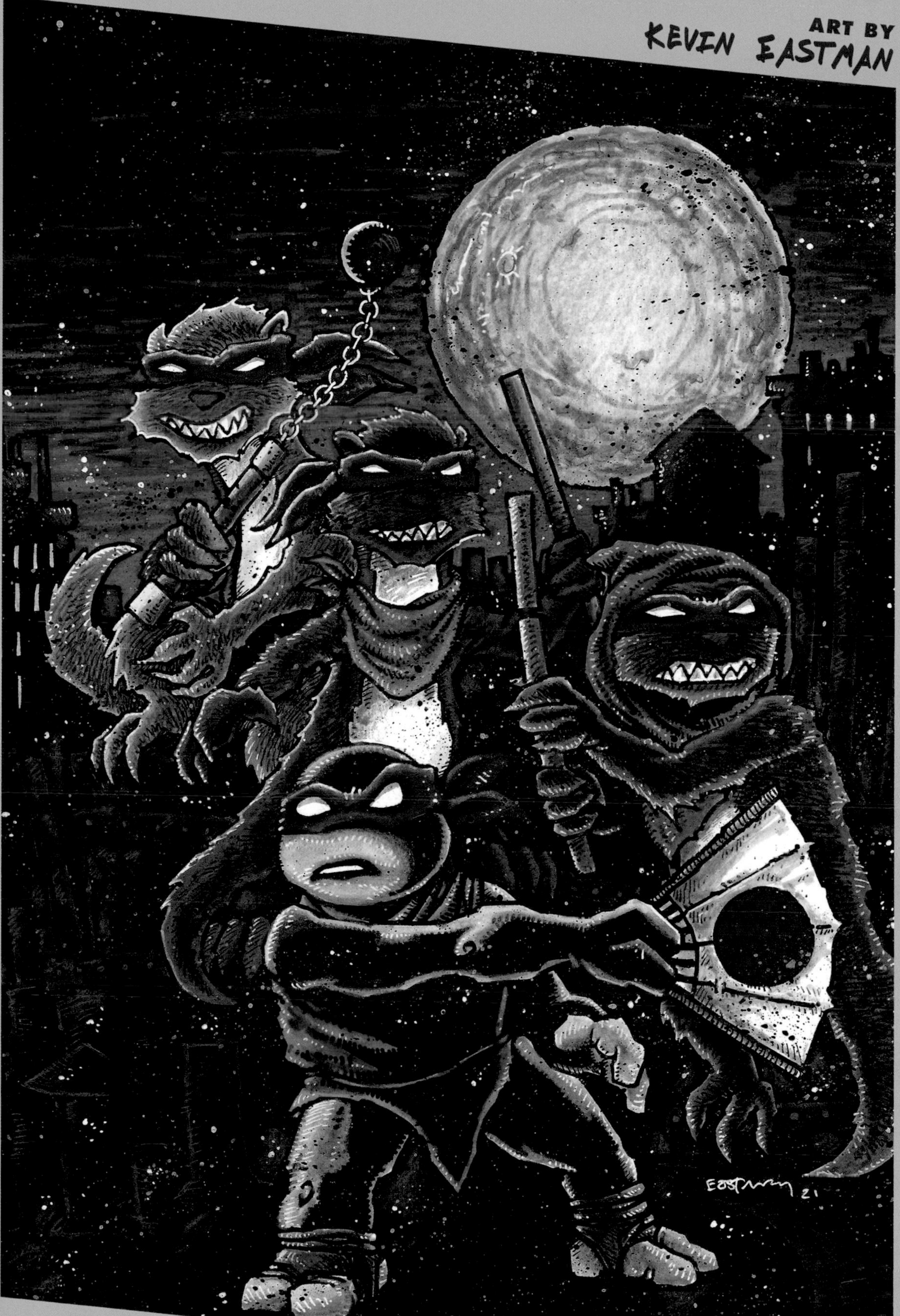
EASTMAN 21

COLORS BY
FAHRIZA KAMAPUTRA

ART BY
JODI NISHIJIMA

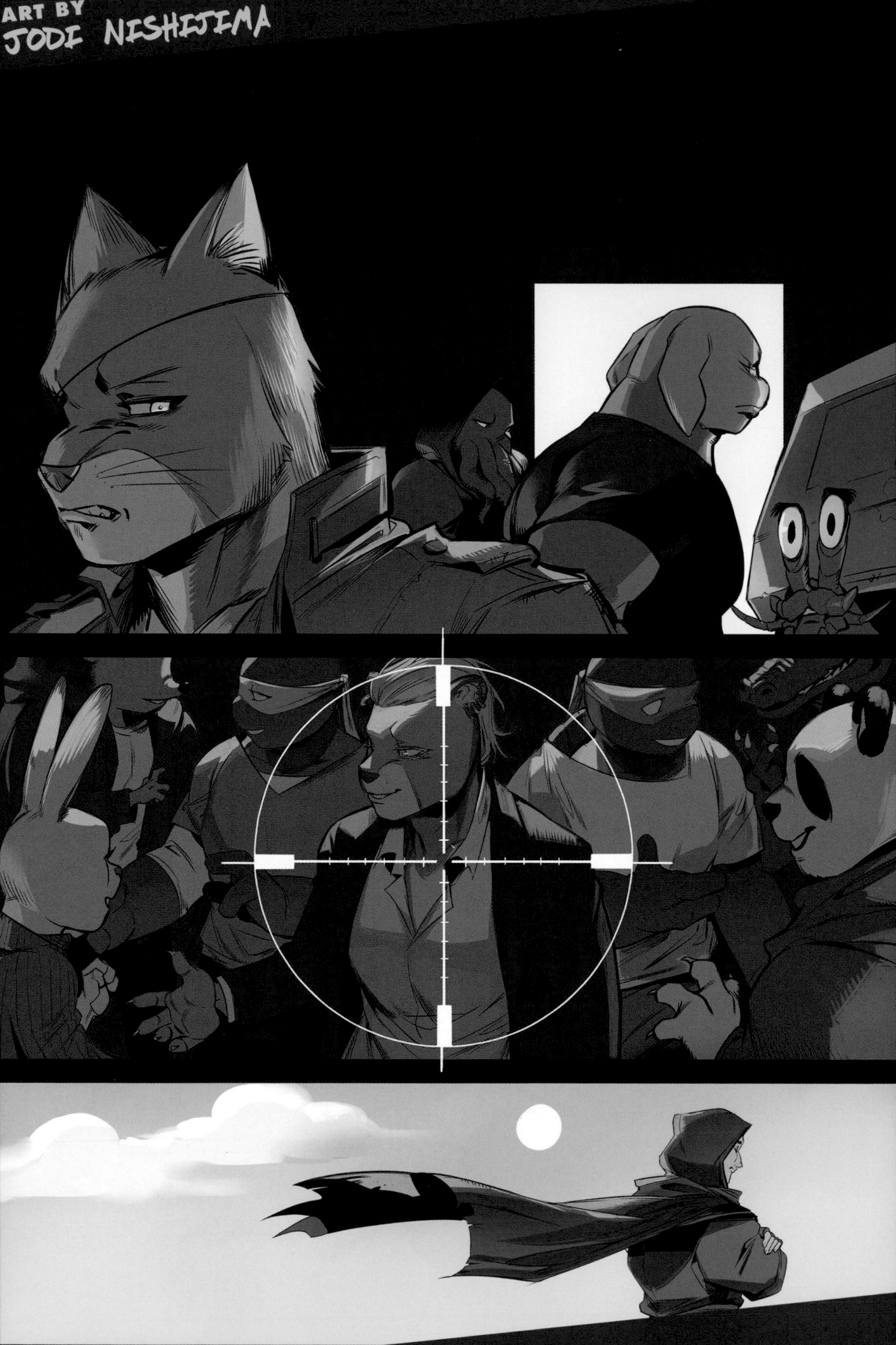

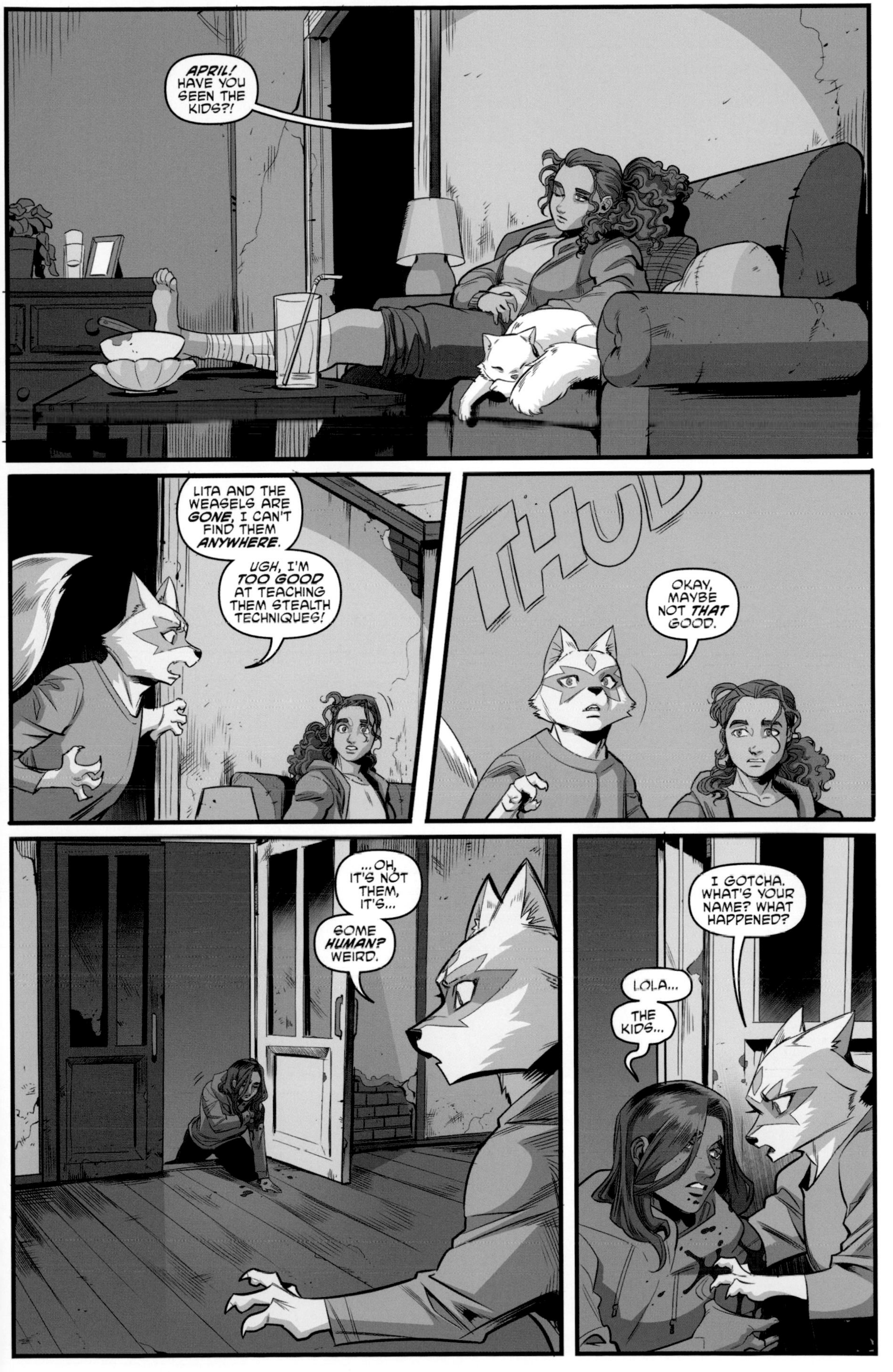
APRIL! HAVE YOU SEEN THE KIDS?!
LITA AND THE WEASELS ARE GONE, I CAN'T FIND THEM ANYWHERE.
UGH, I'M TOO GOOD AT TEACHING THEM STEALTH TECHNIQUES!
THUD
OKAY, MAYBE NOT THAT GOOD.
...OH, IT'S NOT THEM, IT'S...
SOME HUMAN? WEIRD.
I GOTCHA. WHAT'S YOUR NAME? WHAT HAPPENED?
LOLA...
THE KIDS...

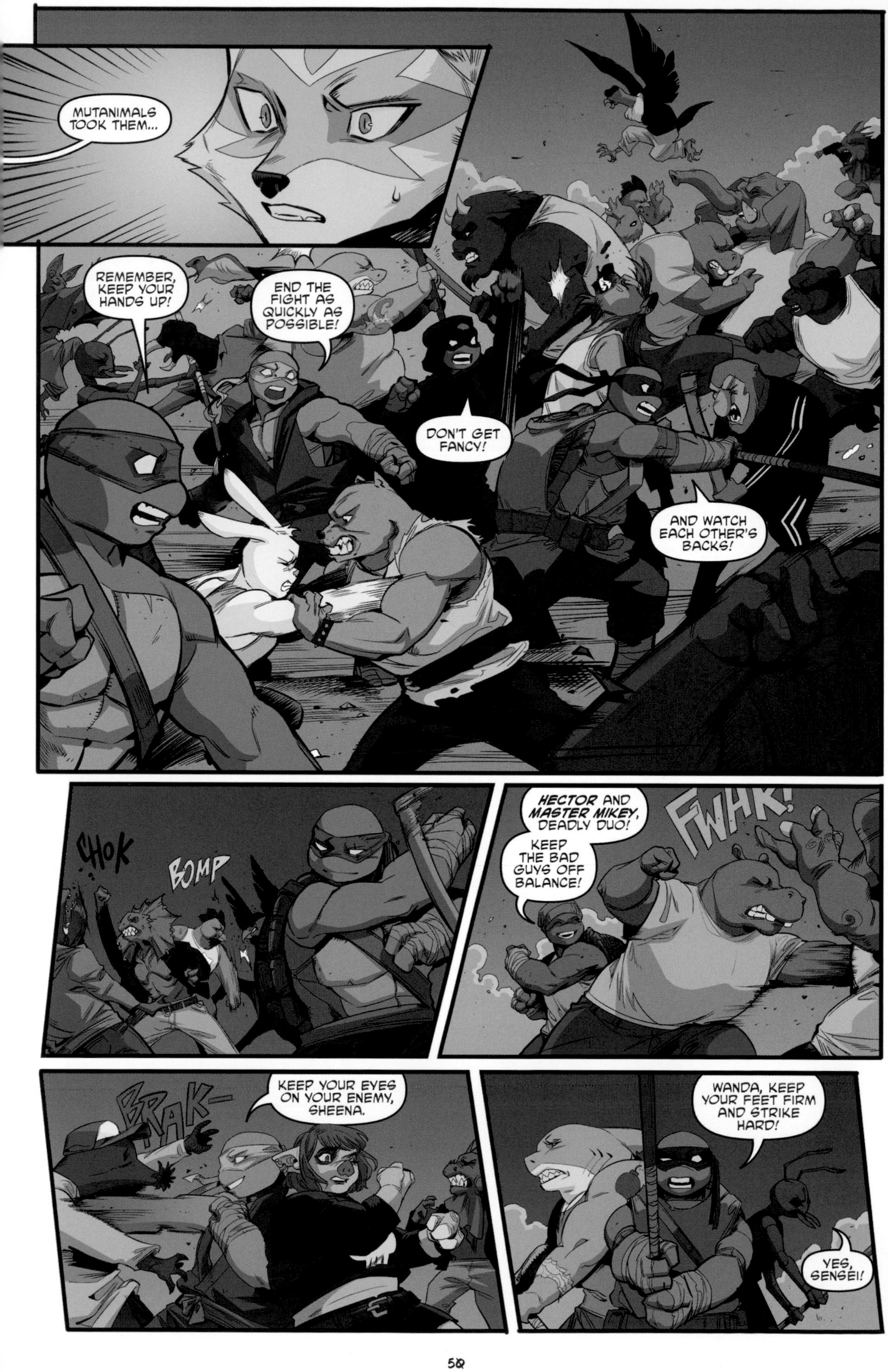

MUTANIMALS TOOK THEM...
REMEMBER, KEEP YOUR HANDS UP!
END THE FIGHT AS QUICKLY AS POSSIBLE!
DON'T GET FANCY!
AND WATCH EACH OTHER'S BACKS!
CHOK
BOMP
HECTOR AND MASTER MIKEY, DEADLY DUO!
KEEP THE BAD GUYS OFF BALANCE!
FWAK!
BRAK-
KEEP YOUR EYES ON YOUR ENEMY, SHEENA.
WANDA, KEEP YOUR FEET FIRM AND STRIKE HARD!
YES, SENSEI!

SMAK!

NICE ONE, IBRAHIM!

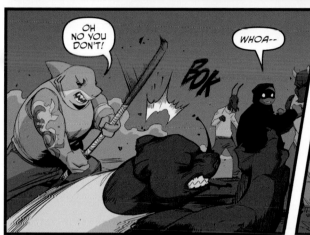

OH NO YOU DON'T!

WHOA--

BOK

BE AWARE OF YOUR SURROUNDINGS, SENSEI!

YEAH, YEAH. THANKS.

CHAK

KRAK!

THOK

HEY, YOUR STUDENTS AIN'T BAD.

THANKS, SALLY.

KRA

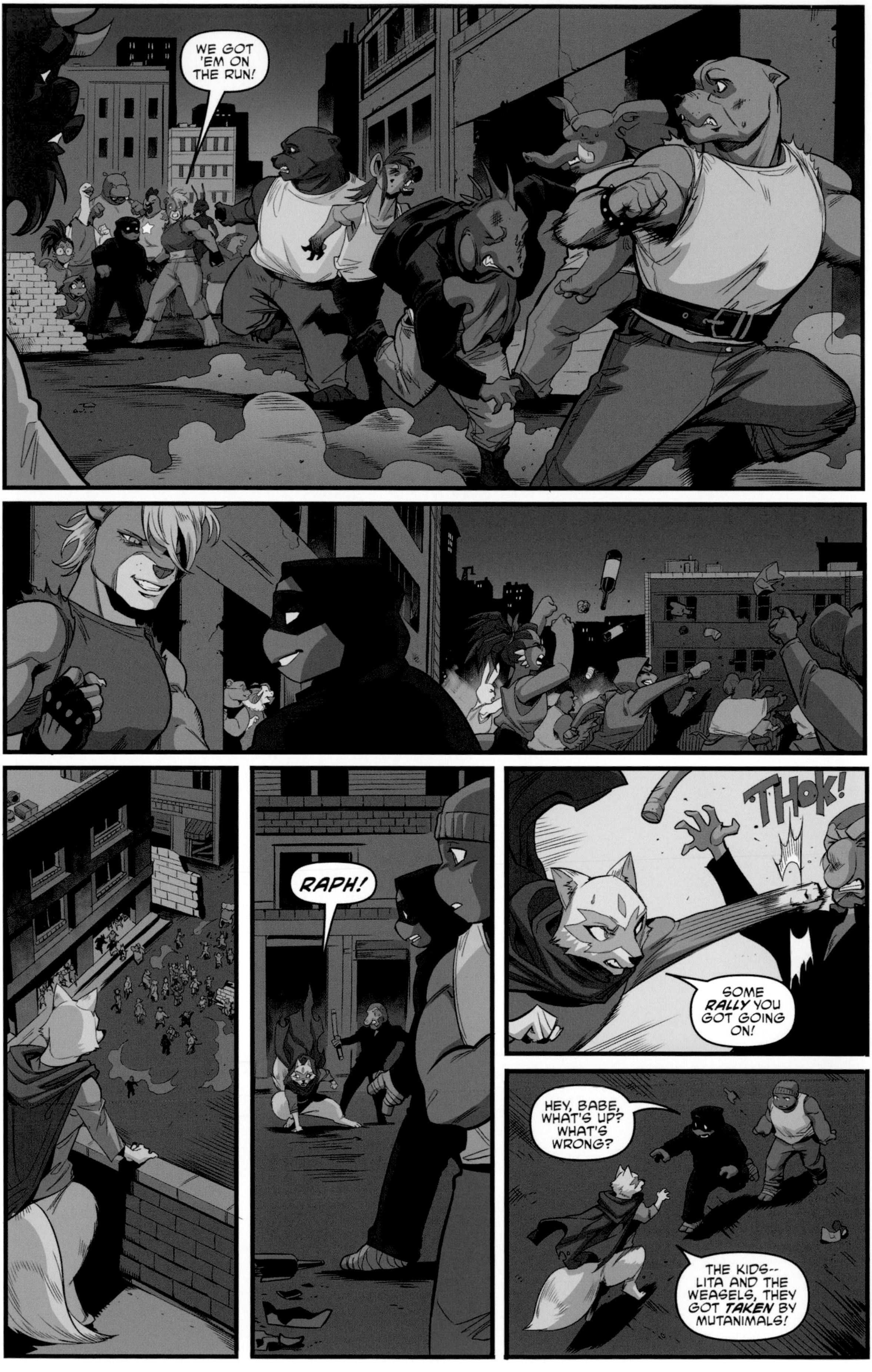
WE GOT 'EM ON THE RUN!
RAPH!
THOK!
SOME RALLY YOU GOT GOING ON!
HEY, BABE, WHAT'S UP? WHAT'S WRONG?
THE KIDS-- LITA AND THE WEASELS, THEY GOT TAKEN BY MUTANIMALS!

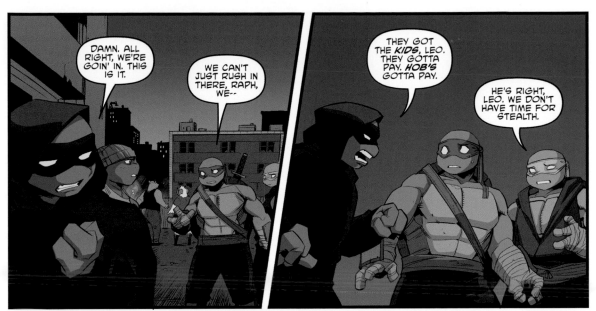

DAMN. ALL RIGHT, WE'RE GOIN' IN. THIS IS IT.

WE CAN'T JUST RUSH IN THERE, RAPH, WE--

THEY GOT THE *KIDS*, LEO. THEY GOTTA PAY. *HOB'S* GOTTA PAY.

HE'S RIGHT, LEO. WE DON'T HAVE TIME FOR STEALTH.

I KNOW.

ALL RIGHT, *LET'S MOVE!*

KRSS-

-SHH

53

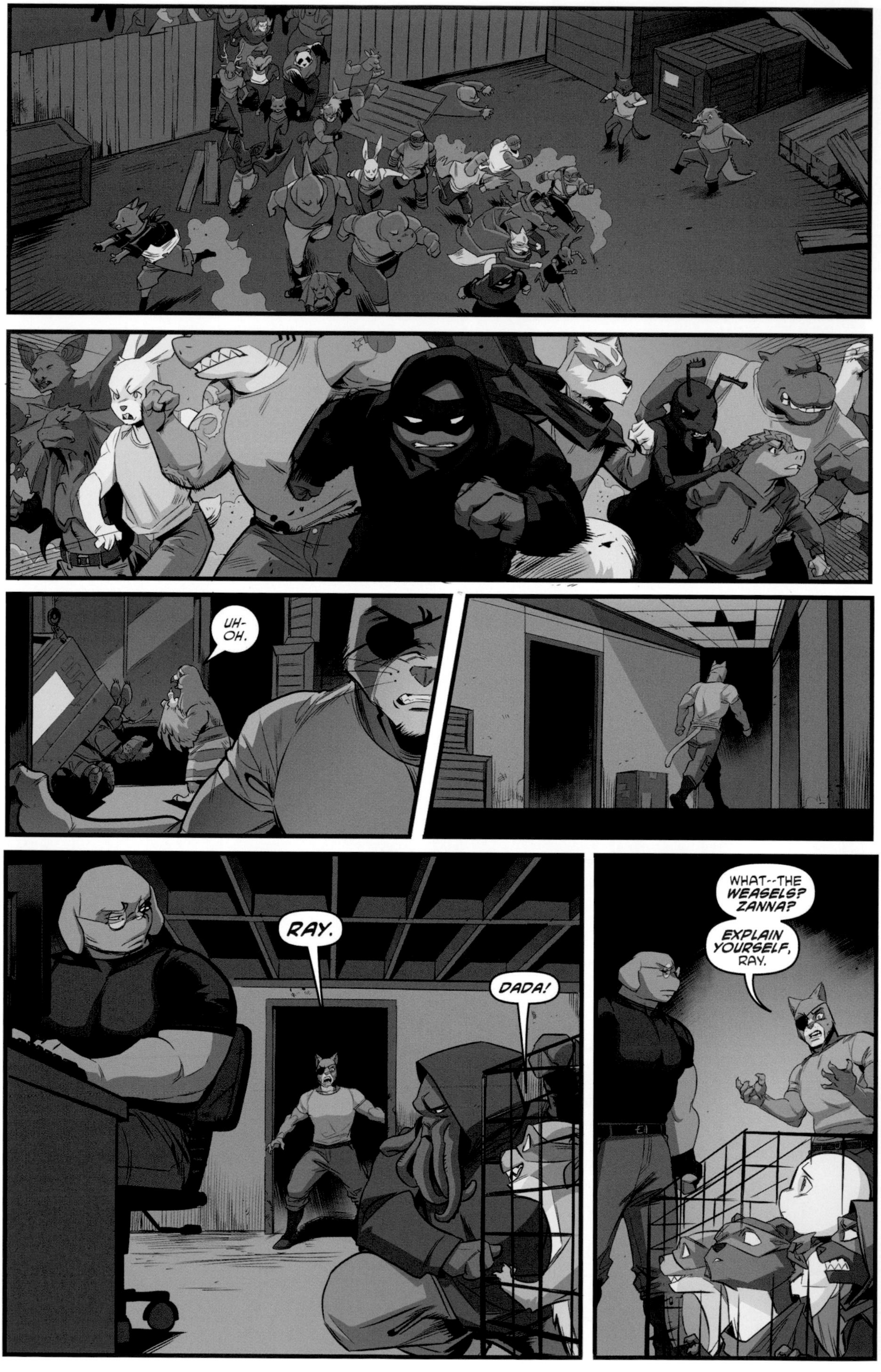
UH-OH.
RAY.
DADA!
WHAT--THE WEASELS? ZANNA?
EXPLAIN YOURSELF, RAY.

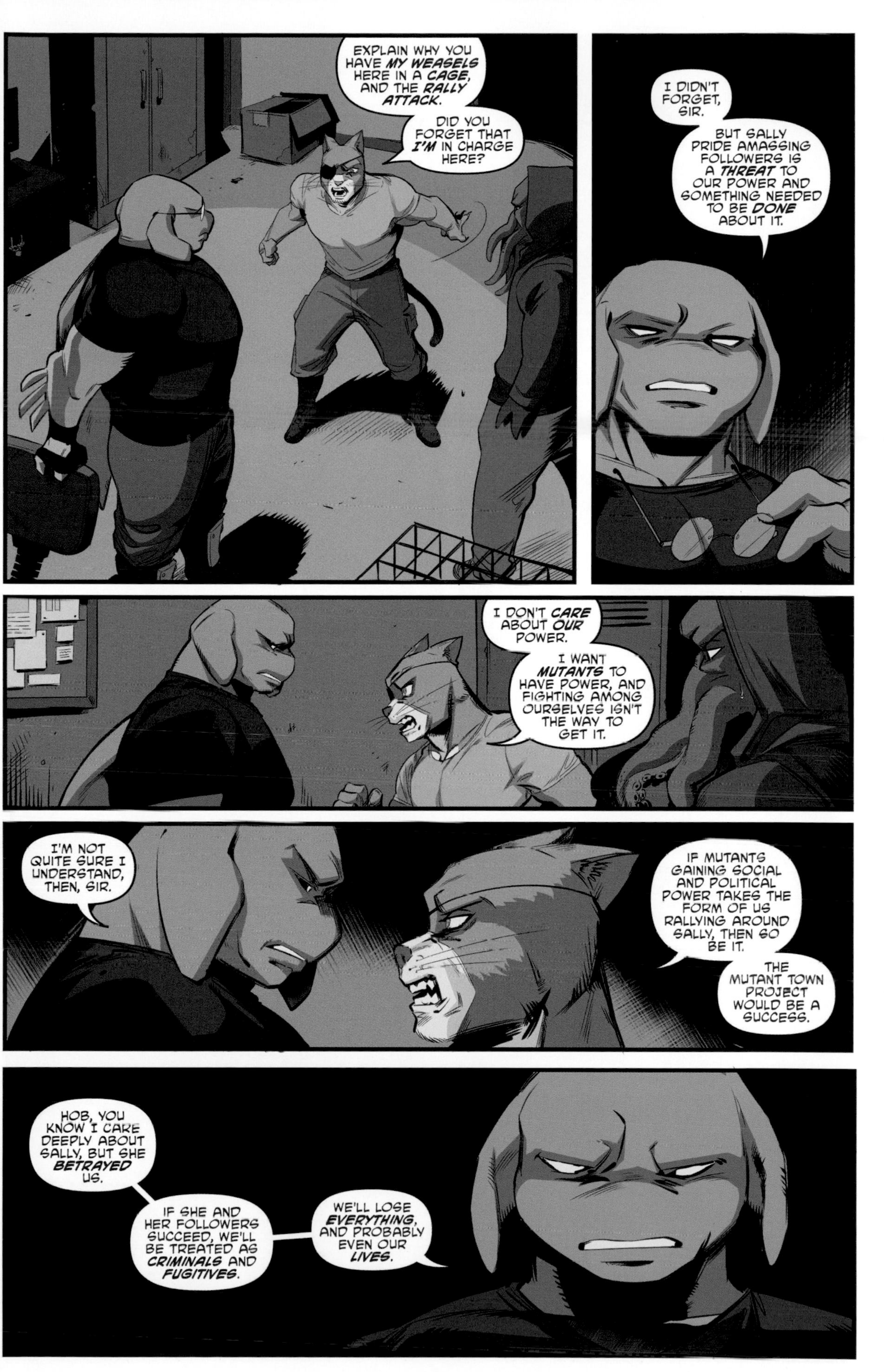
EXPLAIN WHY YOU HAVE MY WEASELS HERE IN A CAGE, AND THE RALLY ATTACK.
DID YOU FORGET THAT I'M IN CHARGE HERE?
I DIDN'T FORGET, SIR.
BUT SALLY PRIDE AMASSING FOLLOWERS IS A THREAT TO OUR POWER AND SOMETHING NEEDED TO BE DONE ABOUT IT.
I DON'T CARE ABOUT OUR POWER.
I WANT MUTANTS TO HAVE POWER, AND FIGHTING AMONG OURSELVES ISN'T THE WAY TO GET IT.
I'M NOT QUITE SURE I UNDERSTAND, THEN, SIR.
IF MUTANTS GAINING SOCIAL AND POLITICAL POWER TAKES THE FORM OF US RALLYING AROUND SALLY, THEN SO BE IT.
THE MUTANT TOWN PROJECT WOULD BE A SUCCESS.
HOB, YOU KNOW I CARE DEEPLY ABOUT SALLY, BUT SHE BETRAYED US.
IF SHE AND HER FOLLOWERS SUCCEED, WE'LL BE TREATED AS CRIMINALS AND FUGITIVES.
WE'LL LOSE EVERYTHING, AND PROBABLY EVEN OUR LIVES.

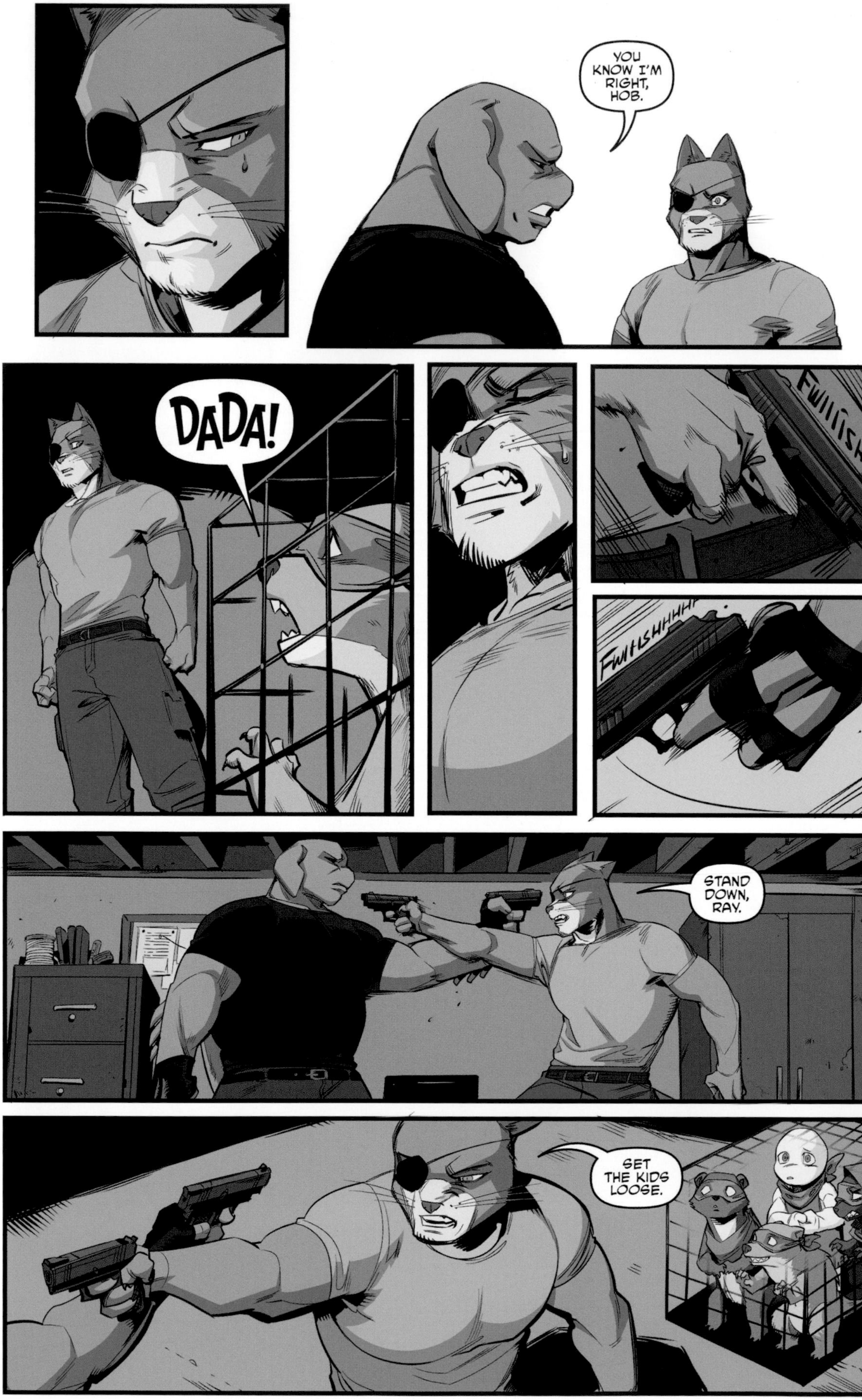
YOU KNOW I'M RIGHT, HOB.
DADA!
FWIIIISHH
FWIIISHHHH
STAND DOWN, RAY.
SET THE KIDS LOOSE.

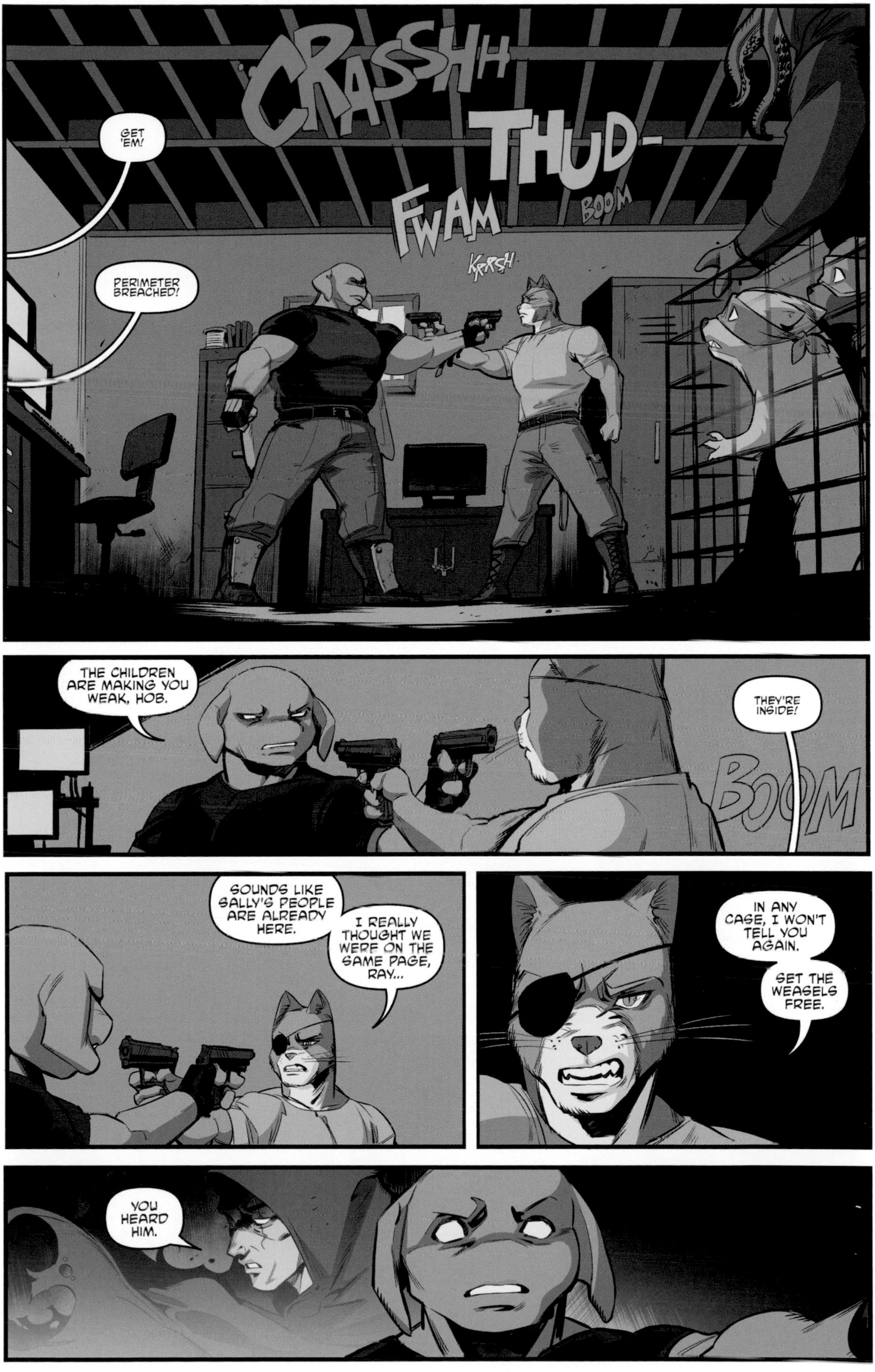
CRASSHH
GET 'EM!
THUD-
FWAM
BOOM
KRRSH
PERIMETER BREACHED!
THE CHILDREN ARE MAKING YOU WEAK, HOB.
THEY'RE INSIDE!
BOOM
SOUNDS LIKE SALLY'S PEOPLE ARE ALREADY HERE.
I REALLY THOUGHT WE WERE ON THE SAME PAGE, RAY...
IN ANY CASE, I WON'T TELL YOU AGAIN.
SET THE WEASELS FREE.
YOU HEARD HIM.

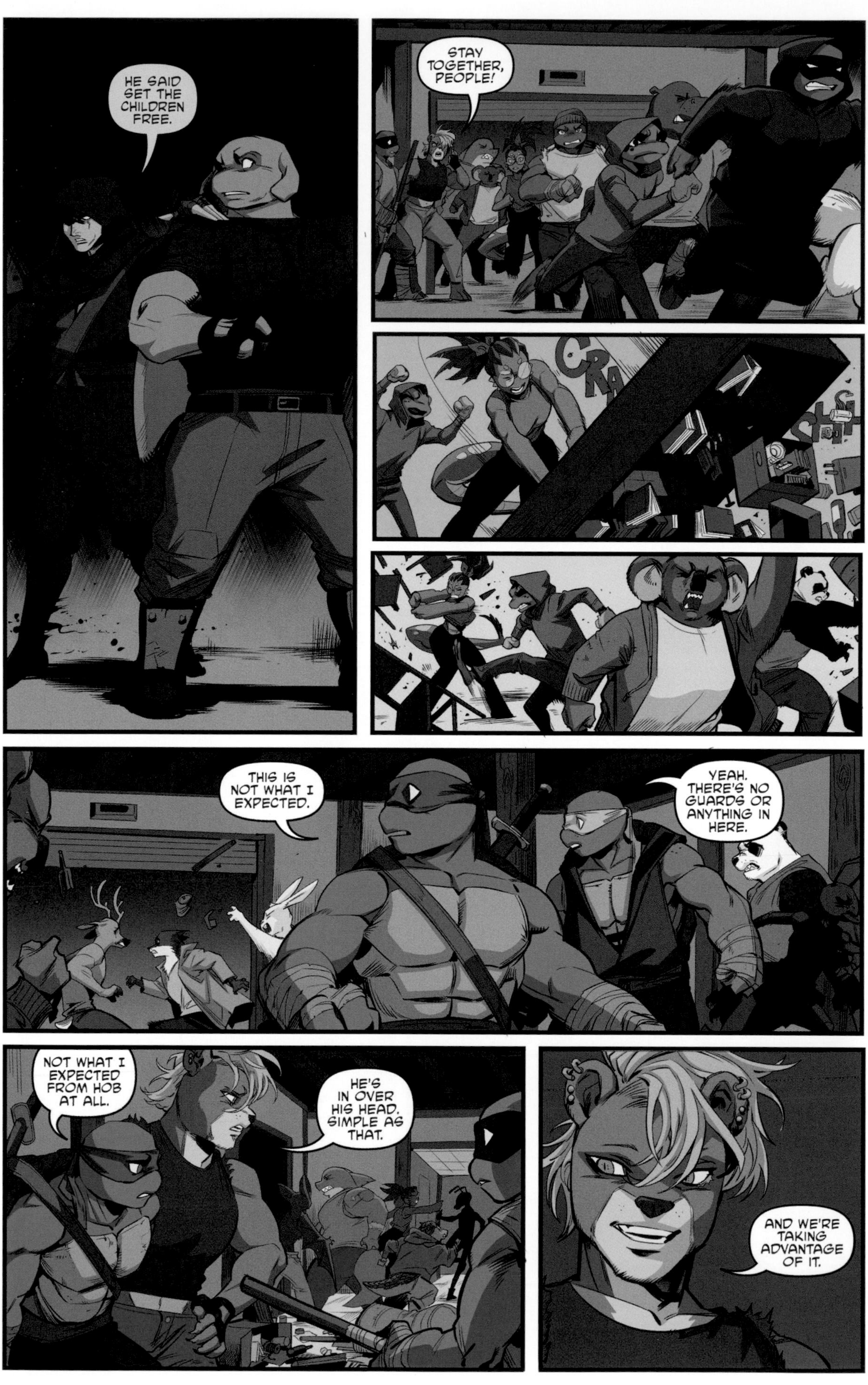
HE SAID SET THE CHILDREN FREE.
STAY TOGETHER, PEOPLE!
CRA
SH
THIS IS NOT WHAT I EXPECTED.
YEAH. THERE'S NO GUARDS OR ANYTHING IN HERE.
NOT WHAT I EXPECTED FROM HOB AT ALL.
HE'S IN OVER HIS HEAD. SIMPLE AS THAT.
AND WE'RE TAKING ADVANTAGE OF IT.

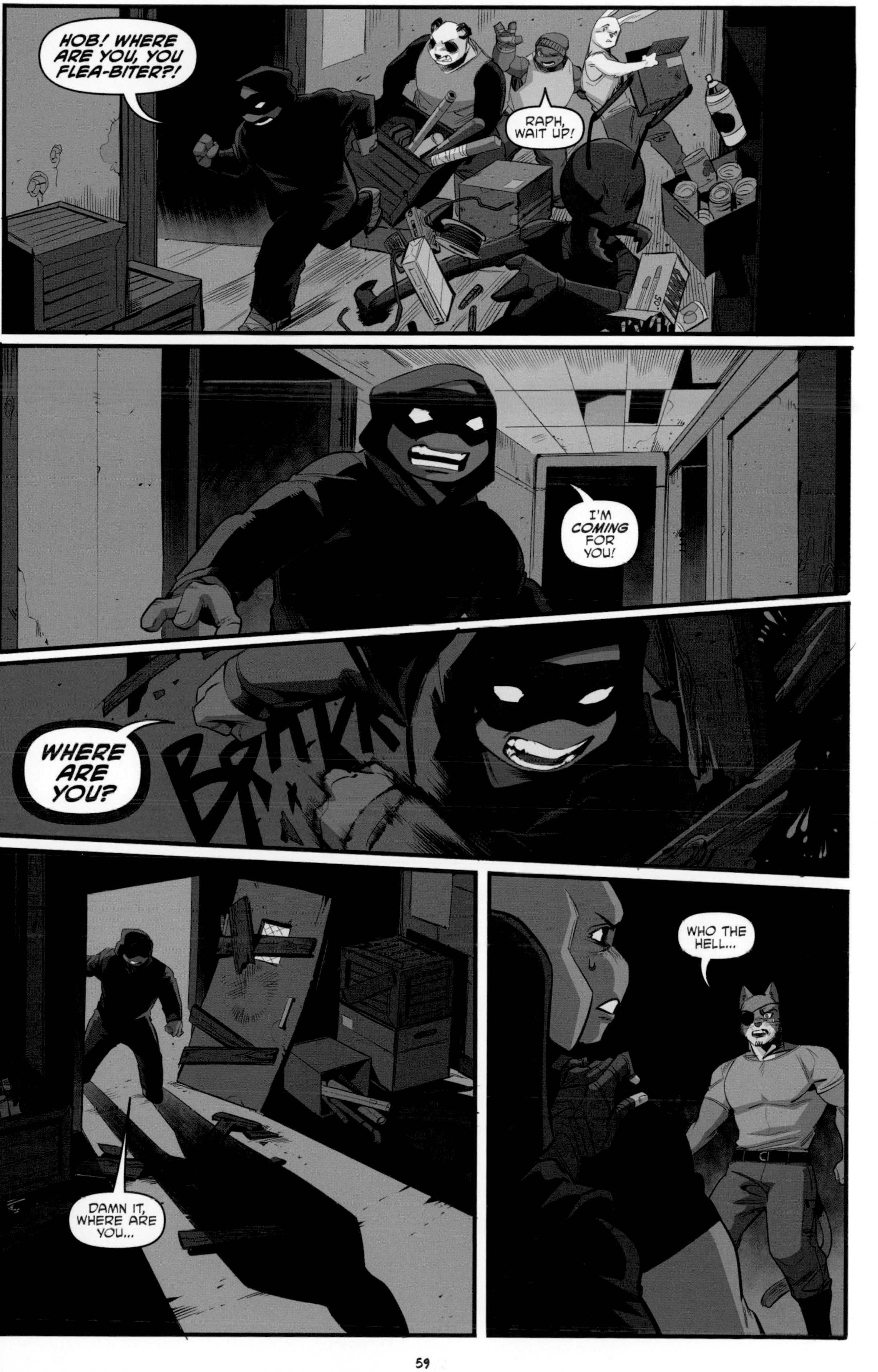
HOB! WHERE ARE YOU, YOU FLEA-BITER?!
RAPH, WAIT UP!
I'M COMING FOR YOU!
WHERE ARE YOU?
DAMN IT, WHERE ARE YOU...
WHO THE HELL...

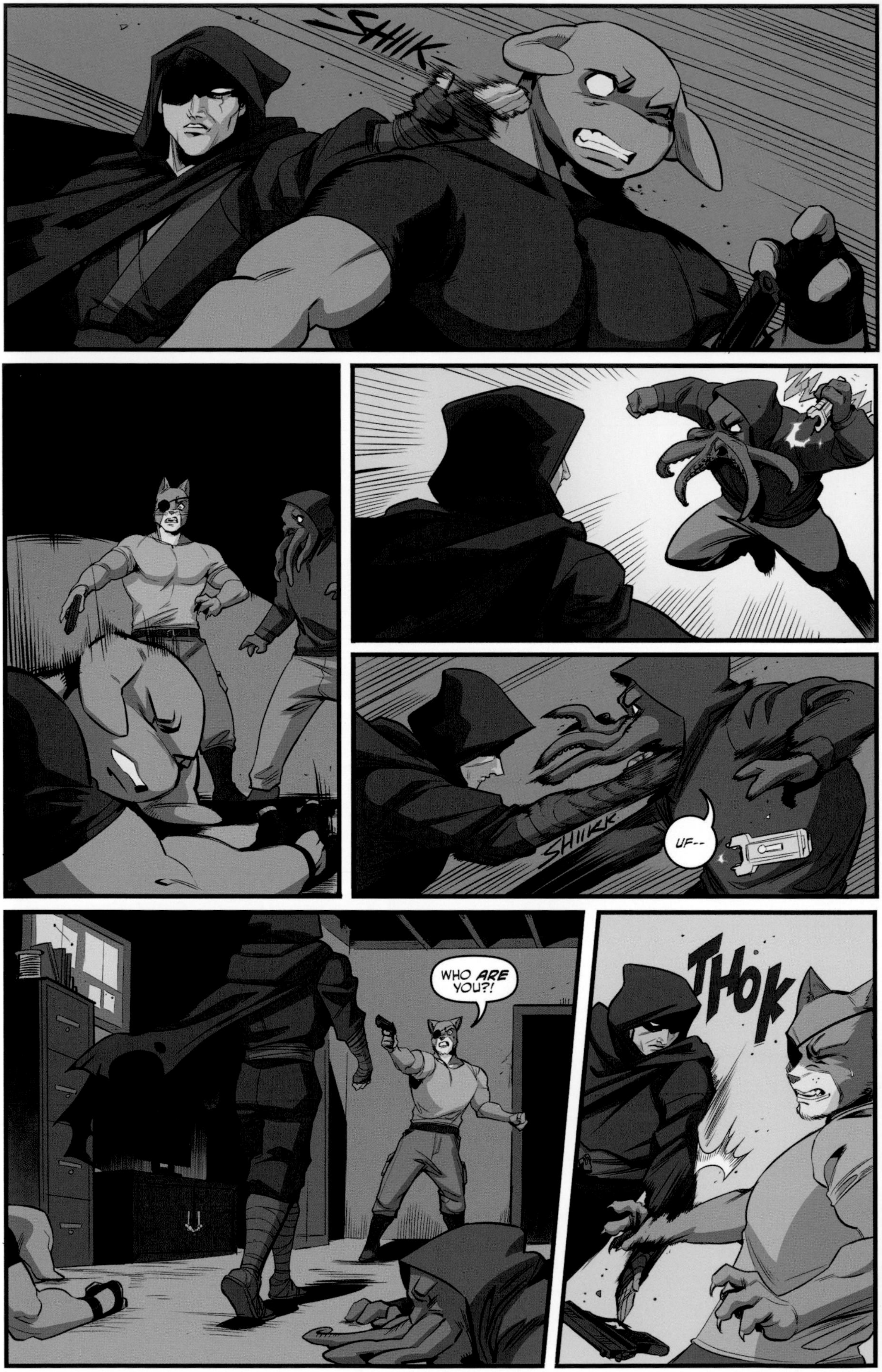
SHIIK
UF--
SHIIRK
WHO ARE YOU?!
THOK

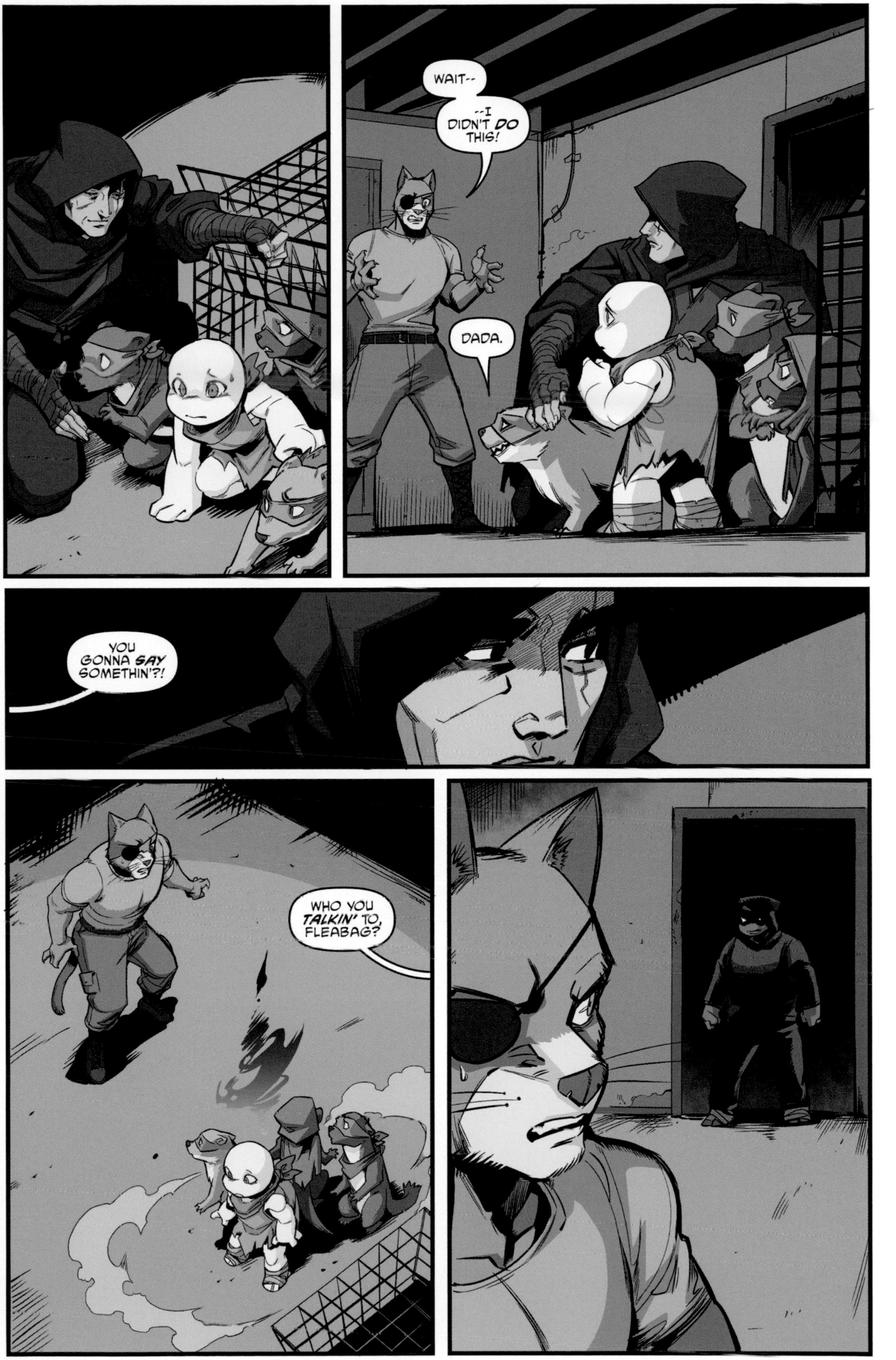
WAIT--
--I DIDN'T DO THIS!
DADA.
YOU GONNA SAY SOMETHIN'?!
WHO YOU TALKIN' TO, FLEABAG?

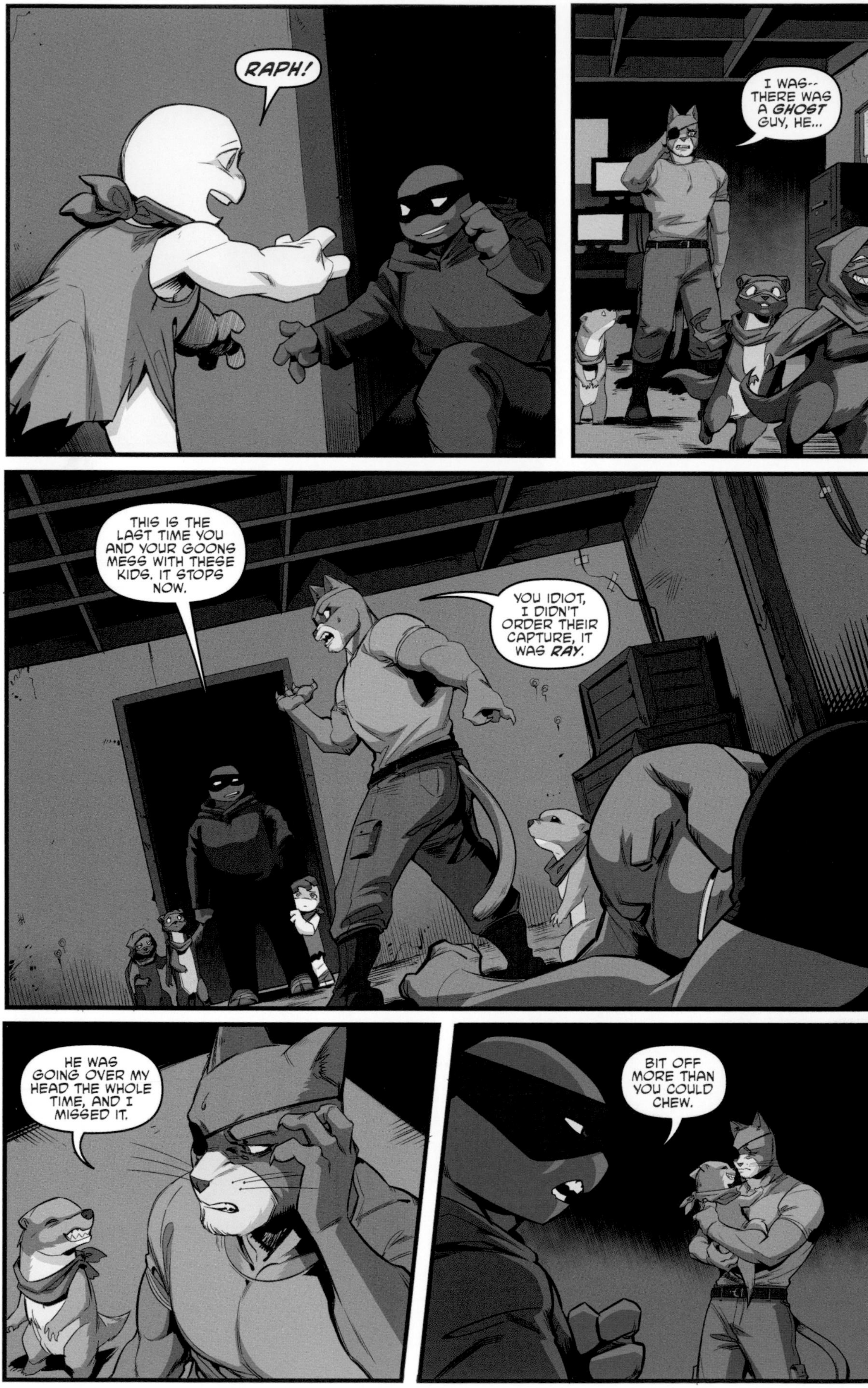
RAPH!
I WAS-- THERE WAS A GHOST GUY, HE...
THIS IS THE LAST TIME YOU AND YOUR GOONS MESS WITH THESE KIDS. IT STOPS NOW.
YOU IDIOT, I DIDN'T ORDER THEIR CAPTURE, IT WAS RAY.
HE WAS GOING OVER MY HEAD THE WHOLE TIME, AND I MISSED IT.
BIT OFF MORE THAN YOU COULD CHEW.

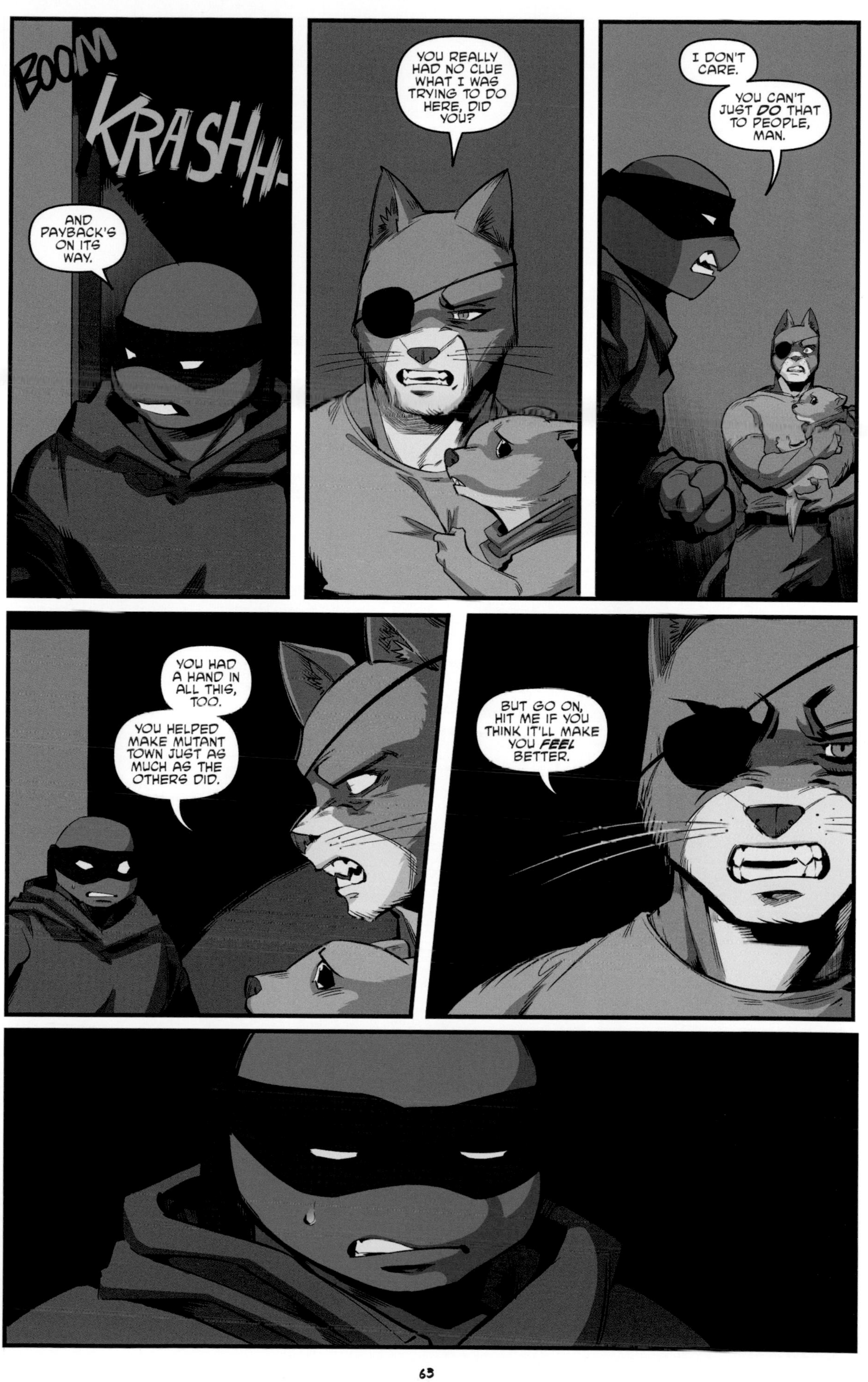
BOOM
KRASHH-
AND PAYBACK'S ON ITS WAY.
YOU REALLY HAD NO CLUE WHAT I WAS TRYING TO DO HERE, DID YOU?
I DON'T CARE.
YOU CAN'T JUST DO THAT TO PEOPLE, MAN.
YOU HAD A HAND IN ALL THIS, TOO.
YOU HELPED MAKE MUTANT TOWN JUST AS MUCH AS THE OTHERS DID.
BUT GO ON, HIT ME IF YOU THINK IT'LL MAKE YOU FEEL BETTER.

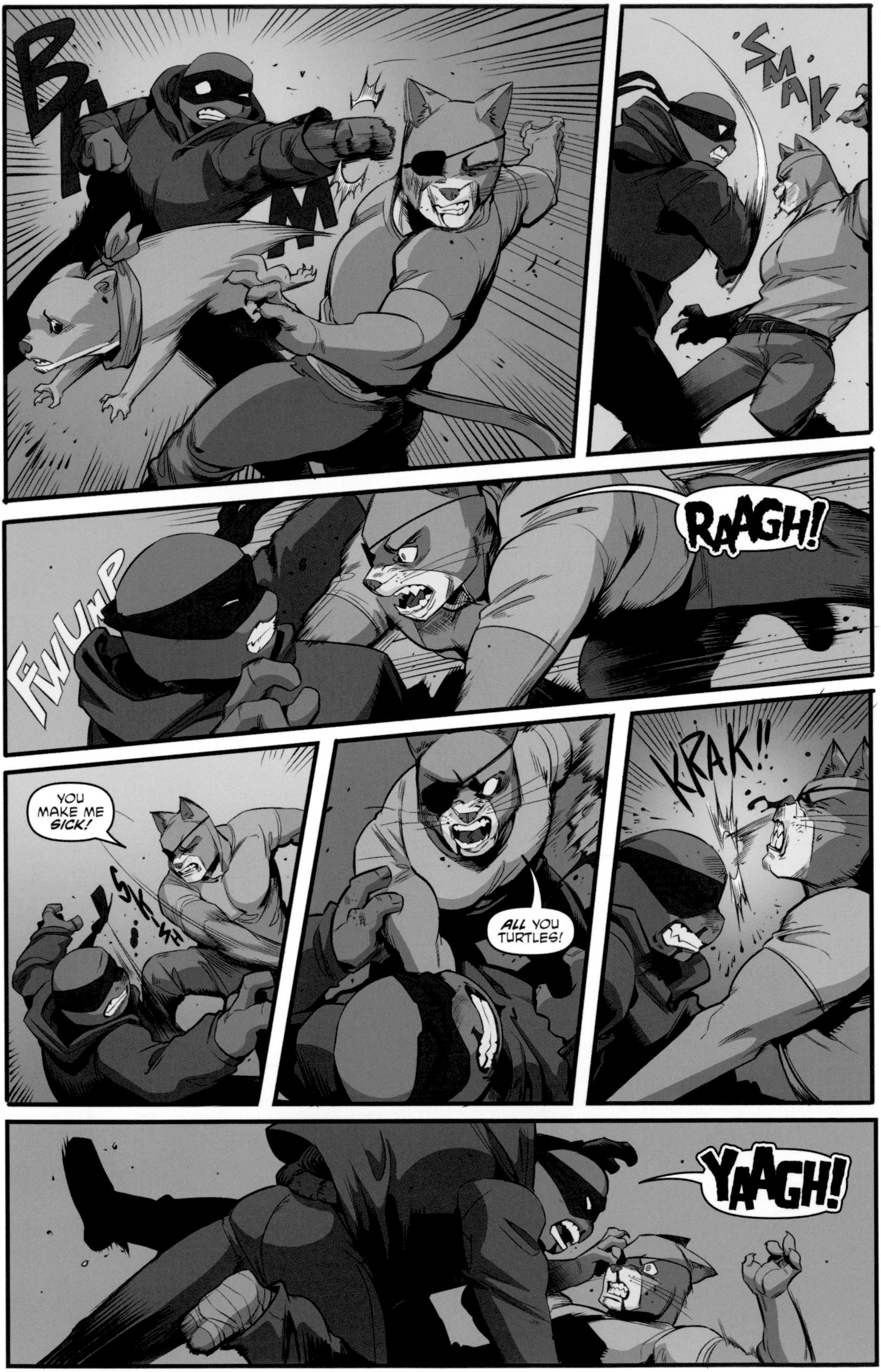
BAMM
SMAK
FWUMP
RAAGH!
YOU MAKE ME SICK!
SK-SH
ALL YOU TURTLES!
KRAK!!
YAAGH!

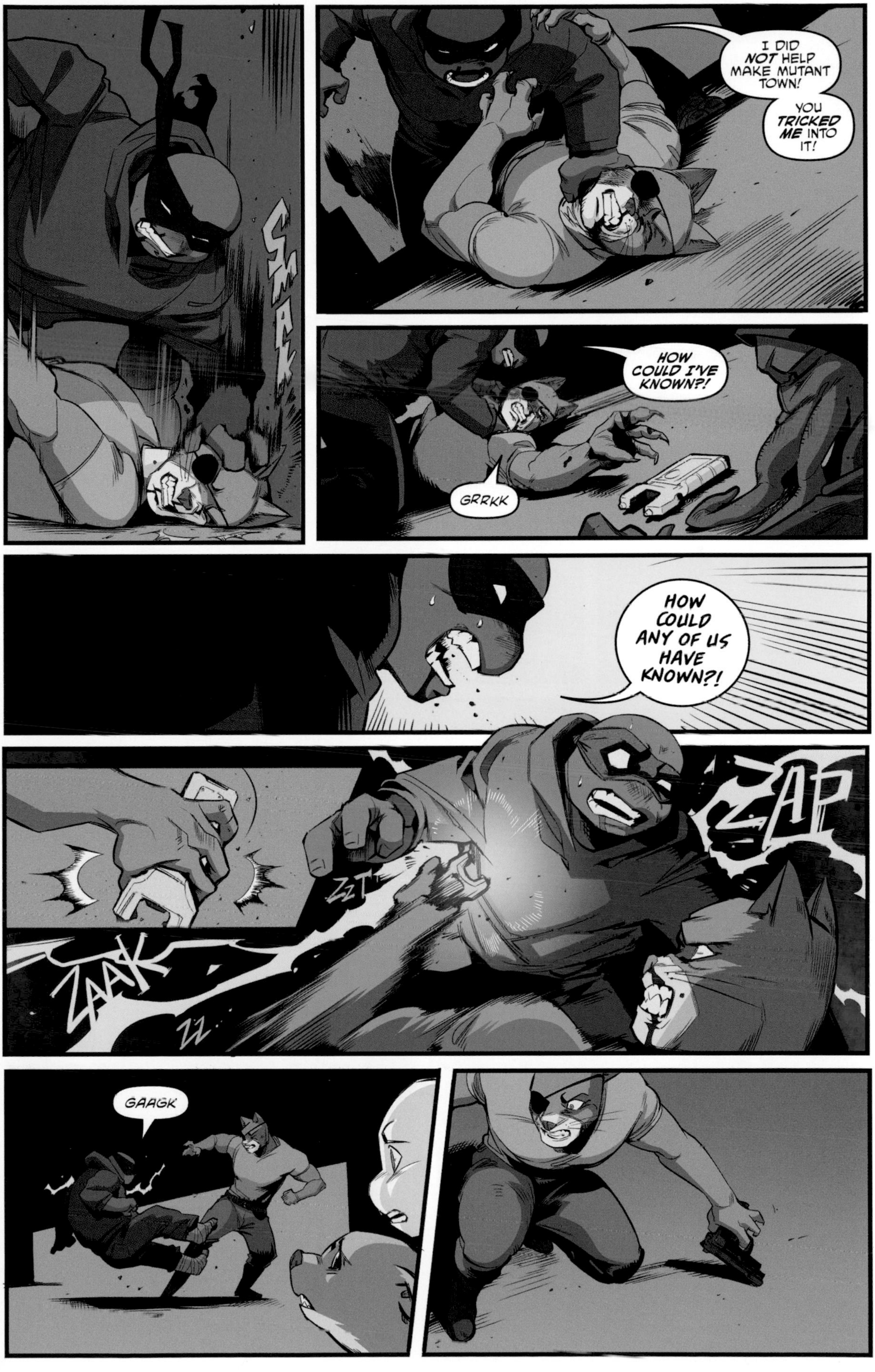
SMAK
I DID NOT HELP MAKE MUTANT TOWN!
YOU TRICKED ME INTO IT!
HOW COULD I'VE KNOWN?!
GRRKK
HOW COULD ANY OF US HAVE KNOWN?!
ZAP
ZZT
ZAAK
ZZ...
GAAGK

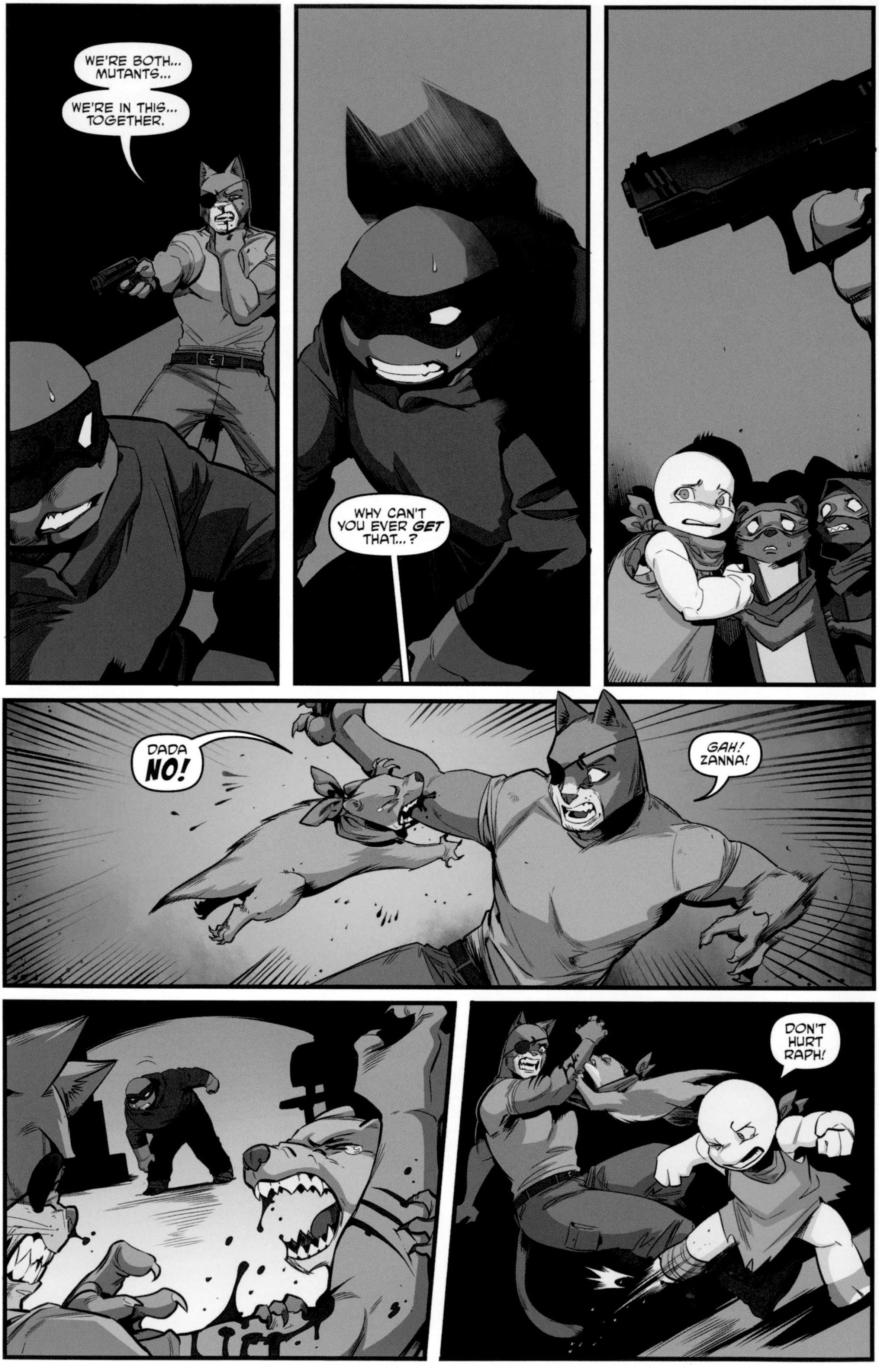
WE'RE BOTH... MUTANTS...
WE'RE IN THIS... TOGETHER.
WHY CAN'T YOU EVER GET THAT...?
DADA NO!
GAH! ZANNA!
DON'T HURT RAPH!

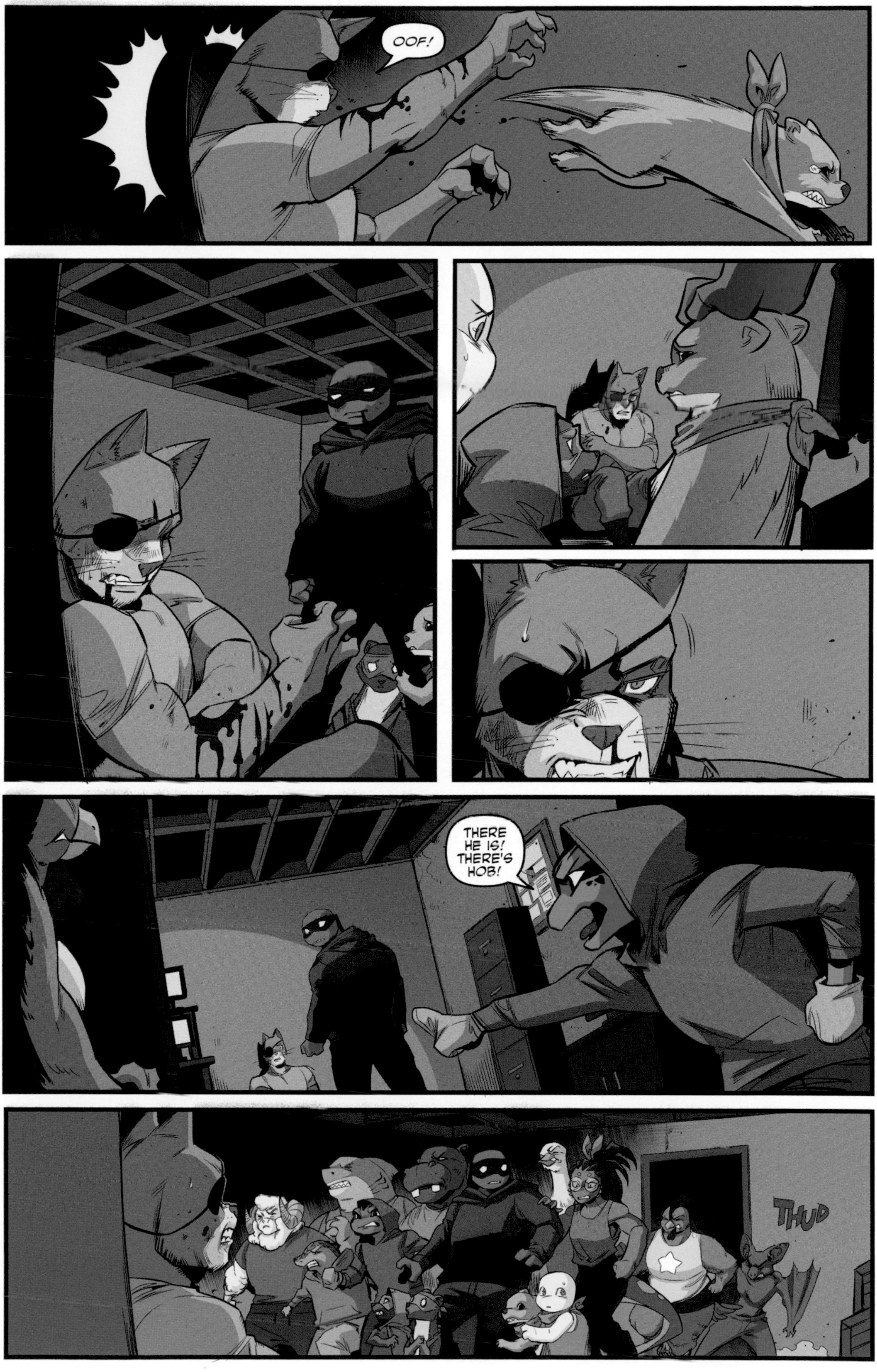
OOF!
THERE HE IS! THERE'S HOB!
THUD

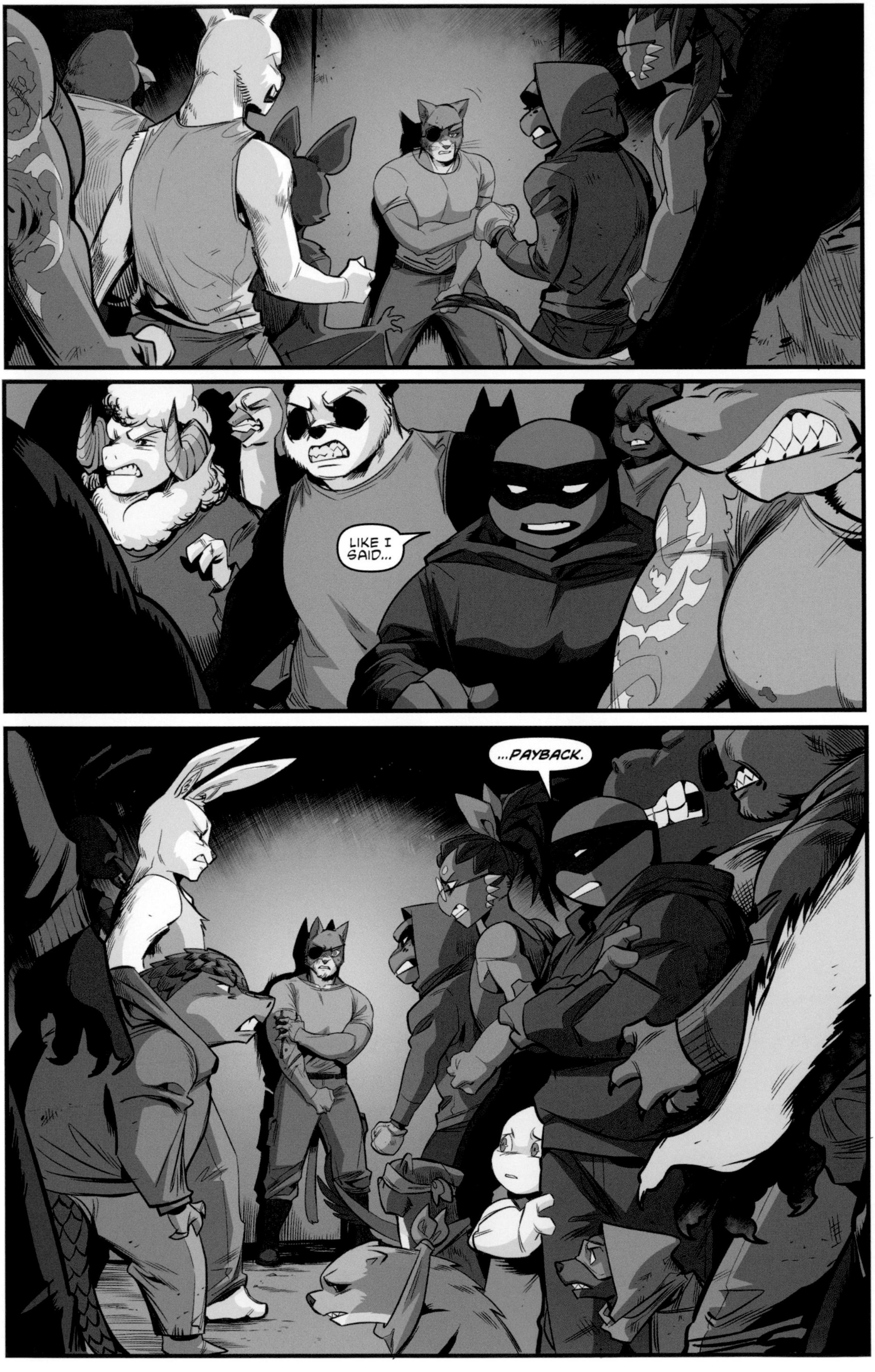
LIKE I SAID...
...PAYBACK.

ART BY
KEVIN EASTMAN

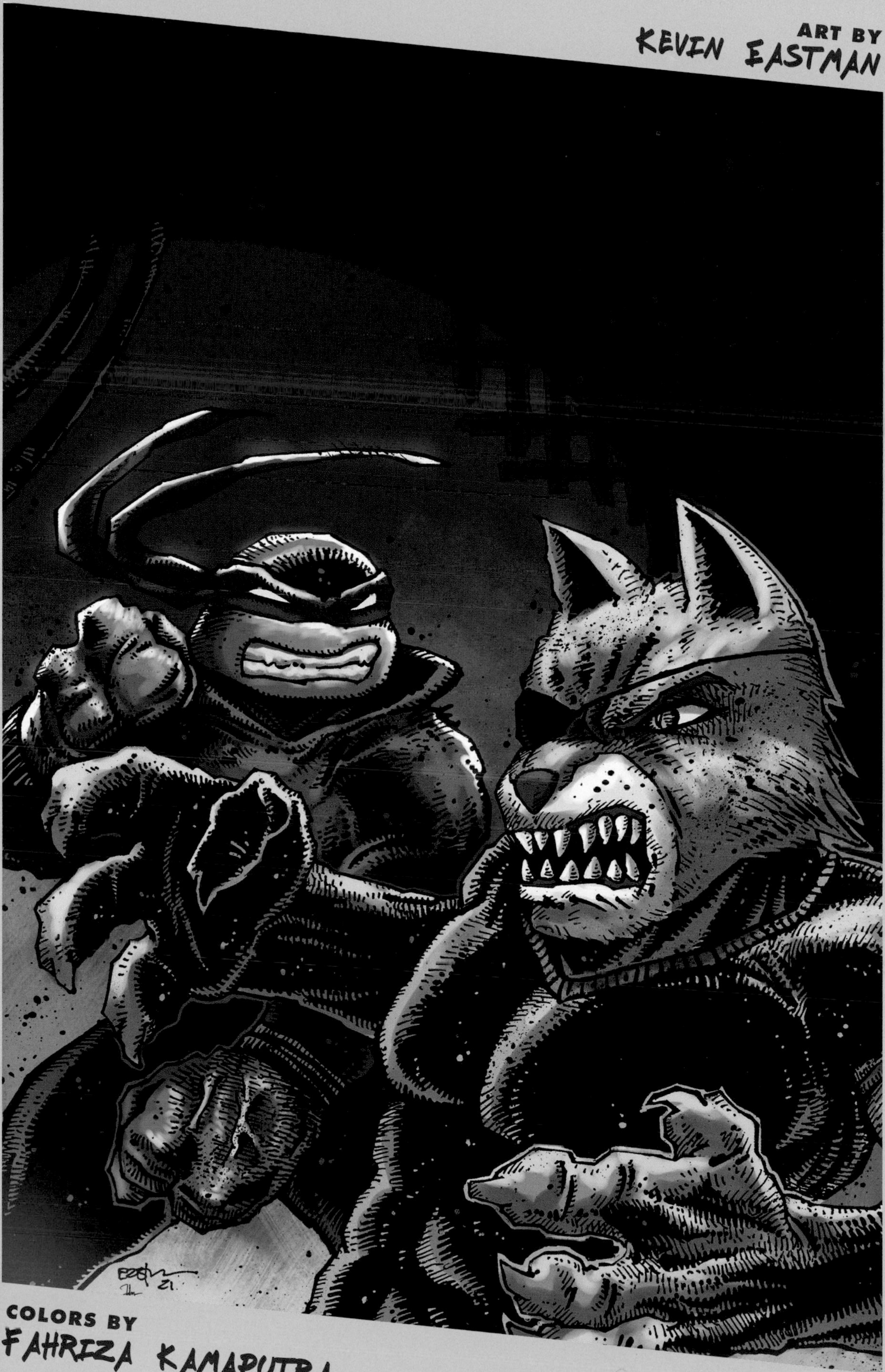

COLORS BY
FAHRIZA KAMAPUTRA

ART BY
JODI NISHIJIMA

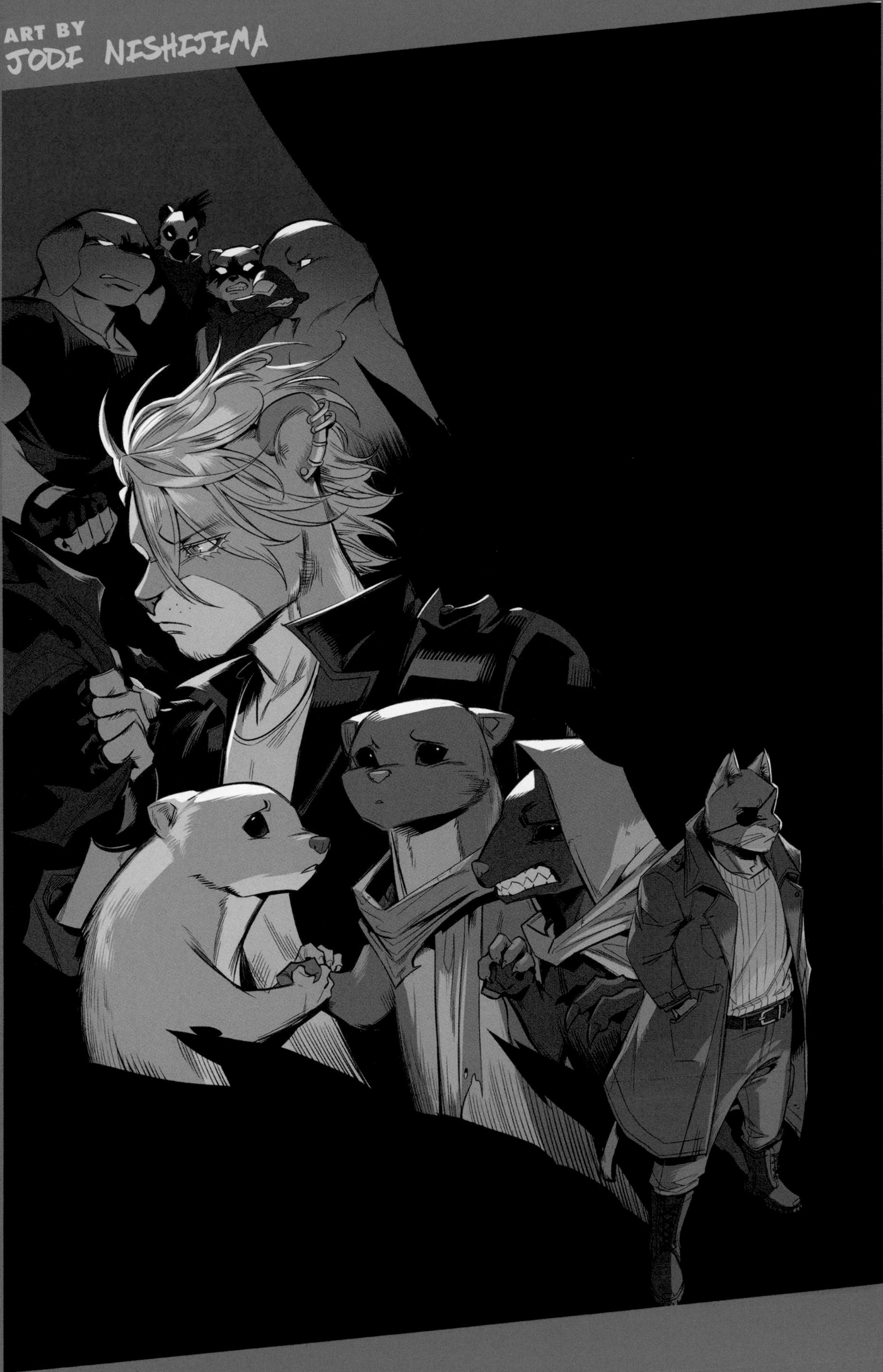

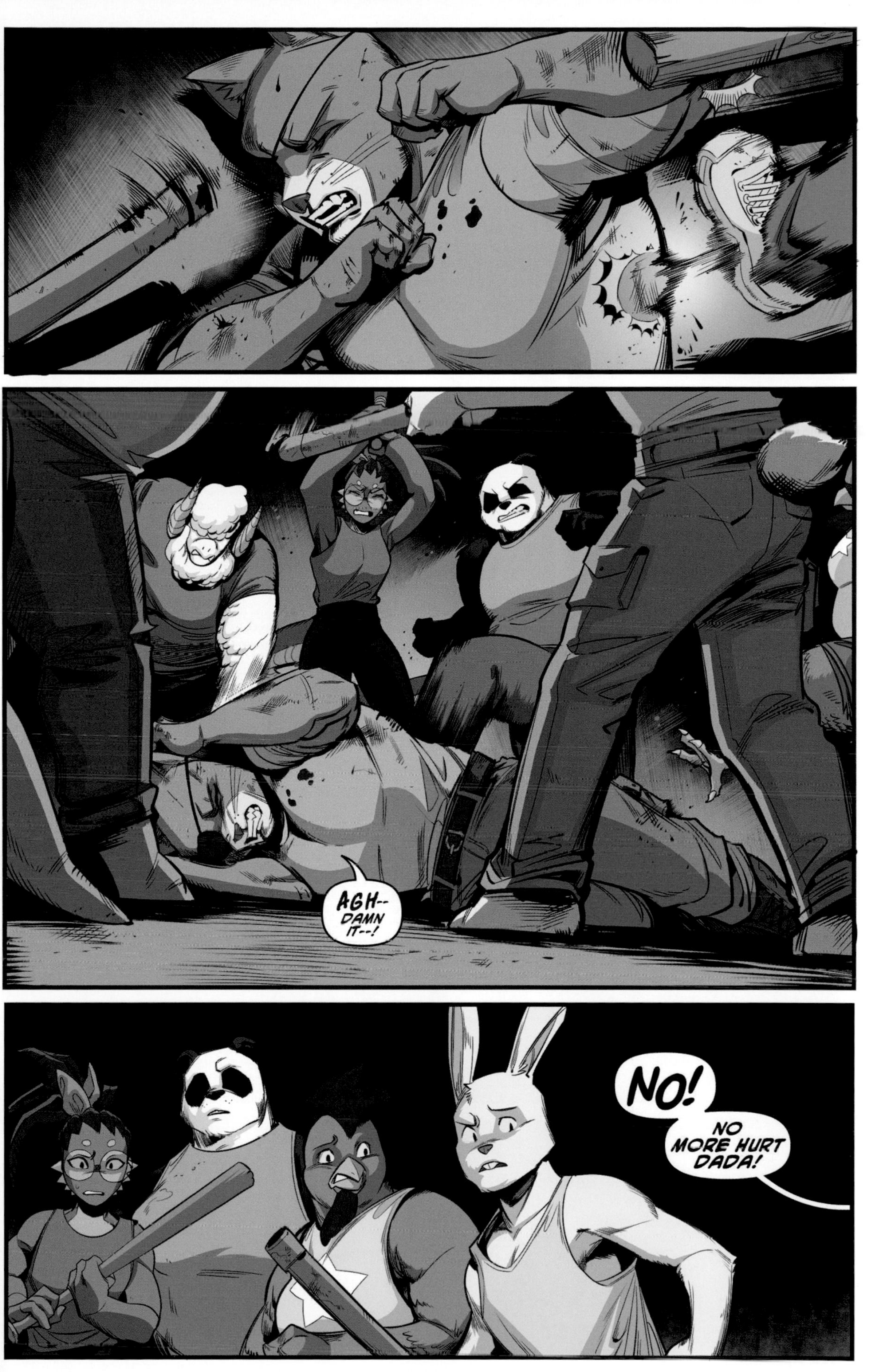
AGH--
DAMN IT--!
NO!
NO MORE HURT DADA!

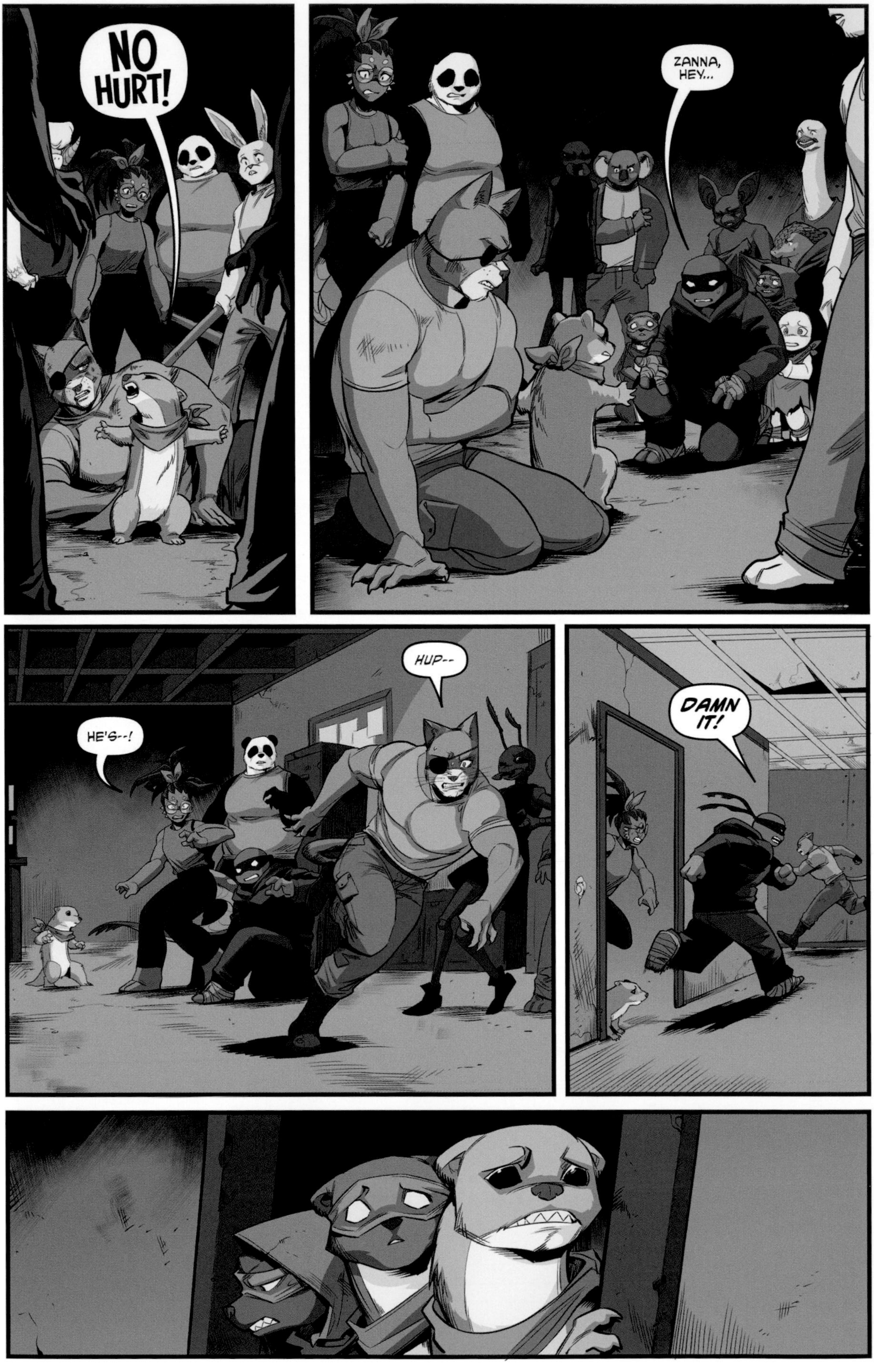
NO HURT!
ZANNA, HEY...
HUP--
HE'S--!
DAMN IT!

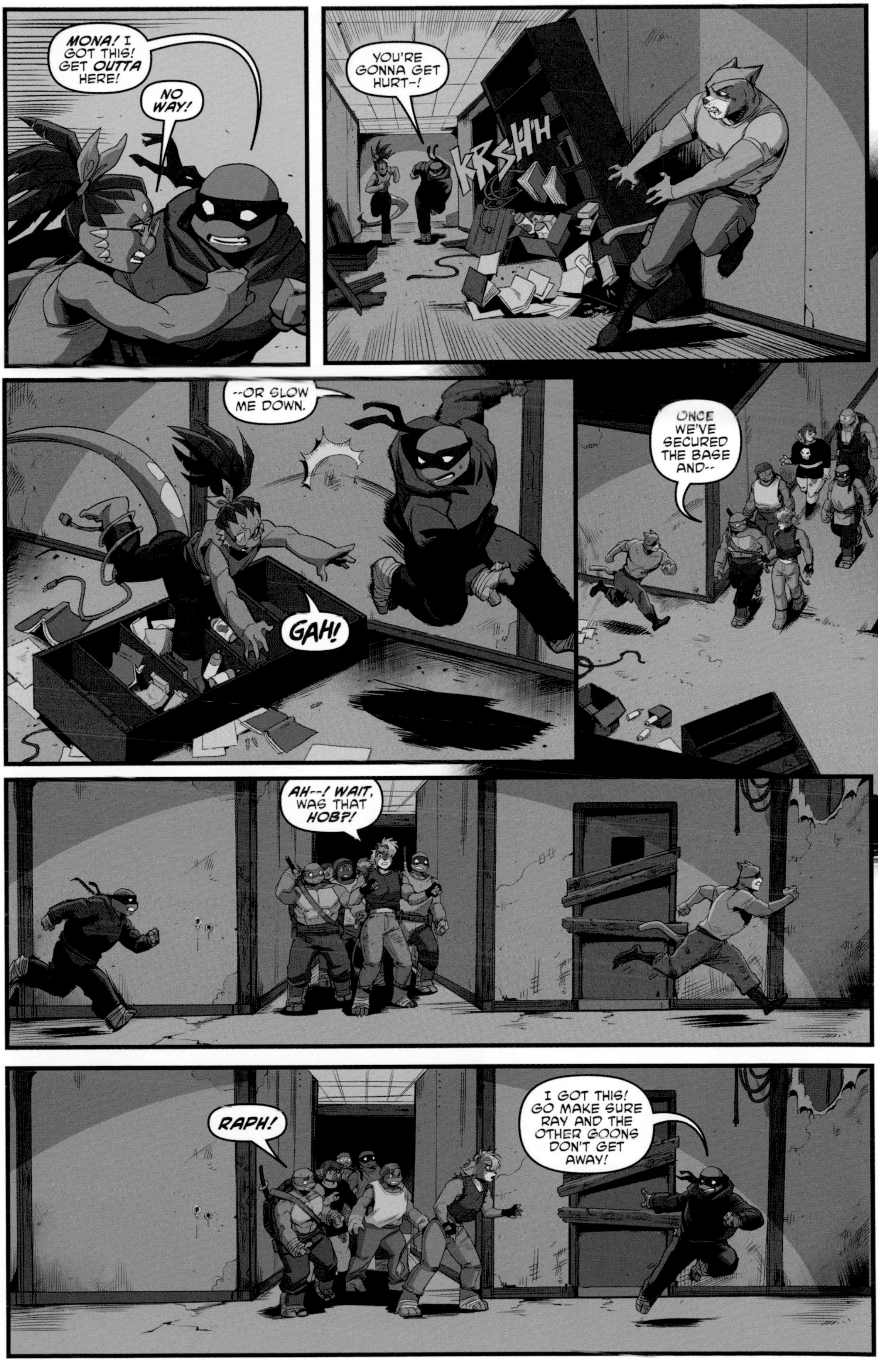
MONA! I GOT THIS! GET OUTTA HERE!
NO WAY!
YOU'RE GONNA GET HURT--!
KRSH'H
--OR SLOW ME DOWN.
GAH!
ONCE WE'VE SECURED THE BASE AND--
AH--! WAIT, WAS THAT HOB?!
RAPH!
I GOT THIS! GO MAKE SURE RAY AND THE OTHER GOONS DON'T GET AWAY!

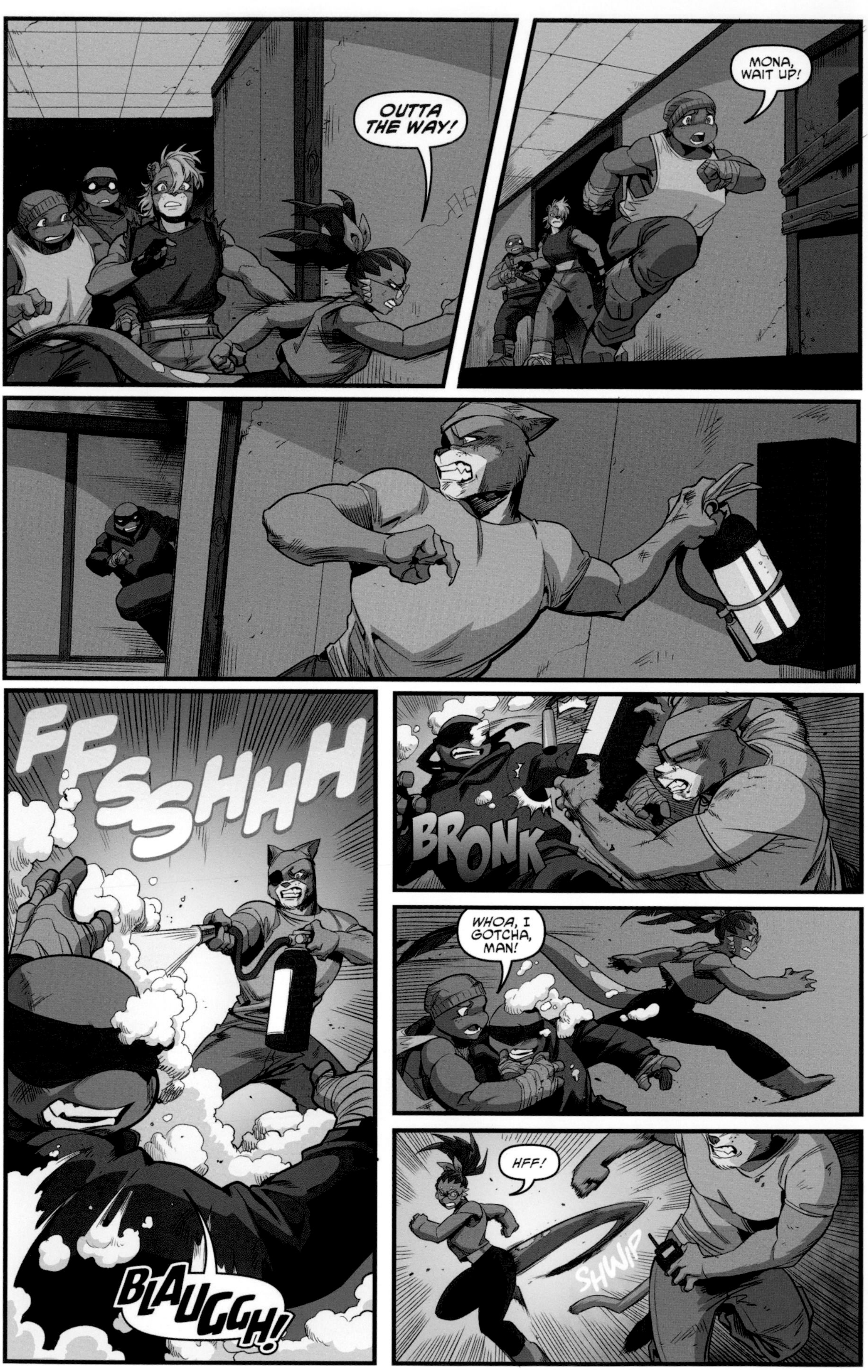
OUTTA THE WAY!
MONA, WAIT UP!
FFSSHHH
BLAUGGH!
BRONK
WHOA, I GOTCHA, MAN!
HFF!
SHWIP

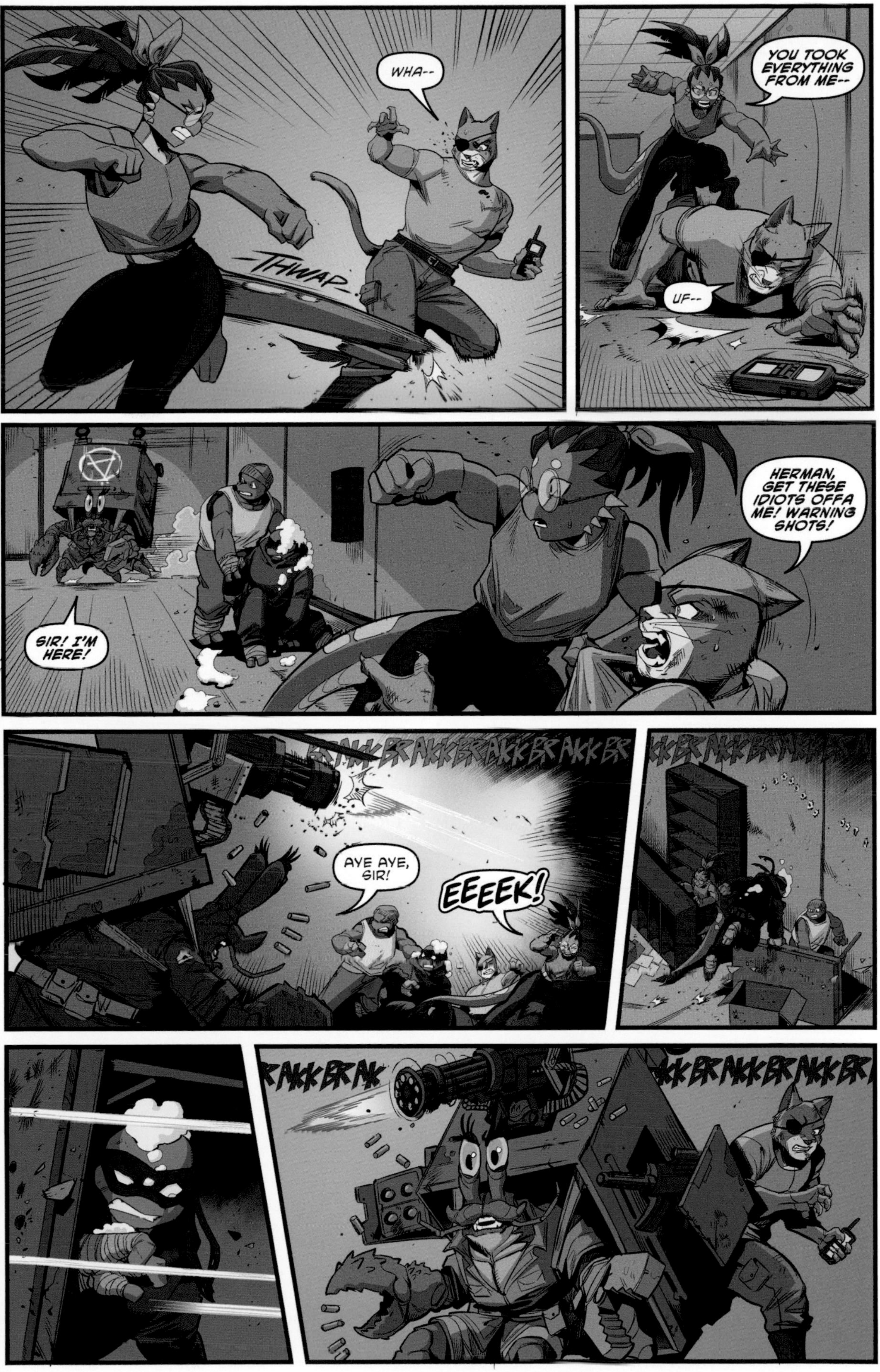
WHA--
THWAP
YOU TOOK EVERYTHING FROM ME--
UF--
HERMAN, GET THESE IDIOTS OFFA ME! WARNING SHOTS!
SIR! I'M HERE!
BRAKK BRAKK BRAKK BRAKK BR
AYE AYE, SIR!
EEEEK!
BRAKK BRAK
BRAKK BRAKK BR

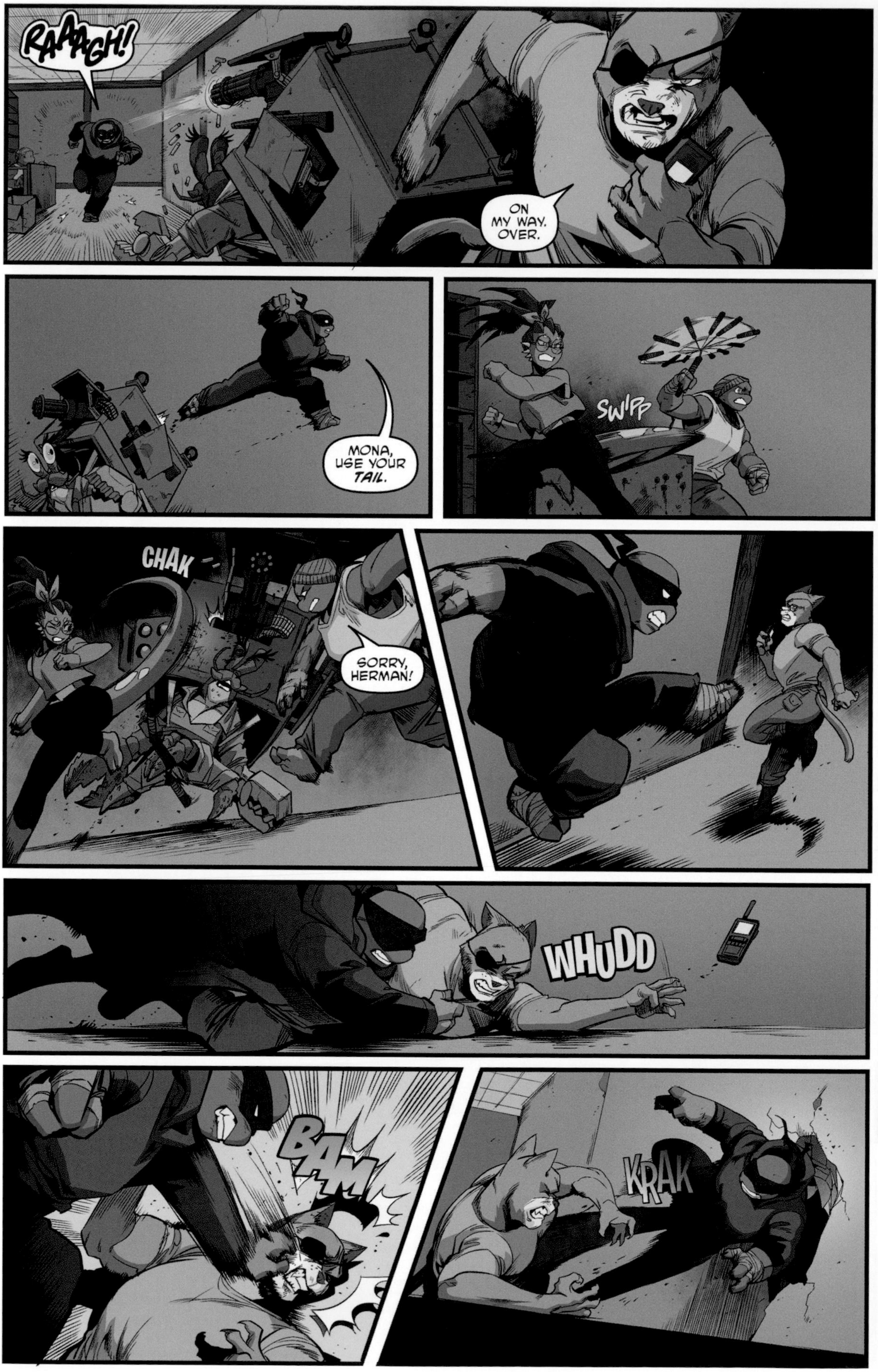
RAAAGH!
ON MY WAY. OVER.
MONA, USE YOUR TAIL.
SWIPP
CHAK
SORRY, HERMAN!
WHUDD
BAM
KRAK

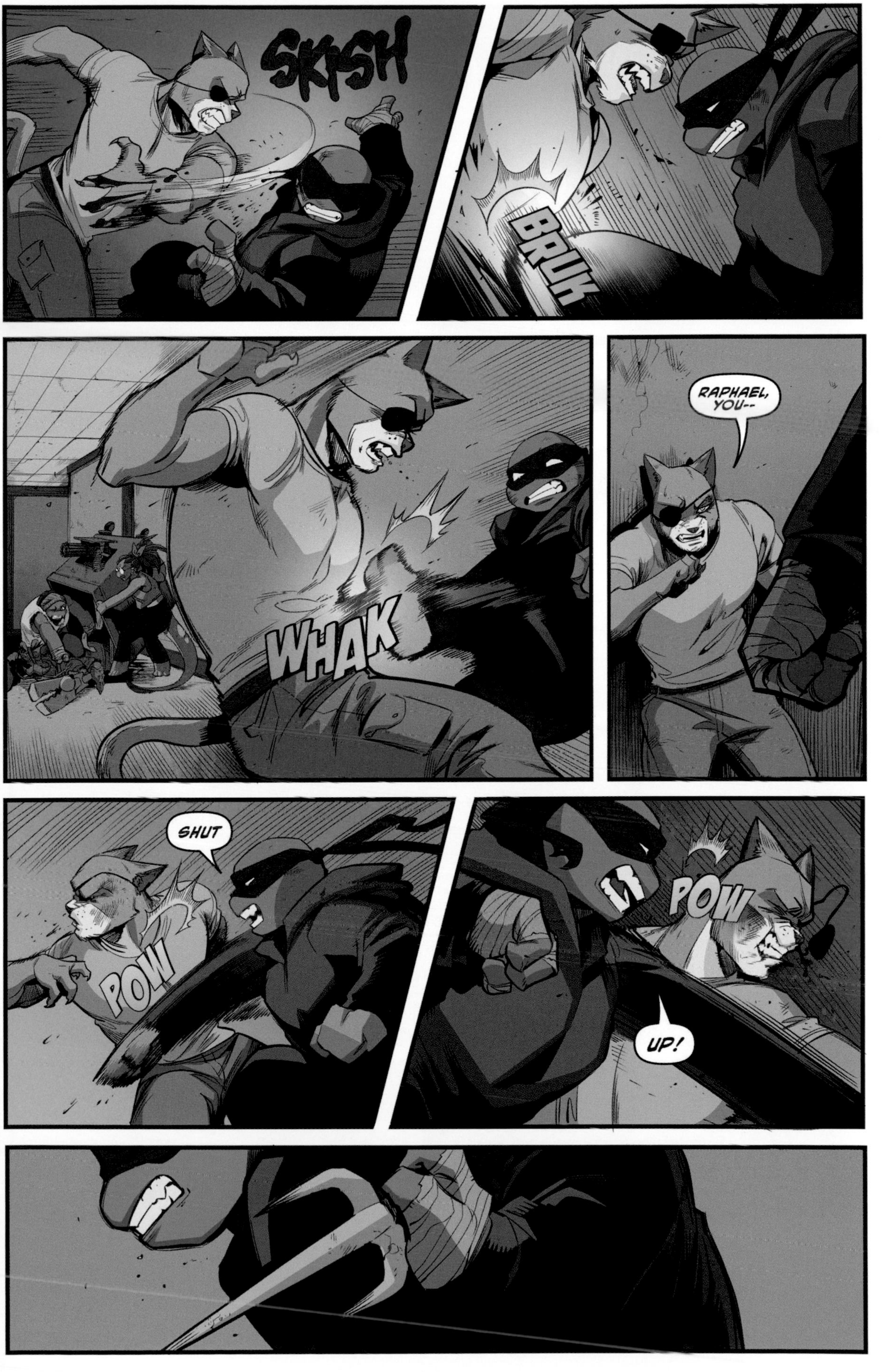
SKISH
BRUK
WHAK
RAPHAEL, YOU--
SHUT
POW
POW
UP!

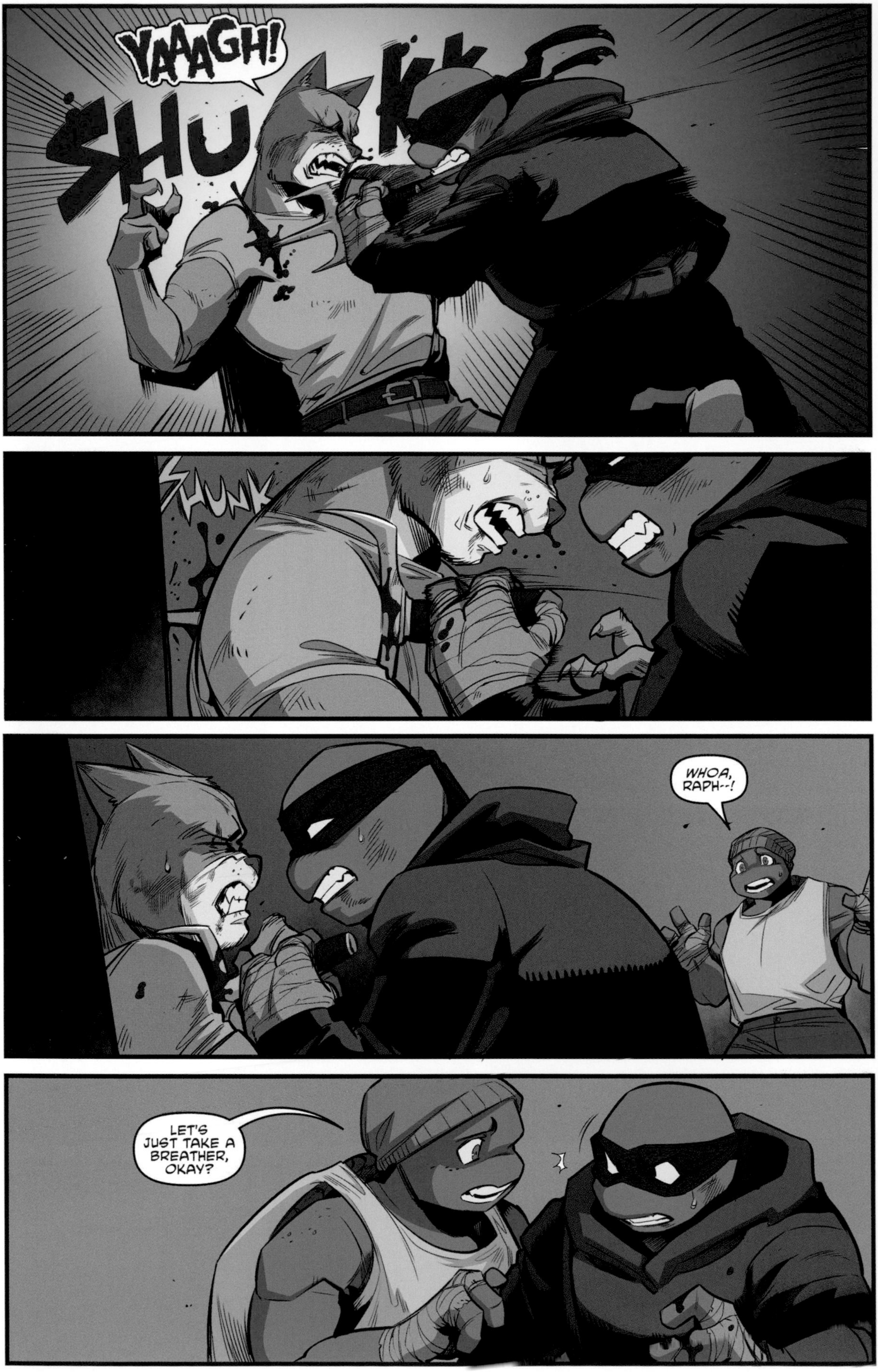
YAAAGH!
SHUKKK
SHUNK
WHOA, RAPH--!
LET'S JUST TAKE A BREATHER, OKAY?

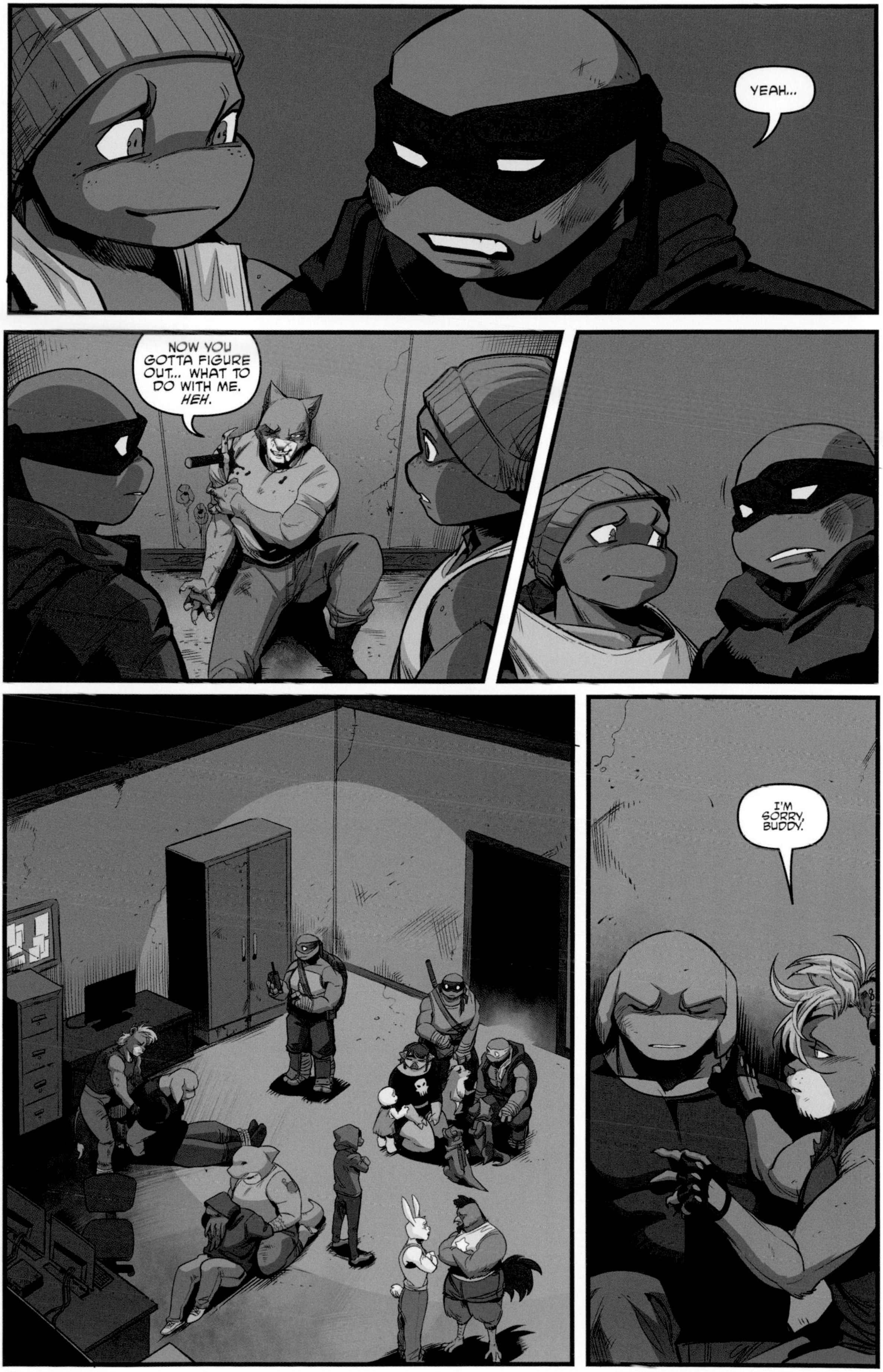
YEAH...
NOW YOU GOTTA FIGURE OUT... WHAT TO DO WITH ME. *HEH*.
I'M SORRY, BUDDY.

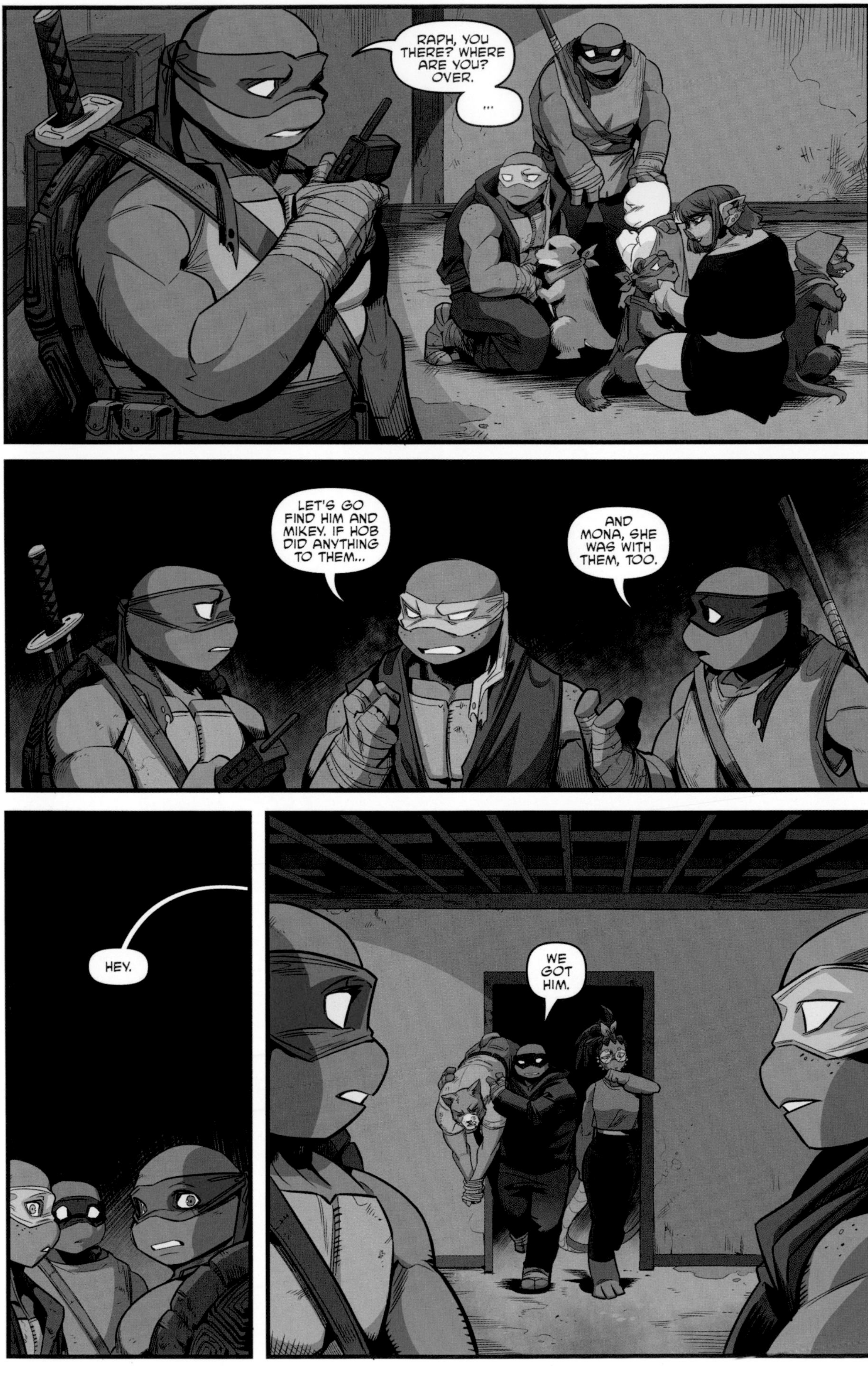
RAPH, YOU THERE? WHERE ARE YOU? OVER.
...
LET'S GO FIND HIM AND MIKEY. IF HOB DID ANYTHING TO THEM...
AND MONA, SHE WAS WITH THEM, TOO.
HEY.
WE GOT HIM.

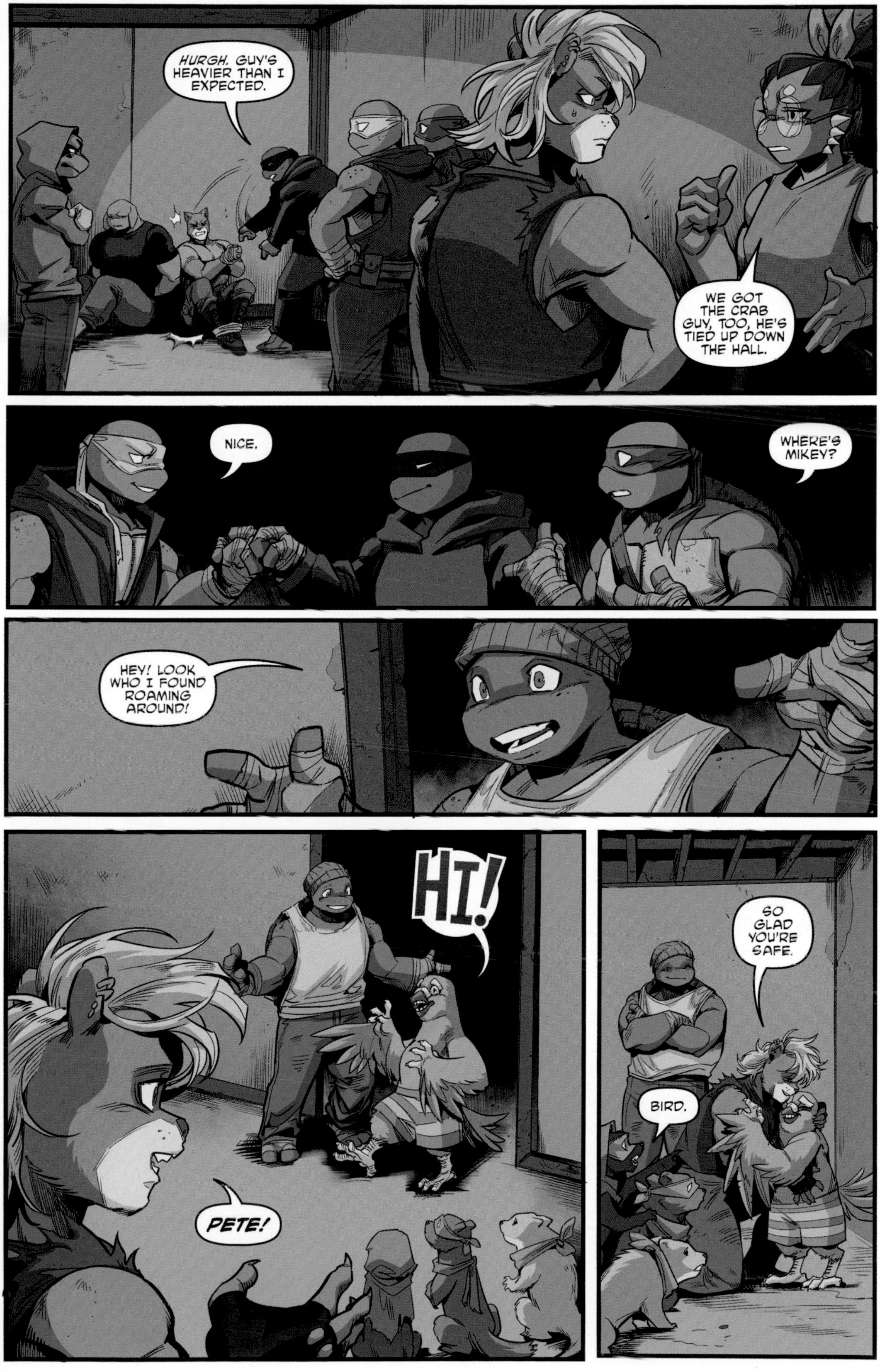
HURGH. GUY'S HEAVIER THAN I EXPECTED.
WE GOT THE CRAB GUY, TOO, HE'S TIED UP DOWN THE HALL.
NICE.
WHERE'S MIKEY?
HEY! LOOK WHO I FOUND ROAMING AROUND!
HI!
PETE!
SO GLAD YOU'RE SAFE.
BIRD.

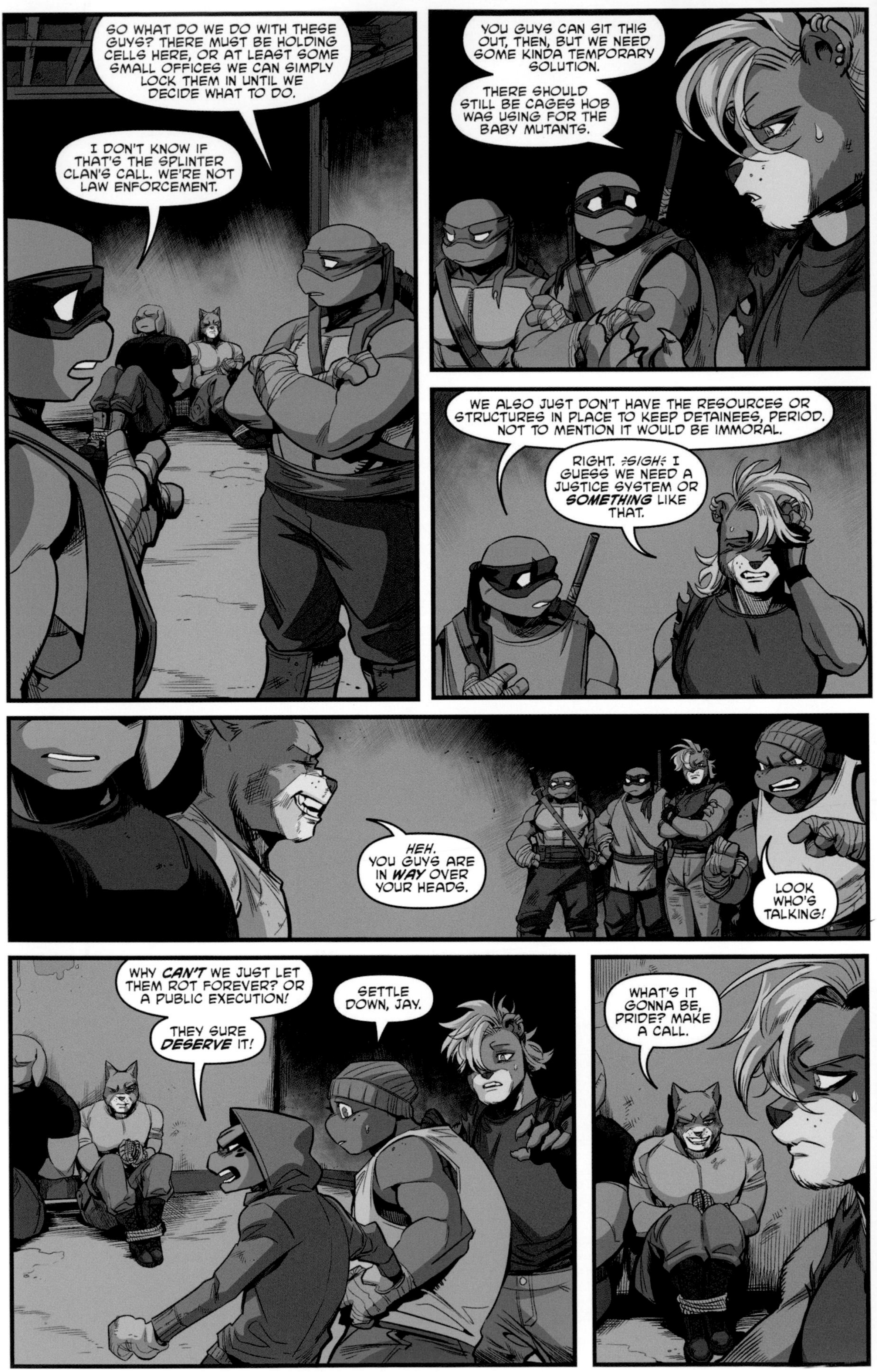
SO WHAT DO WE DO WITH THESE GUYS? THERE MUST BE HOLDING CELLS HERE, OR AT LEAST SOME SMALL OFFICES WE CAN SIMPLY LOCK THEM IN UNTIL WE DECIDE WHAT TO DO.
I DON'T KNOW IF THAT'S THE SPLINTER CLAN'S CALL. WE'RE NOT LAW ENFORCEMENT.
YOU GUYS CAN SIT THIS OUT, THEN, BUT WE NEED SOME KINDA TEMPORARY SOLUTION.
THERE SHOULD STILL BE CAGES HOB WAS USING FOR THE BABY MUTANTS.
WE ALSO JUST DON'T HAVE THE RESOURCES OR STRUCTURES IN PLACE TO KEEP DETAINEES, PERIOD. NOT TO MENTION IT WOULD BE IMMORAL.
RIGHT. *SIGH* I GUESS WE NEED A JUSTICE SYSTEM OR ***SOMETHING*** LIKE THAT.
HEH. YOU GUYS ARE IN ***WAY*** OVER YOUR HEADS.
LOOK WHO'S TALKING!
WHY ***CAN'T*** WE JUST LET THEM ROT FOREVER? OR A PUBLIC EXECUTION!
THEY SURE ***DESERVE*** IT!
SETTLE DOWN, JAY.
WHAT'S IT GONNA BE, PRIDE? MAKE A CALL.

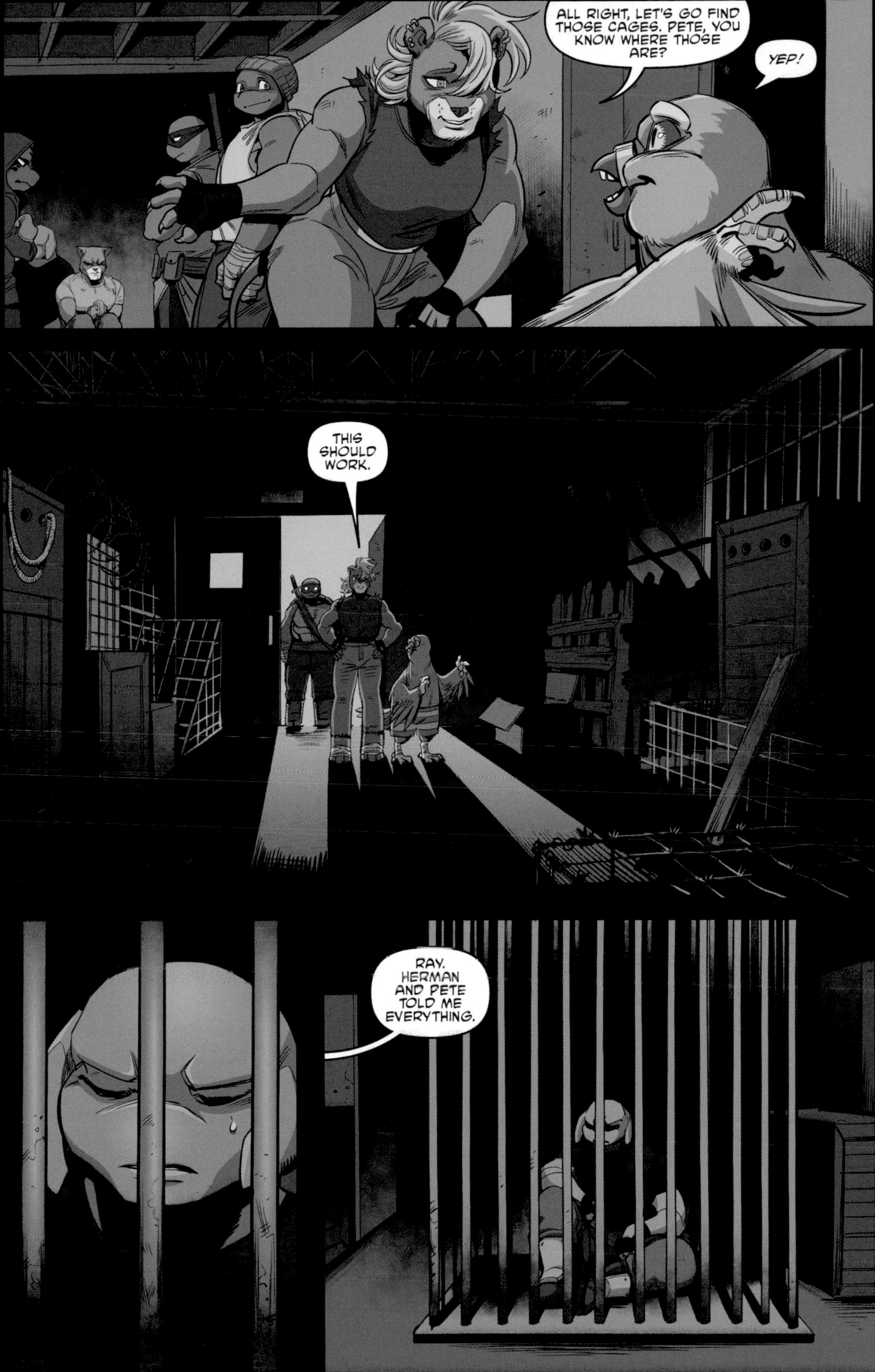
ALL RIGHT, LET'S GO FIND THOSE CAGES. PETE, YOU KNOW WHERE THOSE ARE?
YEP!
THIS SHOULD WORK.
RAY. HERMAN AND PETE TOLD ME EVERYTHING.

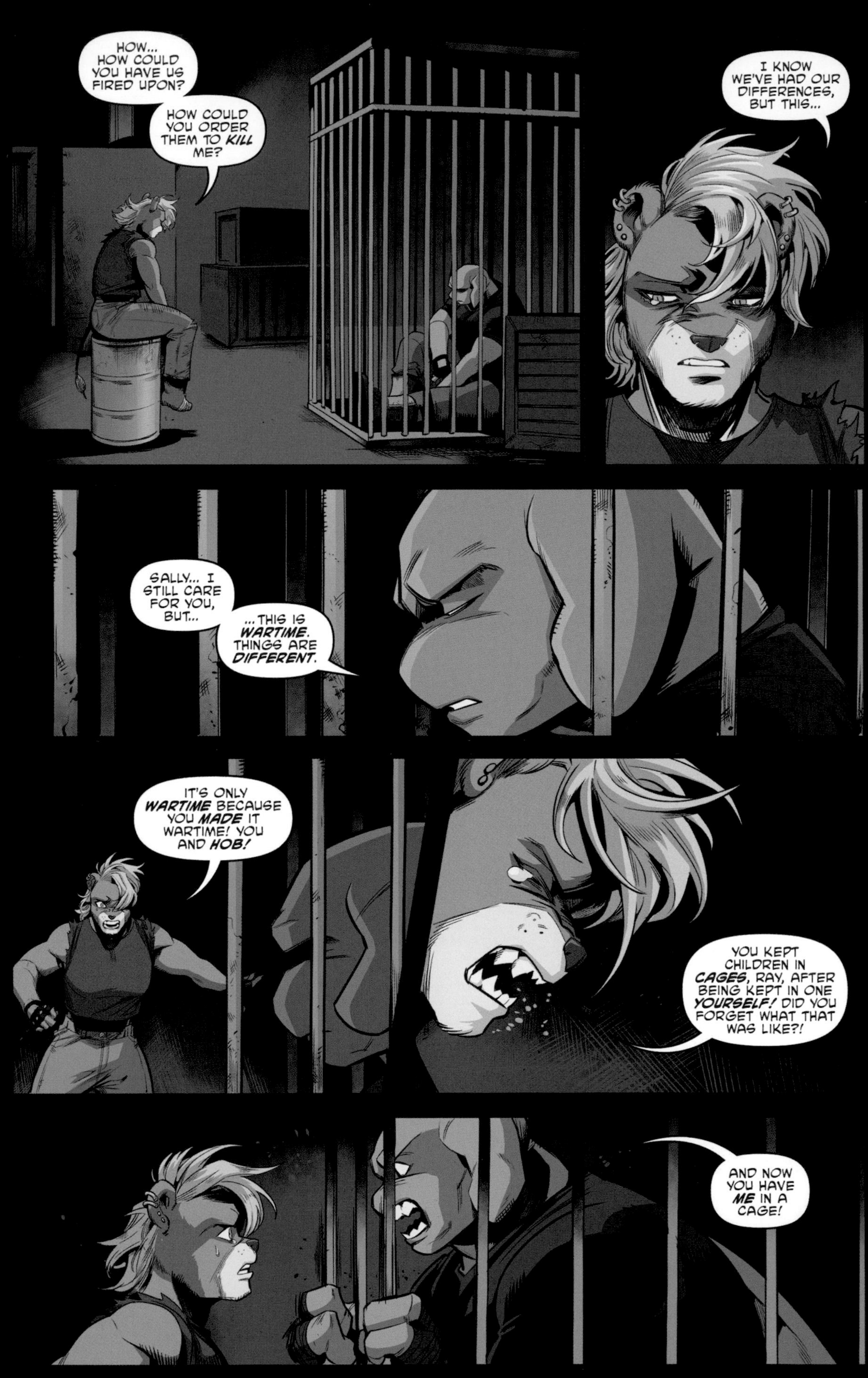
HOW... HOW COULD YOU HAVE US FIRED UPON?
HOW COULD YOU ORDER THEM TO KILL ME?
I KNOW WE'VE HAD OUR DIFFERENCES, BUT THIS...
SALLY... I STILL CARE FOR YOU, BUT...
...THIS IS WARTIME. THINGS ARE DIFFERENT.
IT'S ONLY WARTIME BECAUSE YOU MADE IT WARTIME! YOU AND HOB!
YOU KEPT CHILDREN IN CAGES, RAY, AFTER BEING KEPT IN ONE YOURSELF! DID YOU FORGET WHAT THAT WAS LIKE?!
AND NOW YOU HAVE ME IN A CAGE!

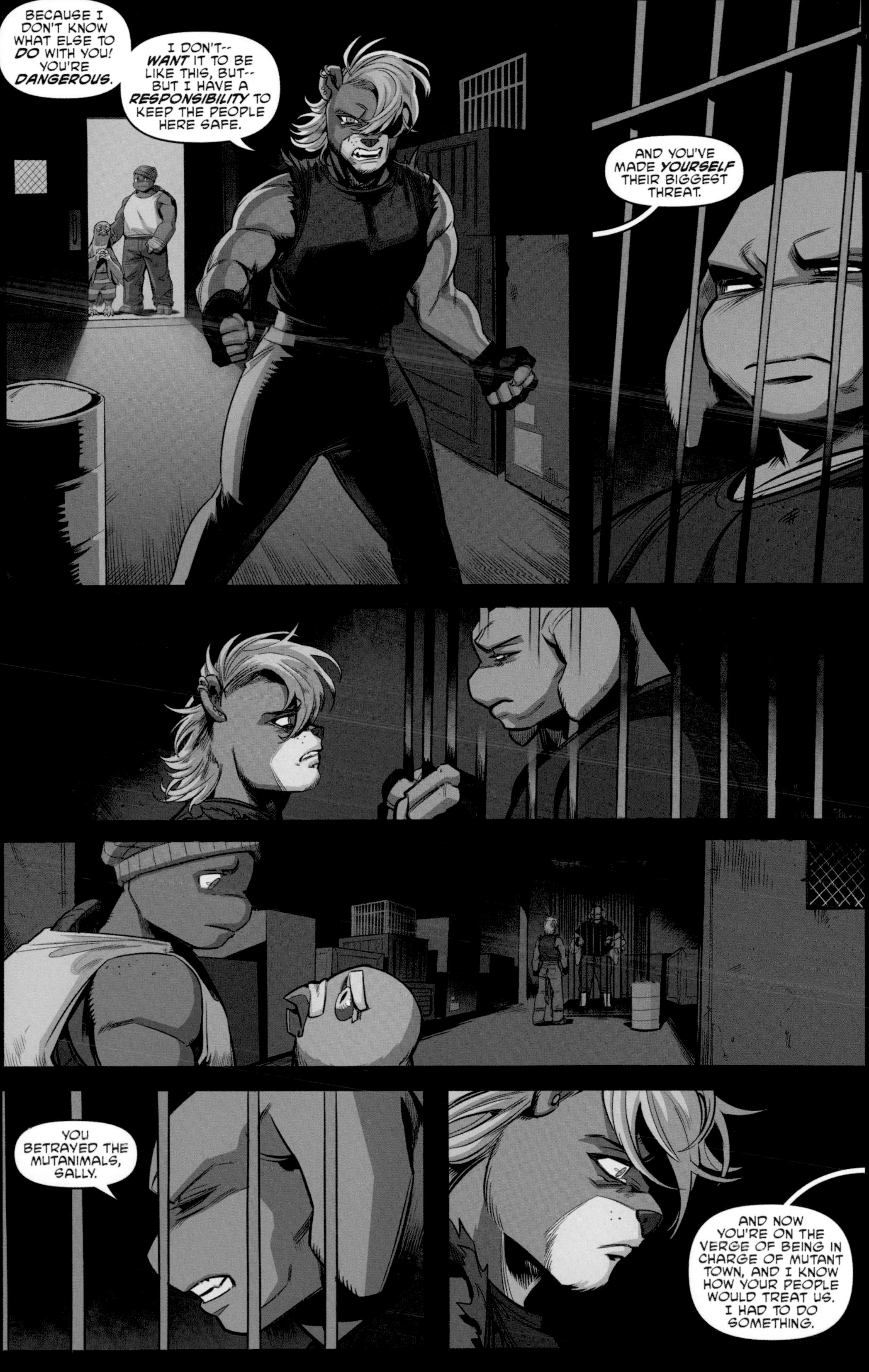
BECAUSE I DON'T KNOW WHAT ELSE TO DO WITH YOU! YOU'RE DANGEROUS.
I DON'T-- WANT IT TO BE LIKE THIS, BUT-- BUT I HAVE A RESPONSIBILITY TO KEEP THE PEOPLE HERE SAFE.
AND YOU'VE MADE YOURSELF THEIR BIGGEST THREAT.
YOU BETRAYED THE MUTANIMALS, SALLY.
AND NOW YOU'RE ON THE VERGE OF BEING IN CHARGE OF MUTANT TOWN, AND I KNOW HOW YOUR PEOPLE WOULD TREAT US. I HAD TO DO SOMETHING.

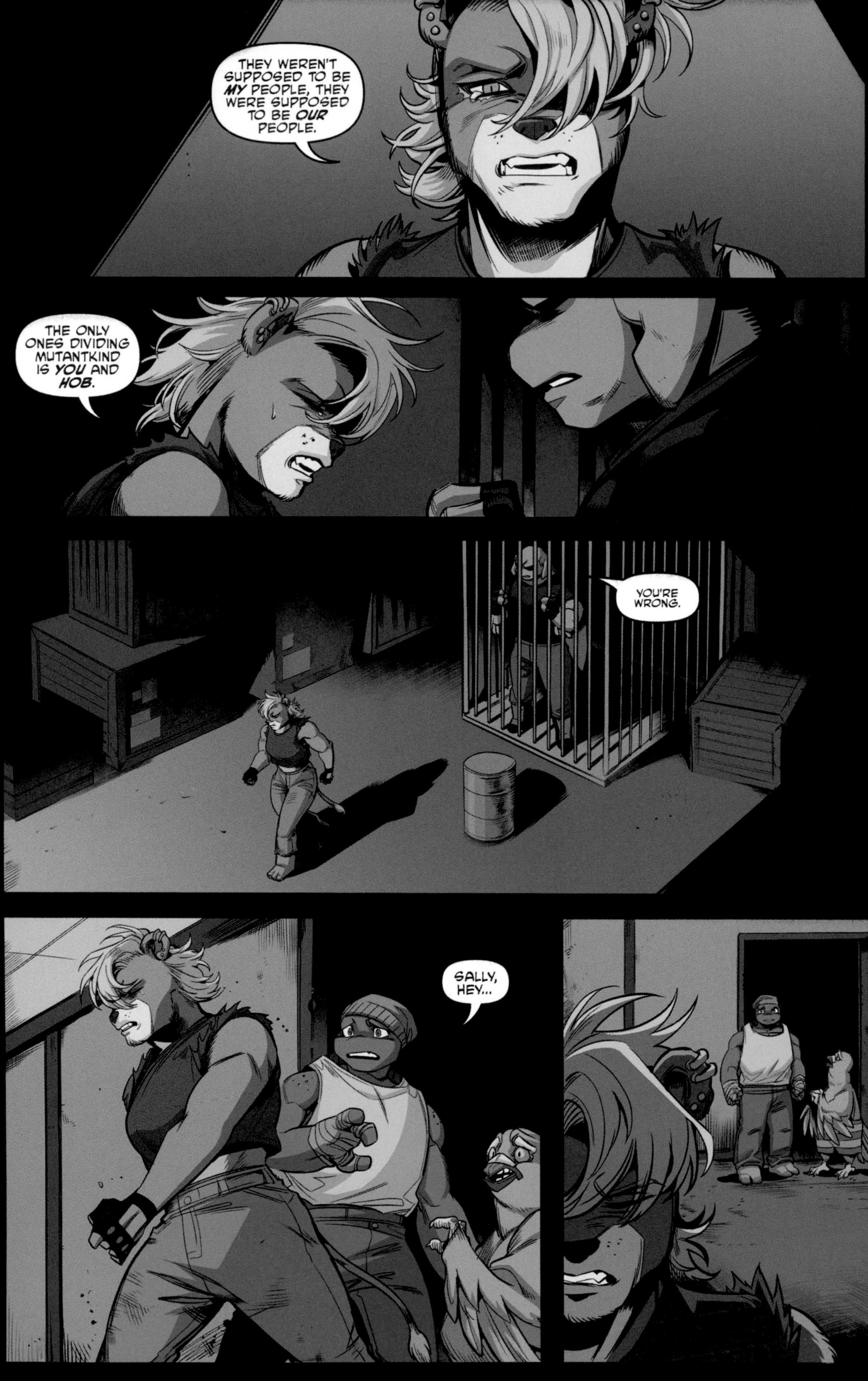

THEY WEREN'T SUPPOSED TO BE MY PEOPLE, THEY WERE SUPPOSED TO BE OUR PEOPLE.
THE ONLY ONES DIVIDING MUTANTKIND IS YOU AND HOB.
YOU'RE WRONG.
SALLY, HEY...

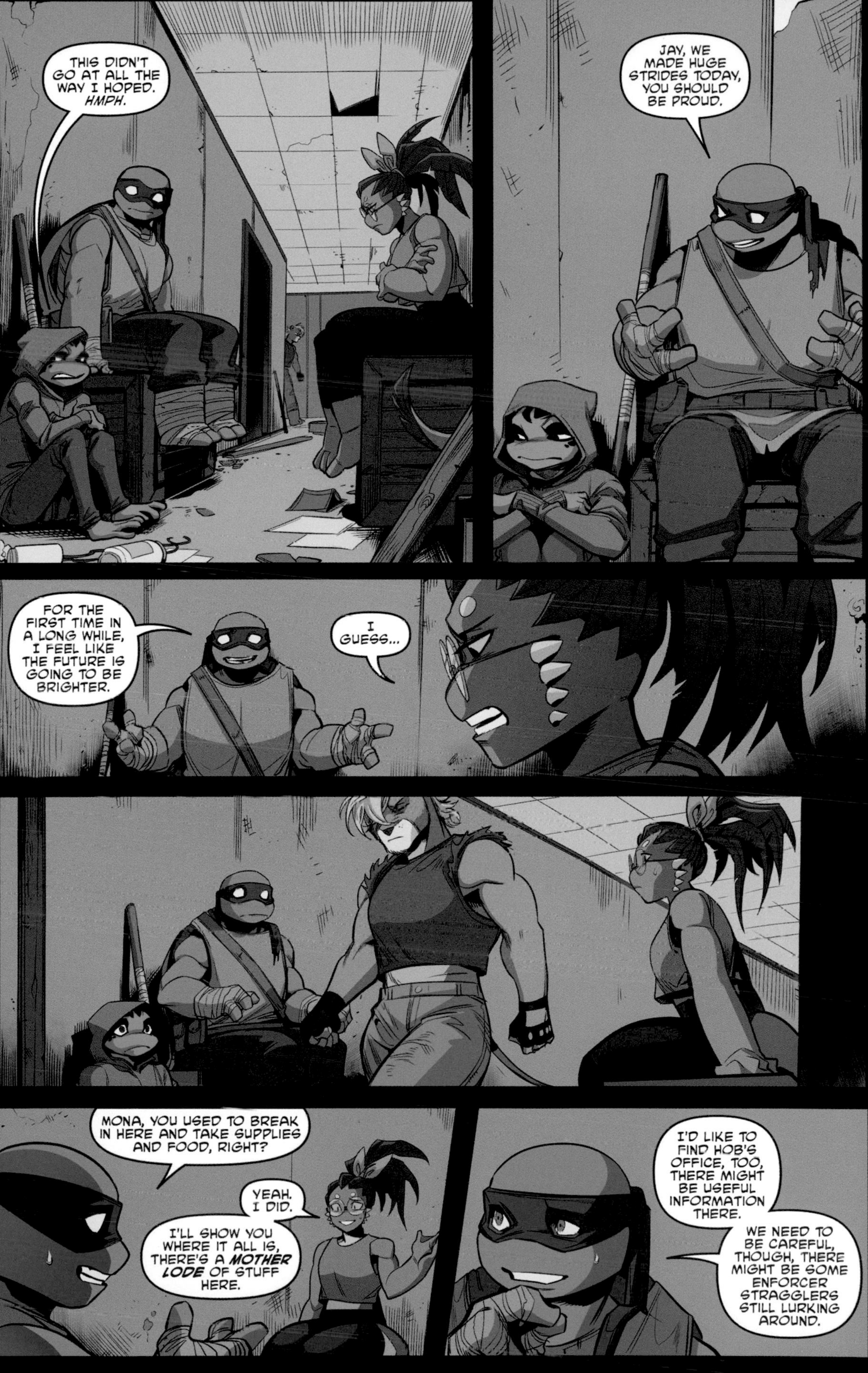

THIS DIDN'T GO AT ALL THE WAY I HOPED. HMPH.
JAY, WE MADE HUGE STRIDES TODAY, YOU SHOULD BE PROUD.
FOR THE FIRST TIME IN A LONG WHILE, I FEEL LIKE THE FUTURE IS GOING TO BE BRIGHTER.
I GUESS...
MONA, YOU USED TO BREAK IN HERE AND TAKE SUPPLIES AND FOOD, RIGHT?
YEAH. I DID.
I'LL SHOW YOU WHERE IT ALL IS, THERE'S A MOTHER LODE OF STUFF HERE.
I'D LIKE TO FIND HOB'S OFFICE, TOO, THERE MIGHT BE USEFUL INFORMATION THERE.
WE NEED TO BE CAREFUL, THOUGH, THERE MIGHT BE SOME ENFORCER STRAGGLERS STILL LURKING AROUND.

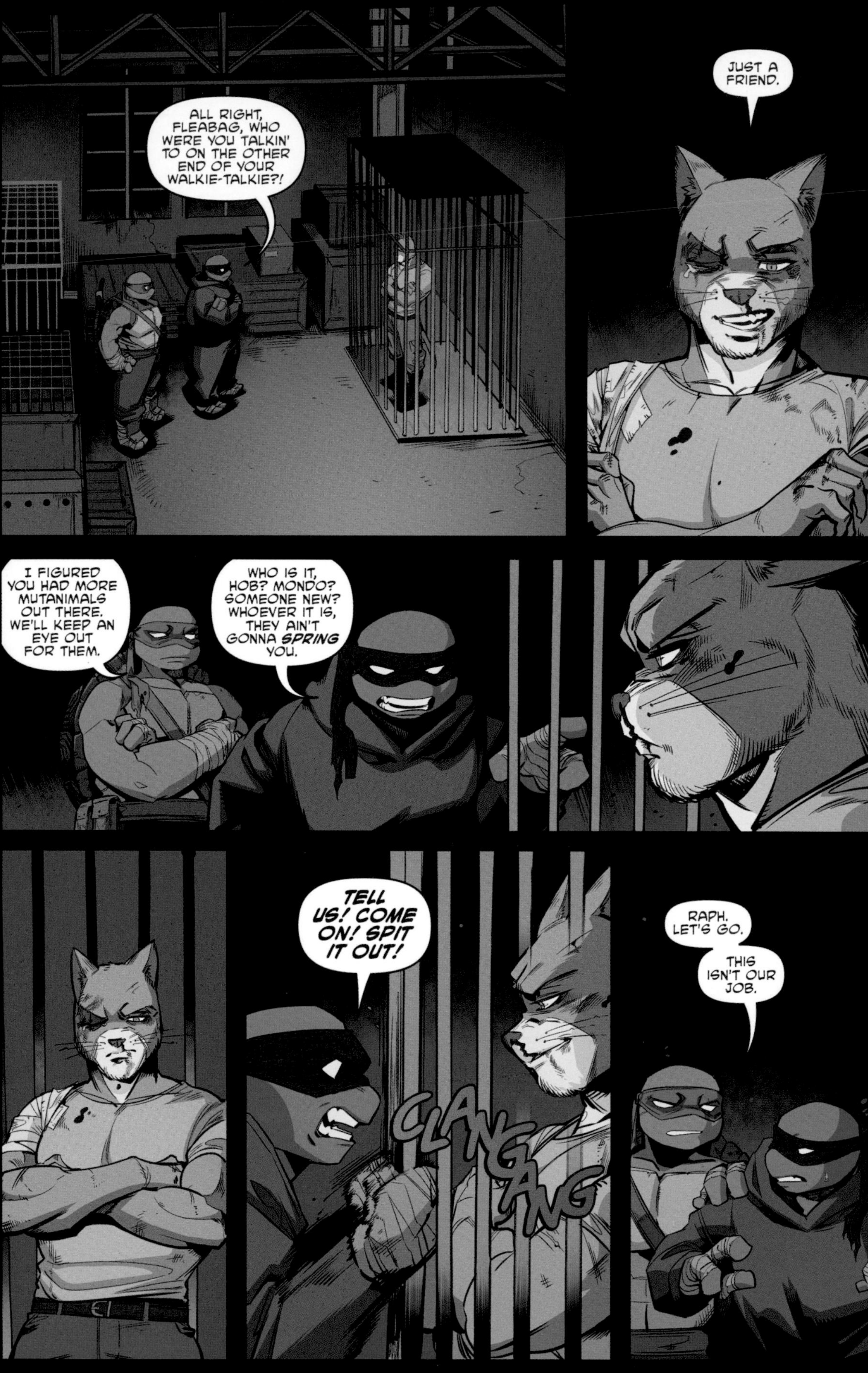
ALL RIGHT, FLEABAG, WHO WERE YOU TALKIN' TO ON THE OTHER END OF YOUR WALKIE-TALKIE?!
JUST A FRIEND.
I FIGURED YOU HAD MORE MUTANIMALS OUT THERE. WE'LL KEEP AN EYE OUT FOR THEM.
WHO IS IT, HOB? MONDO? SOMEONE NEW? WHOEVER IT IS, THEY AIN'T GONNA SPRING YOU.
TELL US! COME ON! SPIT IT OUT!
CLANGANG
RAPH. LET'S GO.
THIS ISN'T OUR JOB.

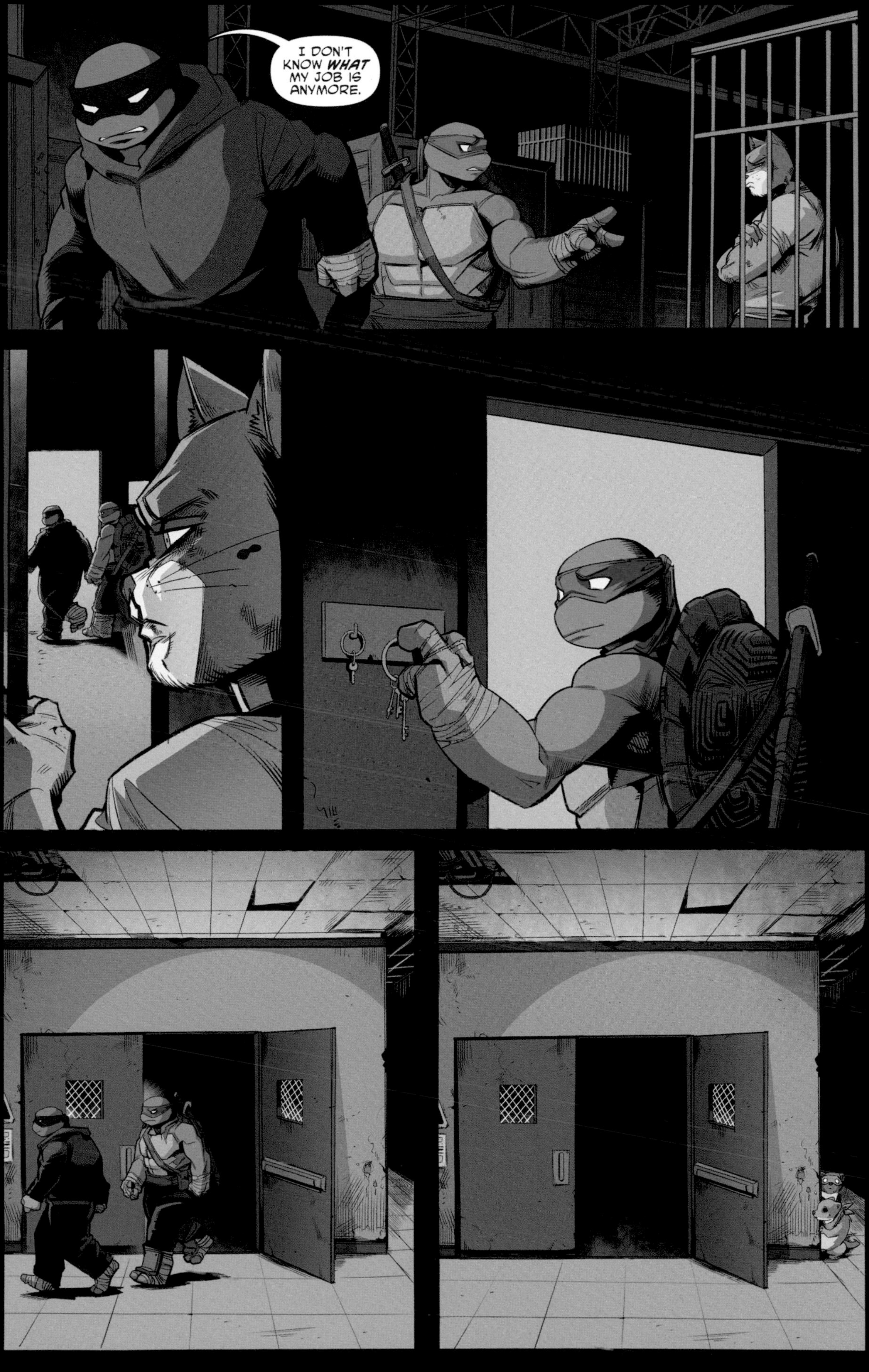
I DON'T KNOW *WHAT* MY JOB IS ANYMORE.

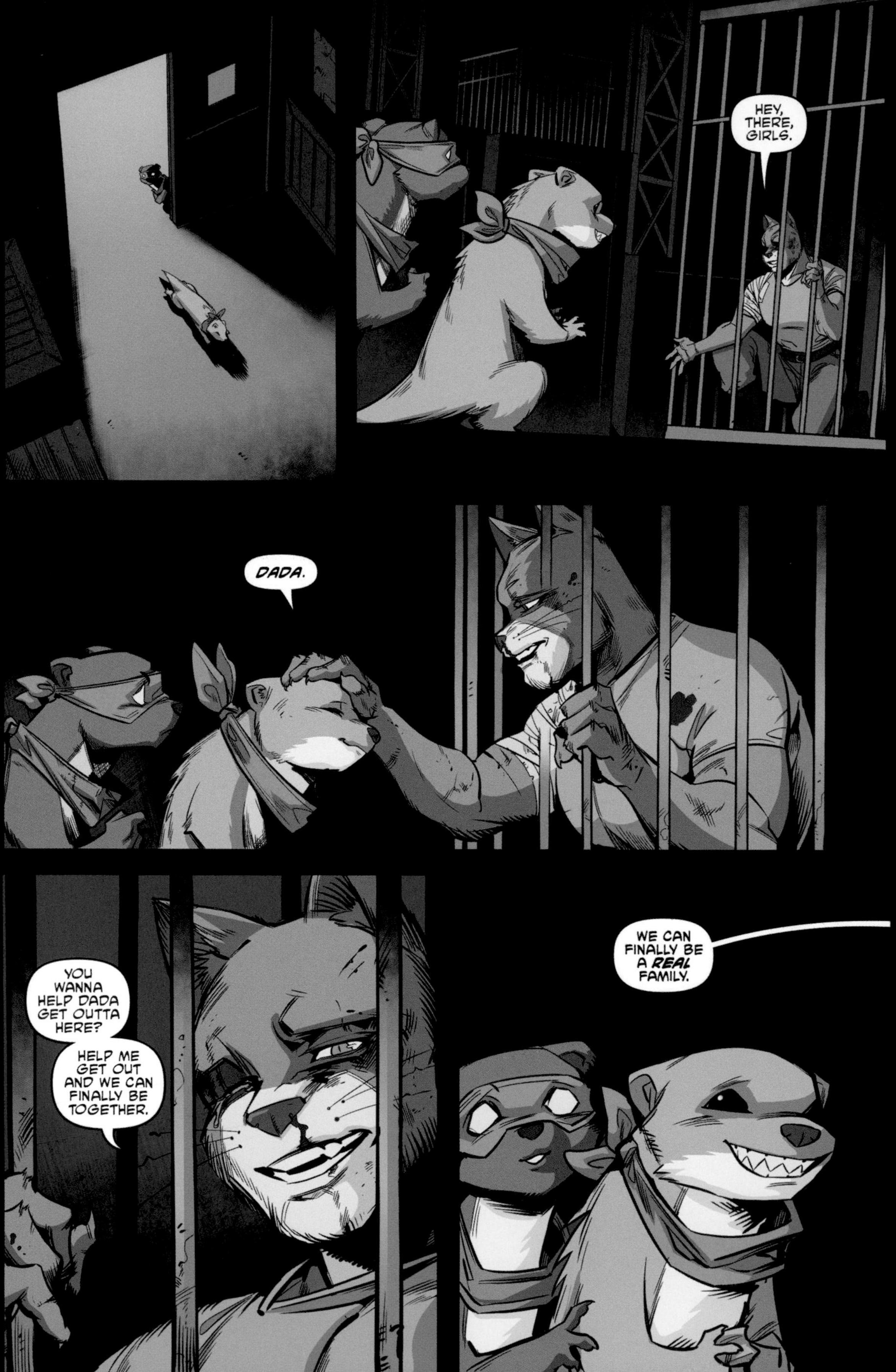

HEY, THERE, GIRLS.
DADA.
YOU WANNA HELP DADA GET OUTTA HERE?
HELP ME GET OUT AND WE CAN FINALLY BE TOGETHER.
WE CAN FINALLY BE A REAL FAMILY.

ART BY
KEVIN EASTMAN

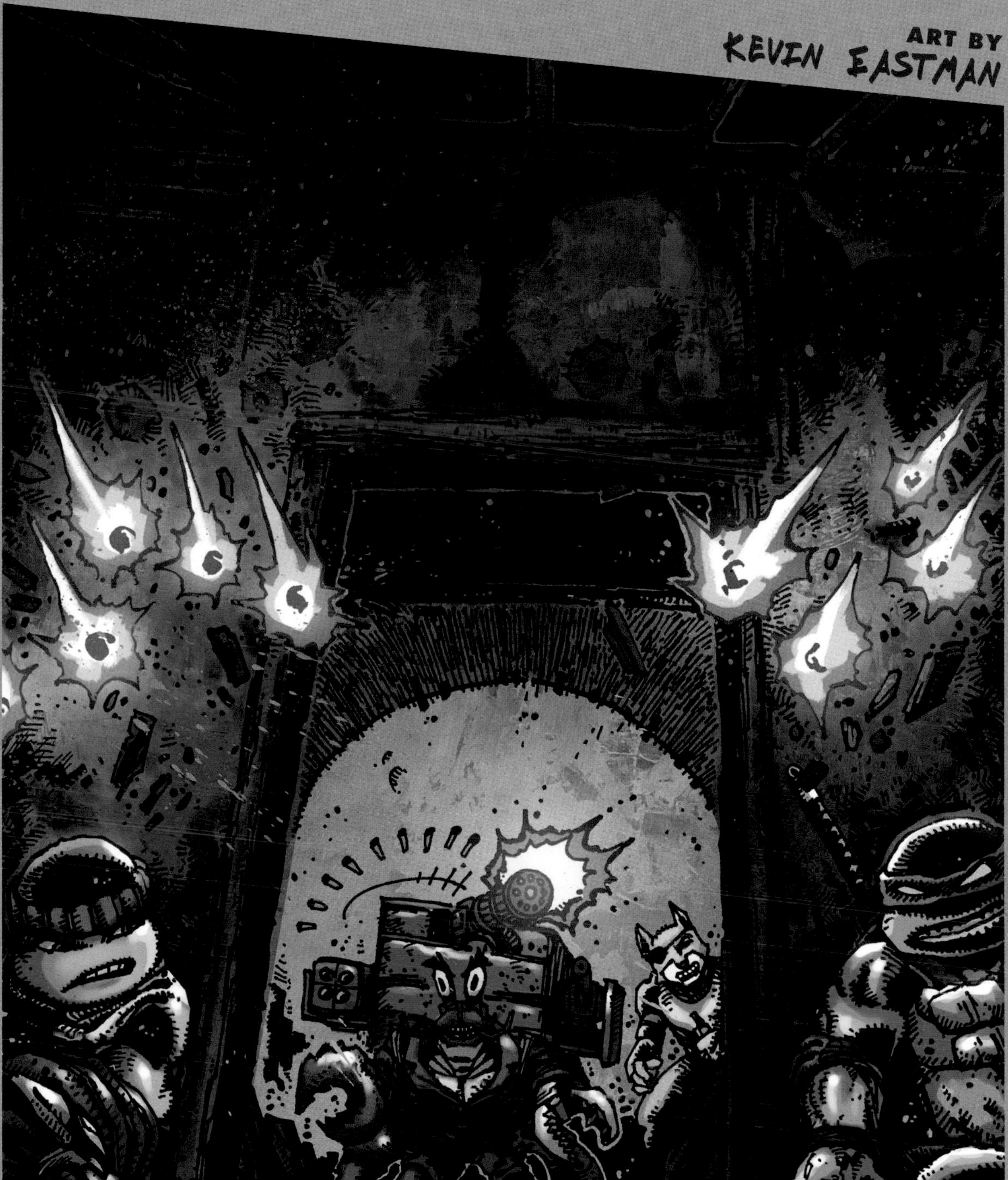

COLORS BY
FAHRIZA KAMAPUTRA

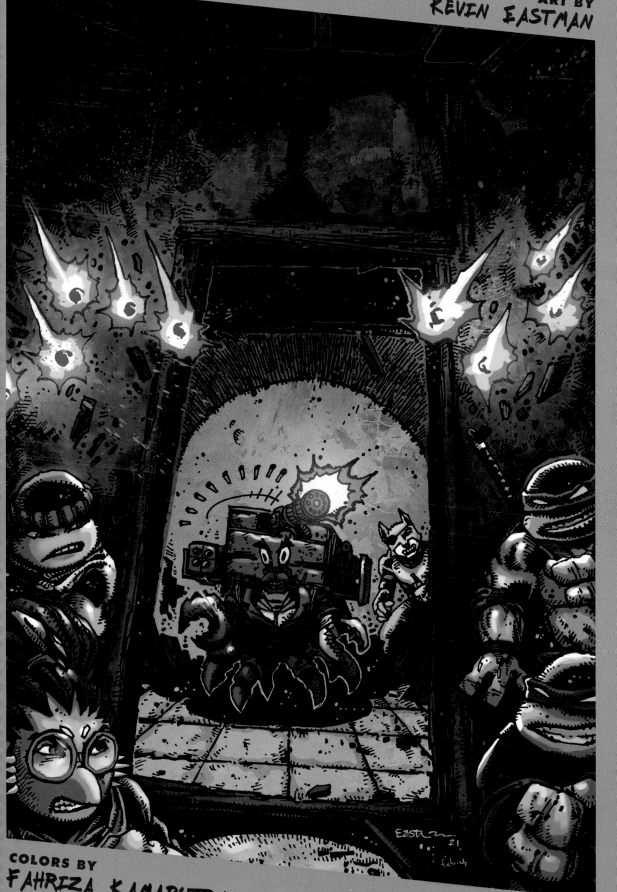

ART BY
JODI NISHIJIMA

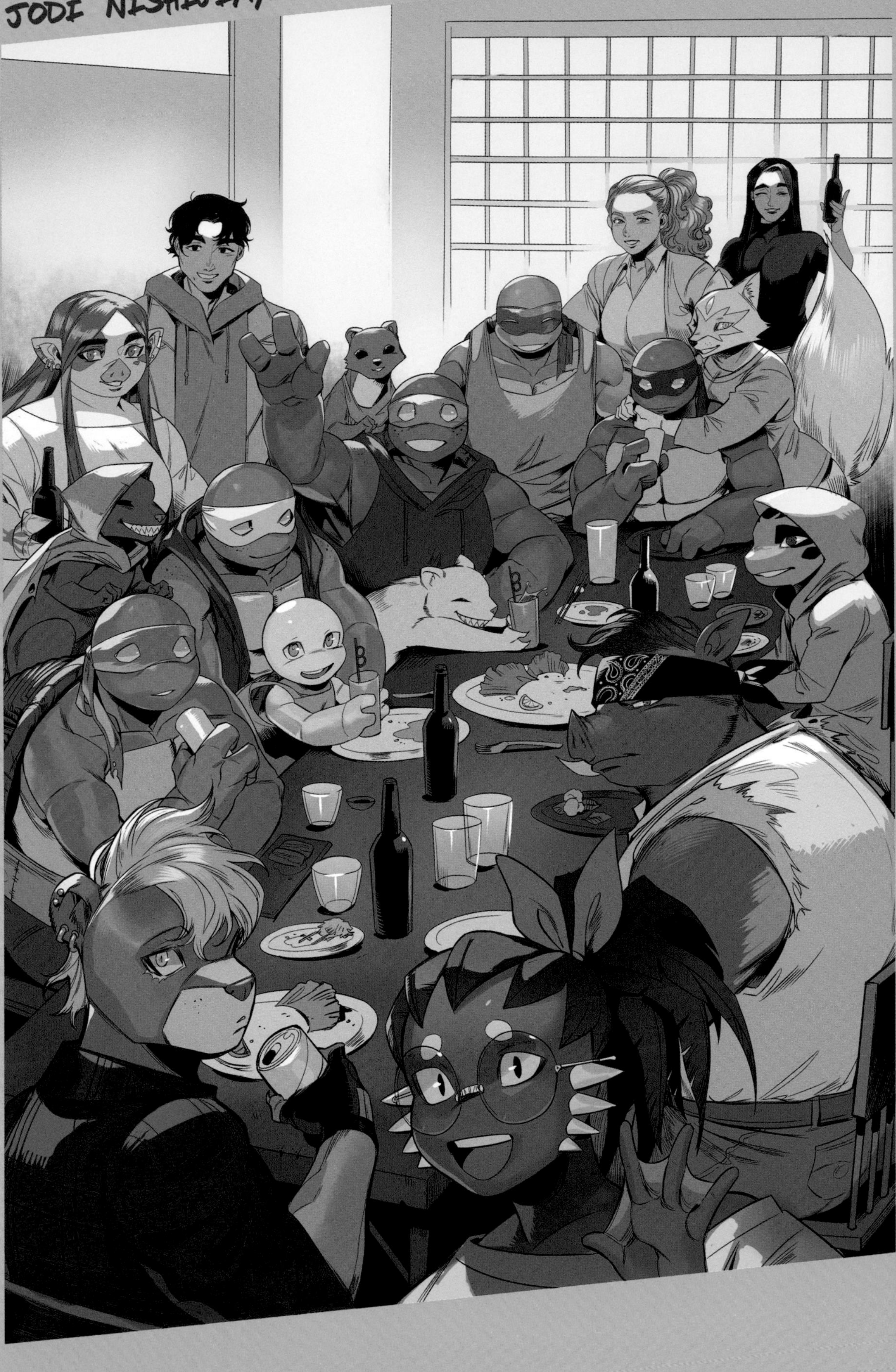

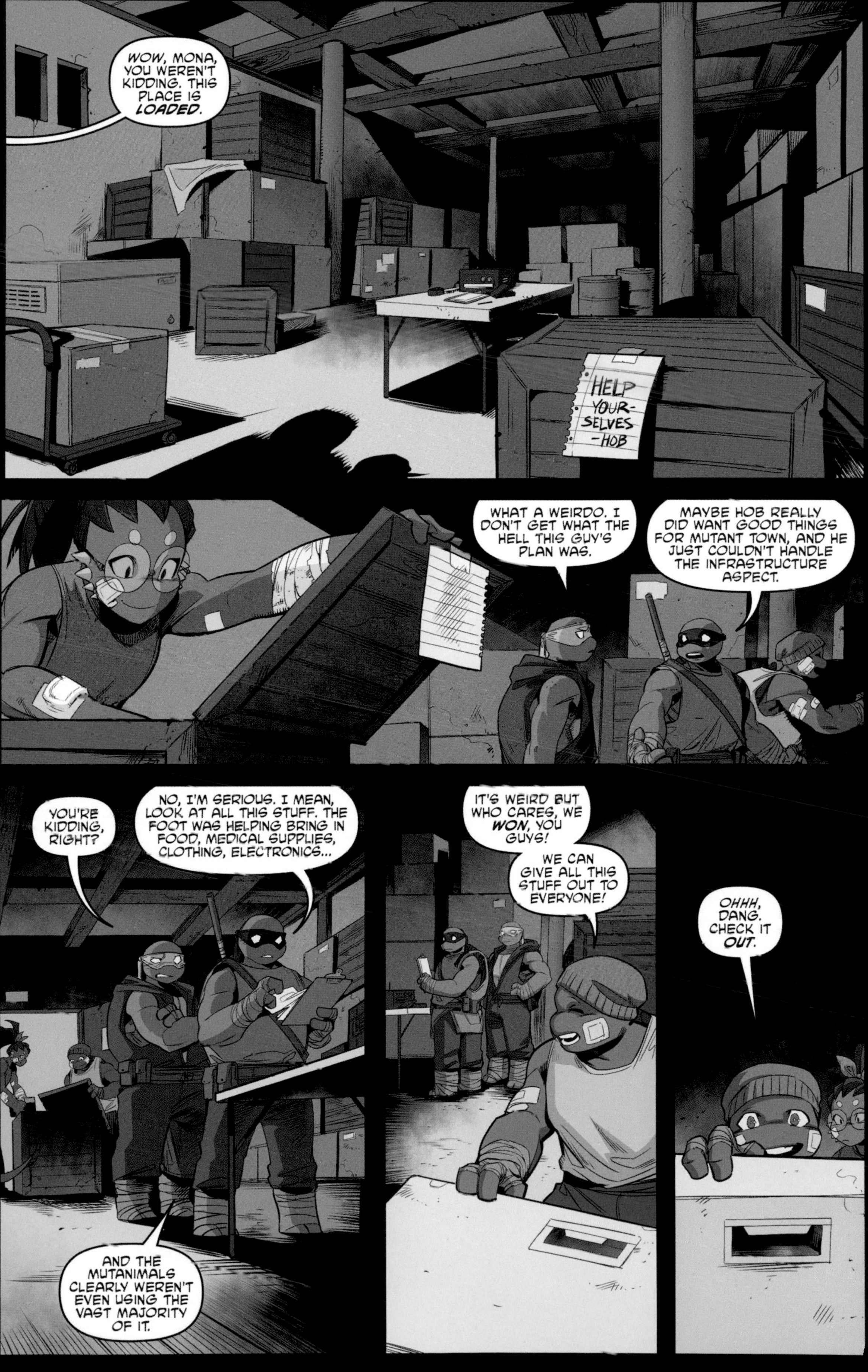
WOW, MONA, YOU WEREN'T KIDDING. THIS PLACE IS *LOADED*.
HELP YOUR-SELVES -HOB
WHAT A WEIRDO. I DON'T GET WHAT THE HELL THIS GUY'S PLAN WAS.
MAYBE HOB REALLY DID WANT GOOD THINGS FOR MUTANT TOWN, AND HE JUST COULDN'T HANDLE THE INFRASTRUCTURE ASPECT.
YOU'RE KIDDING, RIGHT?
NO, I'M SERIOUS. I MEAN, LOOK AT ALL THIS STUFF. THE FOOT WAS HELPING BRING IN FOOD, MEDICAL SUPPLIES, CLOTHING, ELECTRONICS...
AND THE MUTANIMALS CLEARLY WEREN'T EVEN USING THE VAST MAJORITY OF IT.
IT'S WEIRD BUT WHO CARES, WE *WON*, YOU GUYS!
WE CAN GIVE ALL THIS STUFF OUT TO EVERYONE!
OHHH, DANG. CHECK IT *OUT*.

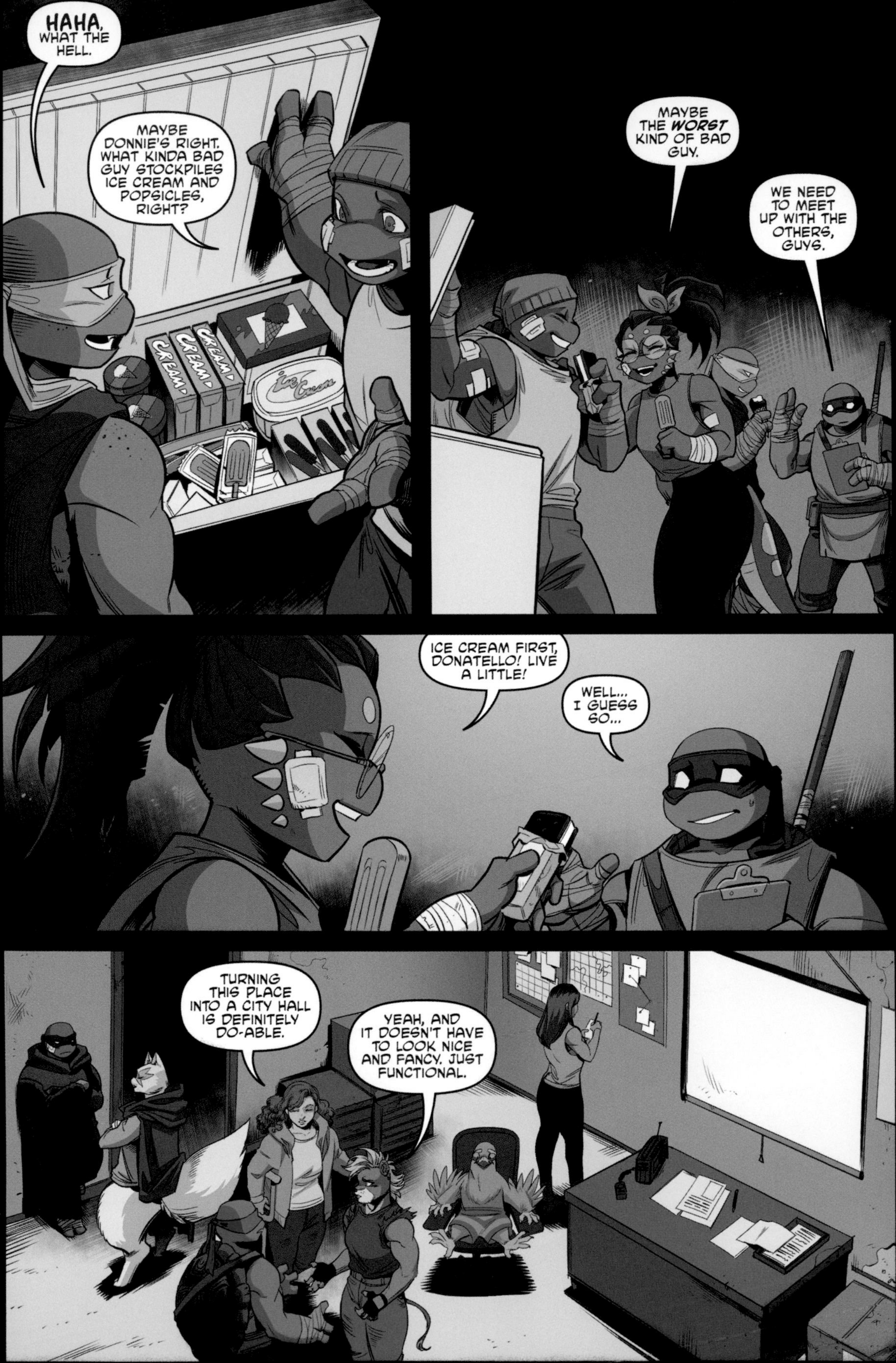
HAHA, WHAT THE HELL.
MAYBE DONNIE'S RIGHT. WHAT KINDA BAD GUY STOCKPILES ICE CREAM AND POPSICLES, RIGHT?
CREAM
CREAM
CREAM
Ice Cream
MAYBE THE WORST KIND OF BAD GUY.
WE NEED TO MEET UP WITH THE OTHERS, GUYS.
ICE CREAM FIRST, DONATELLO! LIVE A LITTLE!
WELL... I GUESS SO...
TURNING THIS PLACE INTO A CITY HALL IS DEFINITELY DO-ABLE.
YEAH, AND IT DOESN'T HAVE TO LOOK NICE AND FANCY. JUST FUNCTIONAL.

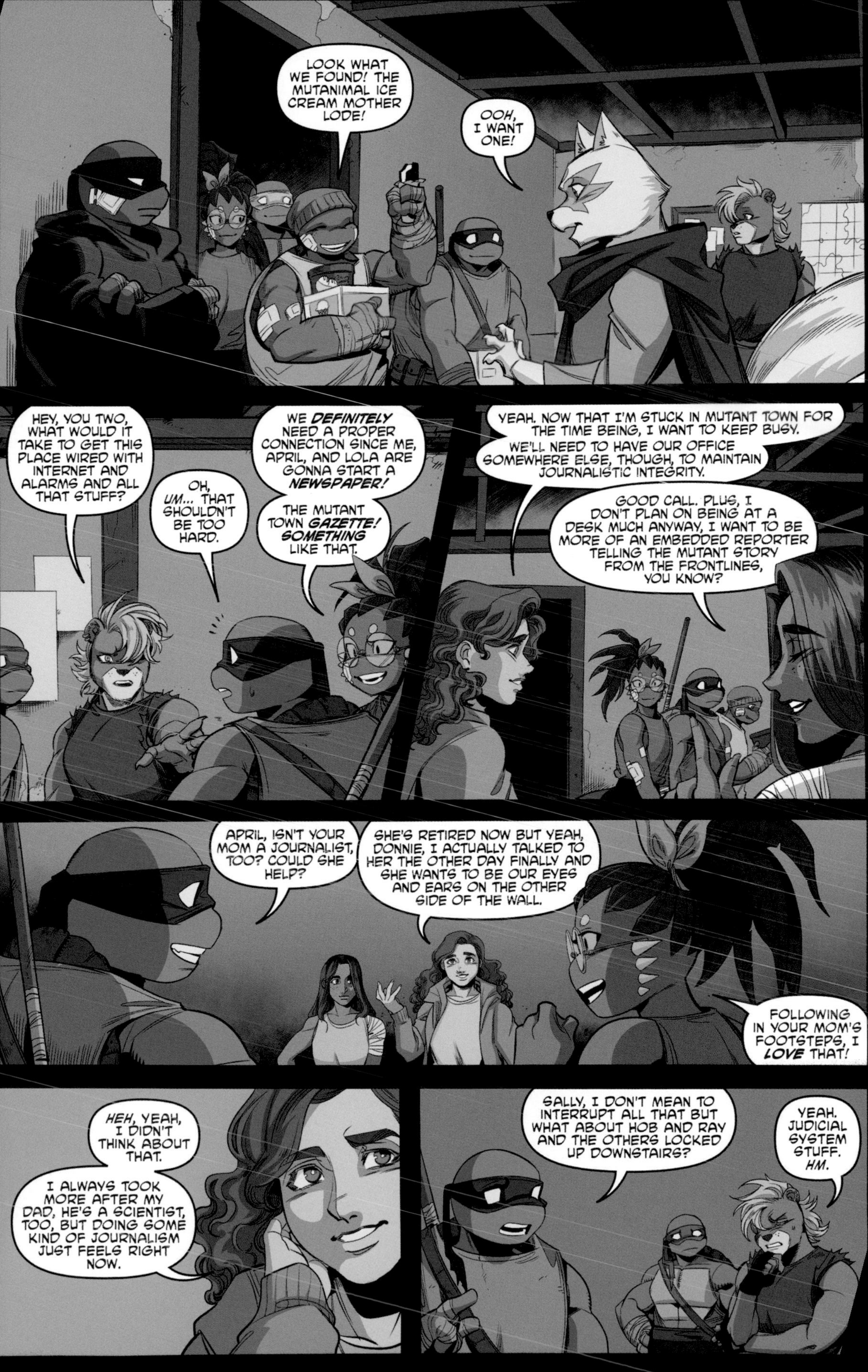

LOOK WHAT WE FOUND! THE MUTANIMAL ICE CREAM MOTHER LODE!
OOH, I WANT ONE!
HEY, YOU TWO, WHAT WOULD IT TAKE TO GET THIS PLACE WIRED WITH INTERNET AND ALARMS AND ALL THAT STUFF?
OH, UM... THAT SHOULDN'T BE TOO HARD.
WE DEFINITELY NEED A PROPER CONNECTION SINCE ME, APRIL, AND LOLA ARE GONNA START A NEWSPAPER!
THE MUTANT TOWN GAZETTE! SOMETHING LIKE THAT.
YEAH. NOW THAT I'M STUCK IN MUTANT TOWN FOR THE TIME BEING, I WANT TO KEEP BUSY.
WE'LL NEED TO HAVE OUR OFFICE SOMEWHERE ELSE, THOUGH, TO MAINTAIN JOURNALISTIC INTEGRITY.
GOOD CALL. PLUS, I DON'T PLAN ON BEING AT A DESK MUCH ANYWAY, I WANT TO BE MORE OF AN EMBEDDED REPORTER TELLING THE MUTANT STORY FROM THE FRONTLINES, YOU KNOW?
APRIL, ISN'T YOUR MOM A JOURNALIST, TOO? COULD SHE HELP?
SHE'S RETIRED NOW BUT YEAH, DONNIE, I ACTUALLY TALKED TO HER THE OTHER DAY FINALLY AND SHE WANTS TO BE OUR EYES AND EARS ON THE OTHER SIDE OF THE WALL.
FOLLOWING IN YOUR MOM'S FOOTSTEPS, I LOVE THAT!
HEH, YEAH, I DIDN'T THINK ABOUT THAT.
I ALWAYS TOOK MORE AFTER MY DAD, HE'S A SCIENTIST, TOO, BUT DOING SOME KIND OF JOURNALISM JUST FEELS RIGHT NOW.
SALLY, I DON'T MEAN TO INTERRUPT ALL THAT BUT WHAT ABOUT HOB AND RAY AND THE OTHERS LOCKED UP DOWNSTAIRS?
YEAH. JUDICIAL SYSTEM STUFF. HM.

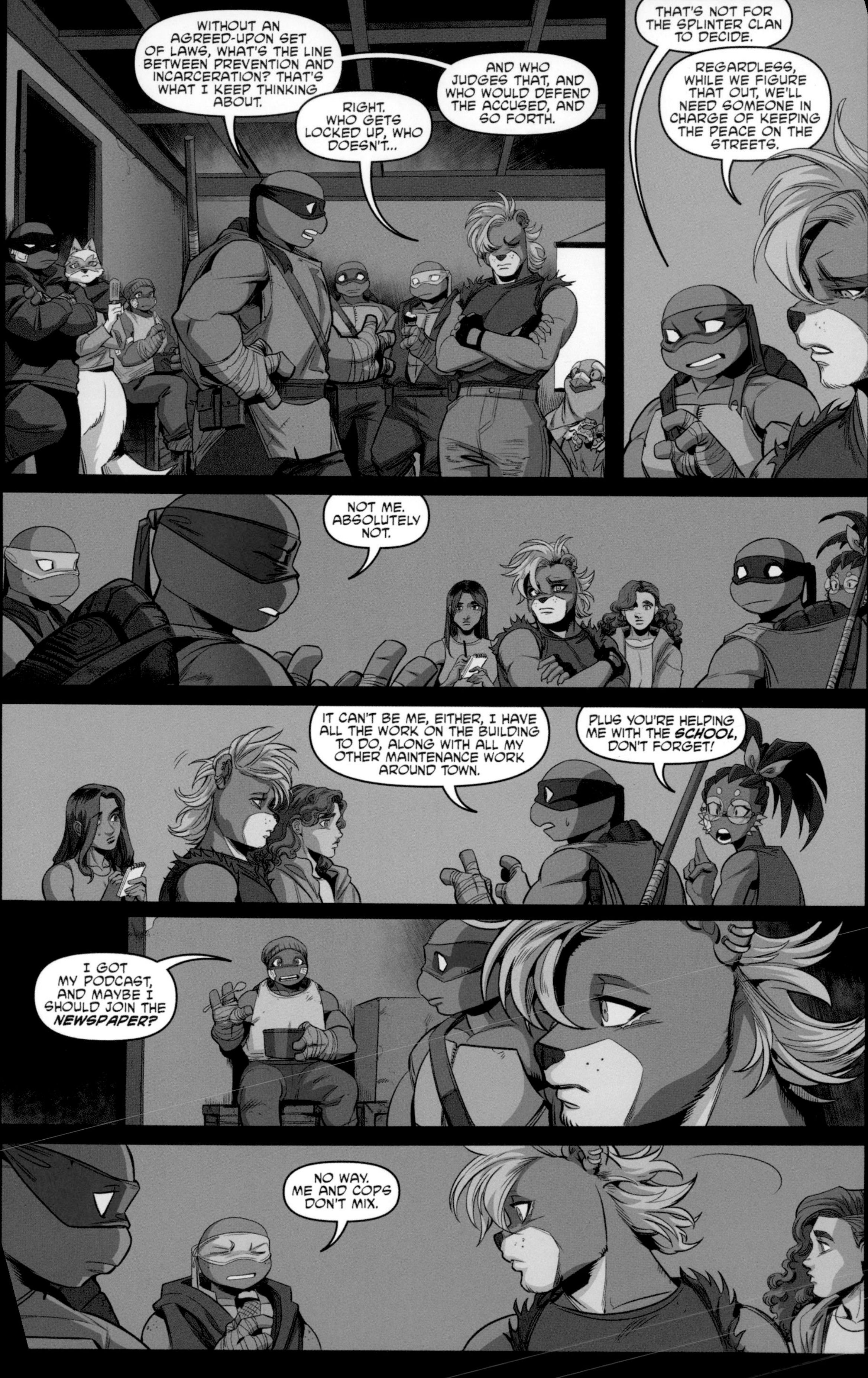
WITHOUT AN AGREED-UPON SET OF LAWS, WHAT'S THE LINE BETWEEN PREVENTION AND INCARCERATION? THAT'S WHAT I KEEP THINKING ABOUT.
RIGHT. WHO GETS LOCKED UP, WHO DOESN'T...
AND WHO JUDGES THAT, AND WHO WOULD DEFEND THE ACCUSED, AND SO FORTH.
THAT'S NOT FOR THE SPLINTER CLAN TO DECIDE.
REGARDLESS, WHILE WE FIGURE THAT OUT, WE'LL NEED SOMEONE IN CHARGE OF KEEPING THE PEACE ON THE STREETS.
NOT ME. ABSOLUTELY NOT.
IT CAN'T BE ME, EITHER, I HAVE ALL THE WORK ON THE BUILDING TO DO, ALONG WITH ALL MY OTHER MAINTENANCE WORK AROUND TOWN.
PLUS YOU'RE HELPING ME WITH THE SCHOOL, DON'T FORGET!
I GOT MY PODCAST, AND MAYBE I SHOULD JOIN THE NEWSPAPER?
NO WAY. ME AND COPS DON'T MIX.

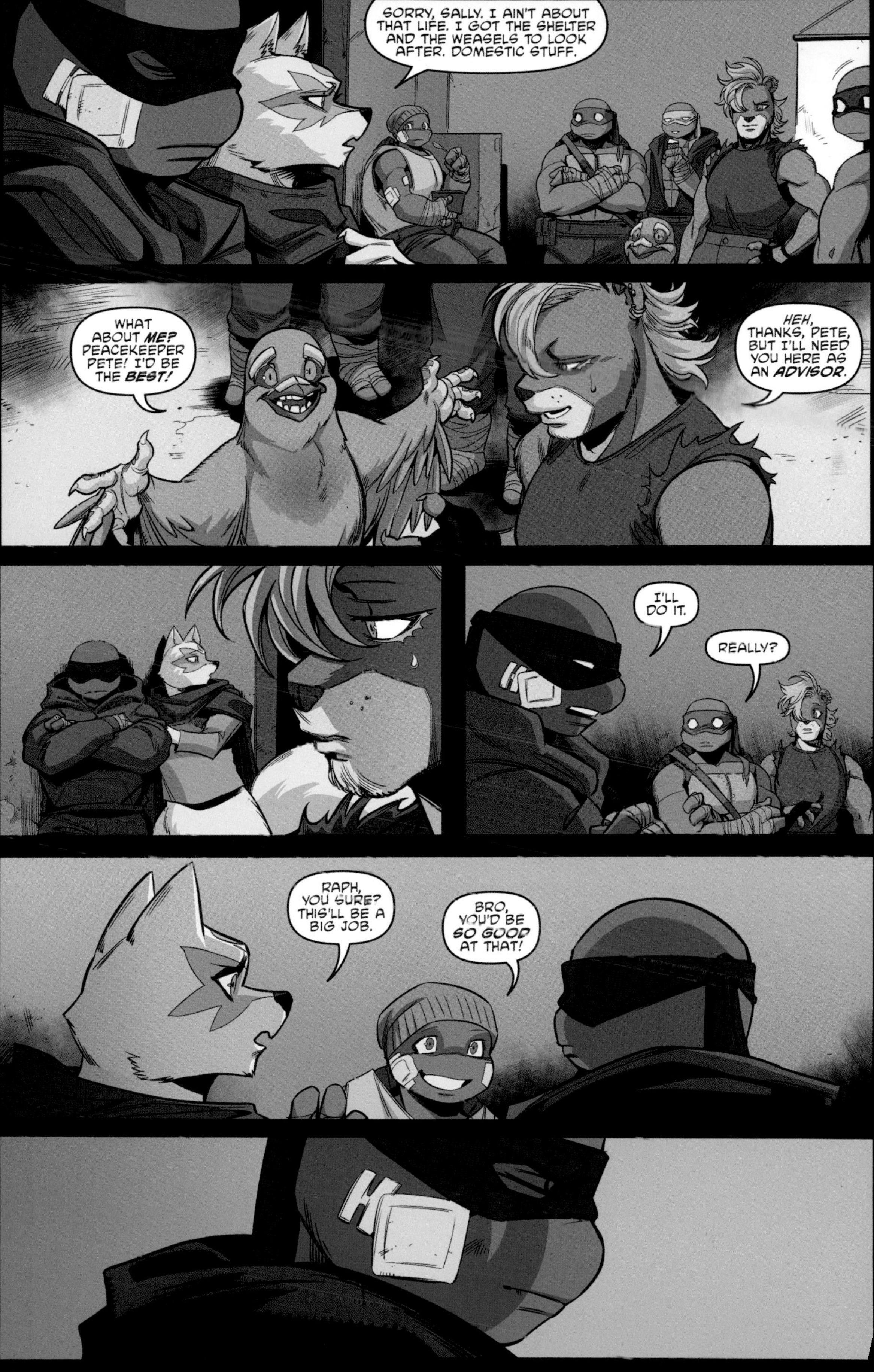
SORRY, SALLY. I AIN'T ABOUT THAT LIFE. I GOT THE SHELTER AND THE WEASELS TO LOOK AFTER. DOMESTIC STUFF.
WHAT ABOUT *ME?* PEACEKEEPER PETE! I'D BE THE *BEST!*
HEH, THANKS, PETE, BUT I'LL NEED YOU HERE AS AN *ADVISOR.*
I'LL DO IT.
REALLY?
RAPH, YOU SURE? THIS'LL BE A BIG JOB.
BRO, YOU'D BE *SO GOOD* AT THAT!

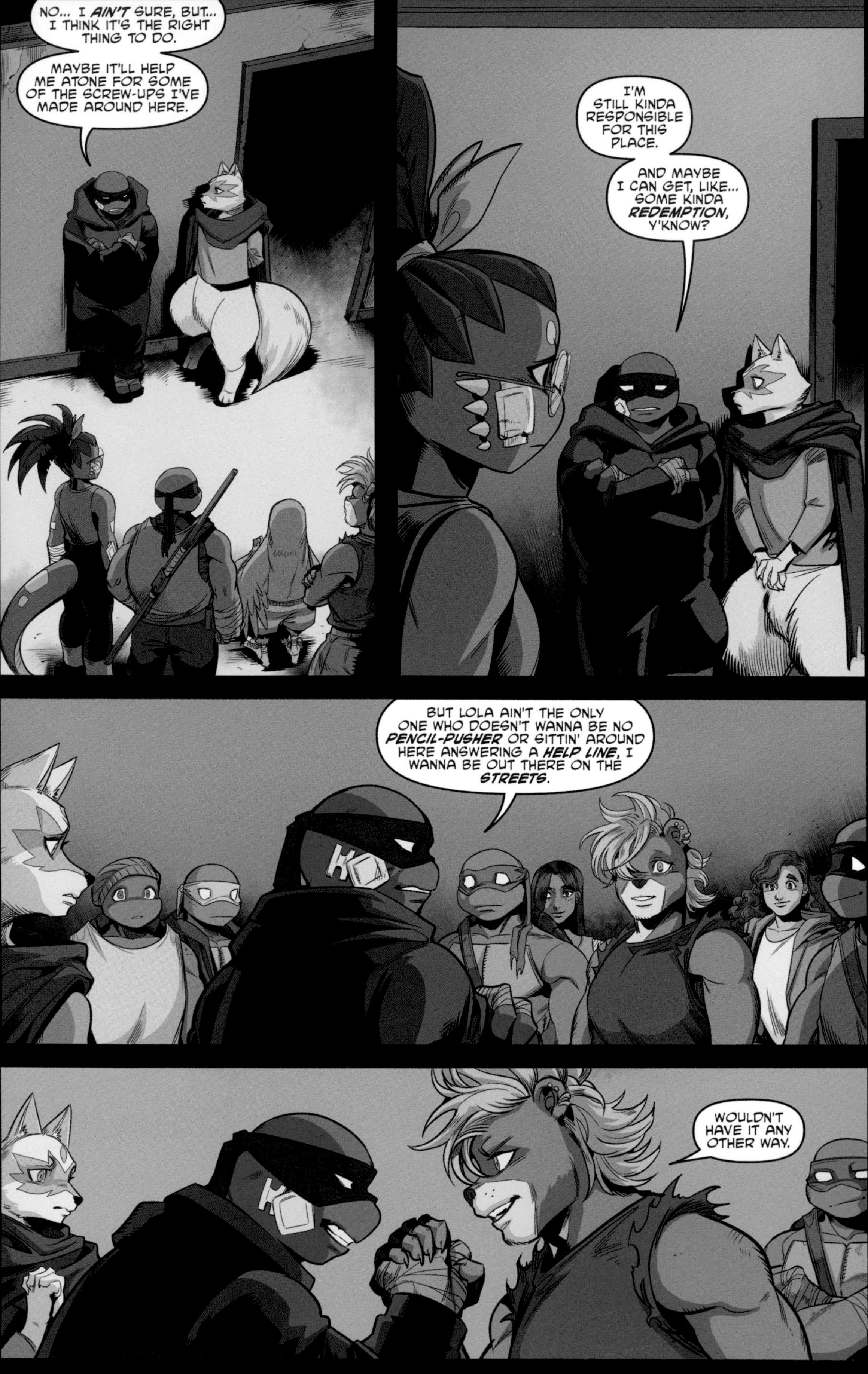
NO... I AIN'T SURE, BUT... I THINK IT'S THE RIGHT THING TO DO.
MAYBE IT'LL HELP ME ATONE FOR SOME OF THE SCREW-UPS I'VE MADE AROUND HERE.
I'M STILL KINDA RESPONSIBLE FOR THIS PLACE.
AND MAYBE I CAN GET, LIKE... SOME KINDA REDEMPTION, Y'KNOW?
BUT LOLA AIN'T THE ONLY ONE WHO DOESN'T WANNA BE NO PENCIL-PUSHER OR SITTIN' AROUND HERE ANSWERING A HELP LINE, I WANNA BE OUT THERE ON THE STREETS.
WOULDN'T HAVE IT ANY OTHER WAY.

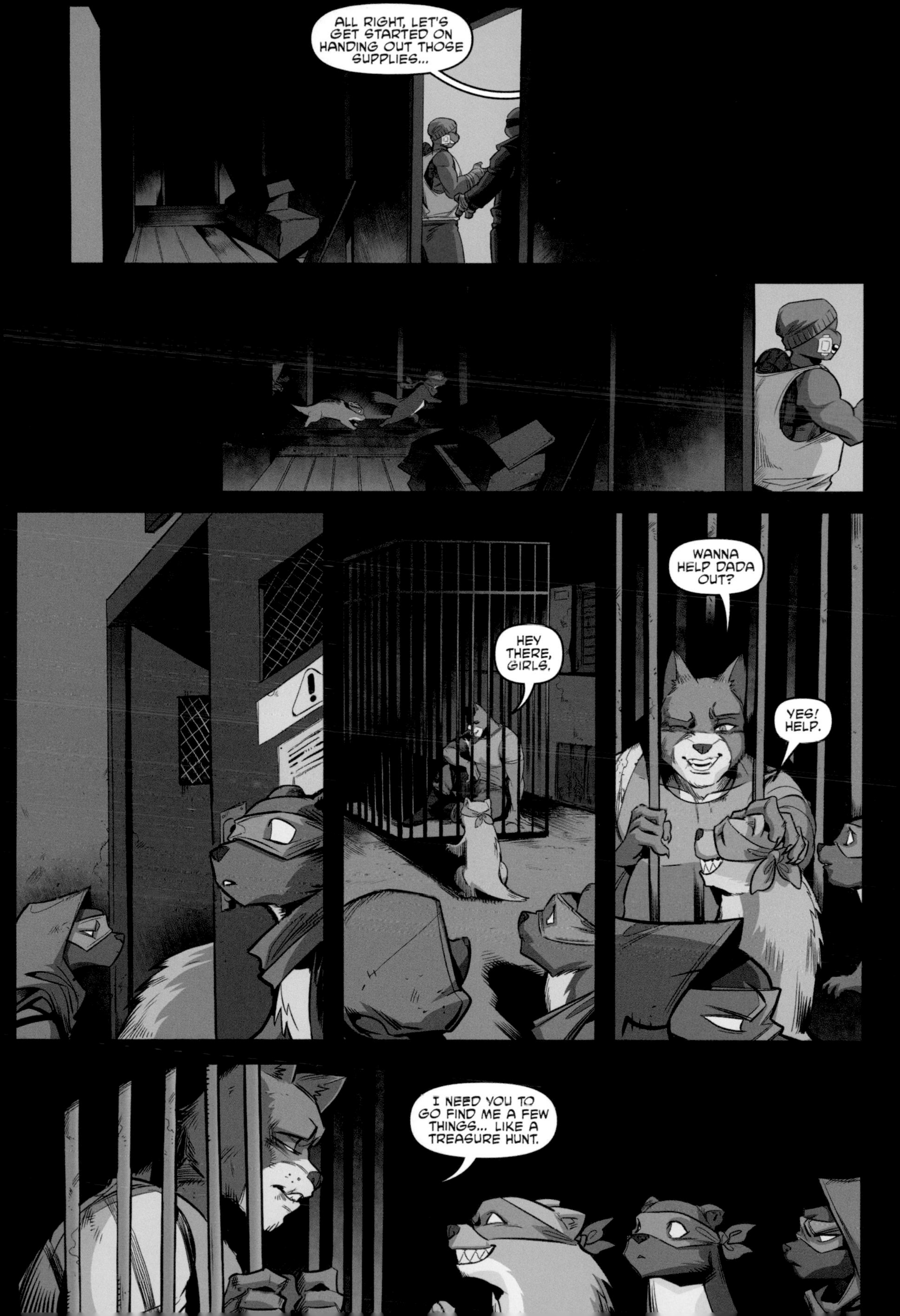
ALL RIGHT, LET'S GET STARTED ON HANDING OUT THOSE SUPPLIES...
HEY THERE, GIRLS.
WANNA HELP DADA OUT?
YES! HELP.
I NEED YOU TO GO FIND ME A FEW THINGS... LIKE A TREASURE HUNT.

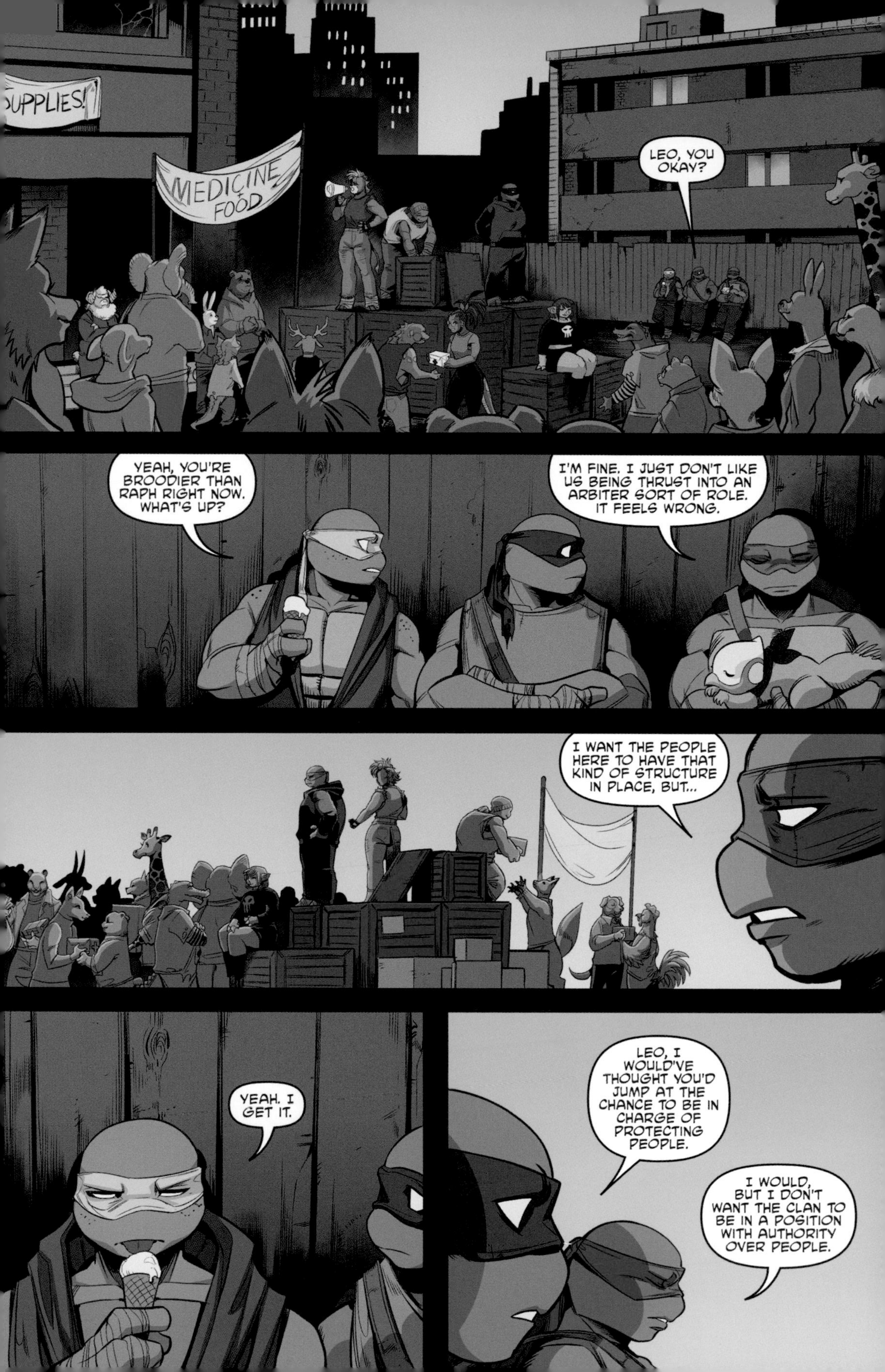
SUPPLIES!
MEDICINE + FOOD
LEO, YOU OKAY?
YEAH, YOU'RE BROODIER THAN RAPH RIGHT NOW. WHAT'S UP?
I'M FINE. I JUST DON'T LIKE US BEING THRUST INTO AN ARBITER SORT OF ROLE. IT FEELS WRONG.
I WANT THE PEOPLE HERE TO HAVE THAT KIND OF STRUCTURE IN PLACE, BUT...
YEAH. I GET IT.
LEO, I WOULD'VE THOUGHT YOU'D JUMP AT THE CHANCE TO BE IN CHARGE OF PROTECTING PEOPLE.
I WOULD, BUT I DON'T WANT THE CLAN TO BE IN A POSITION WITH AUTHORITY OVER PEOPLE.

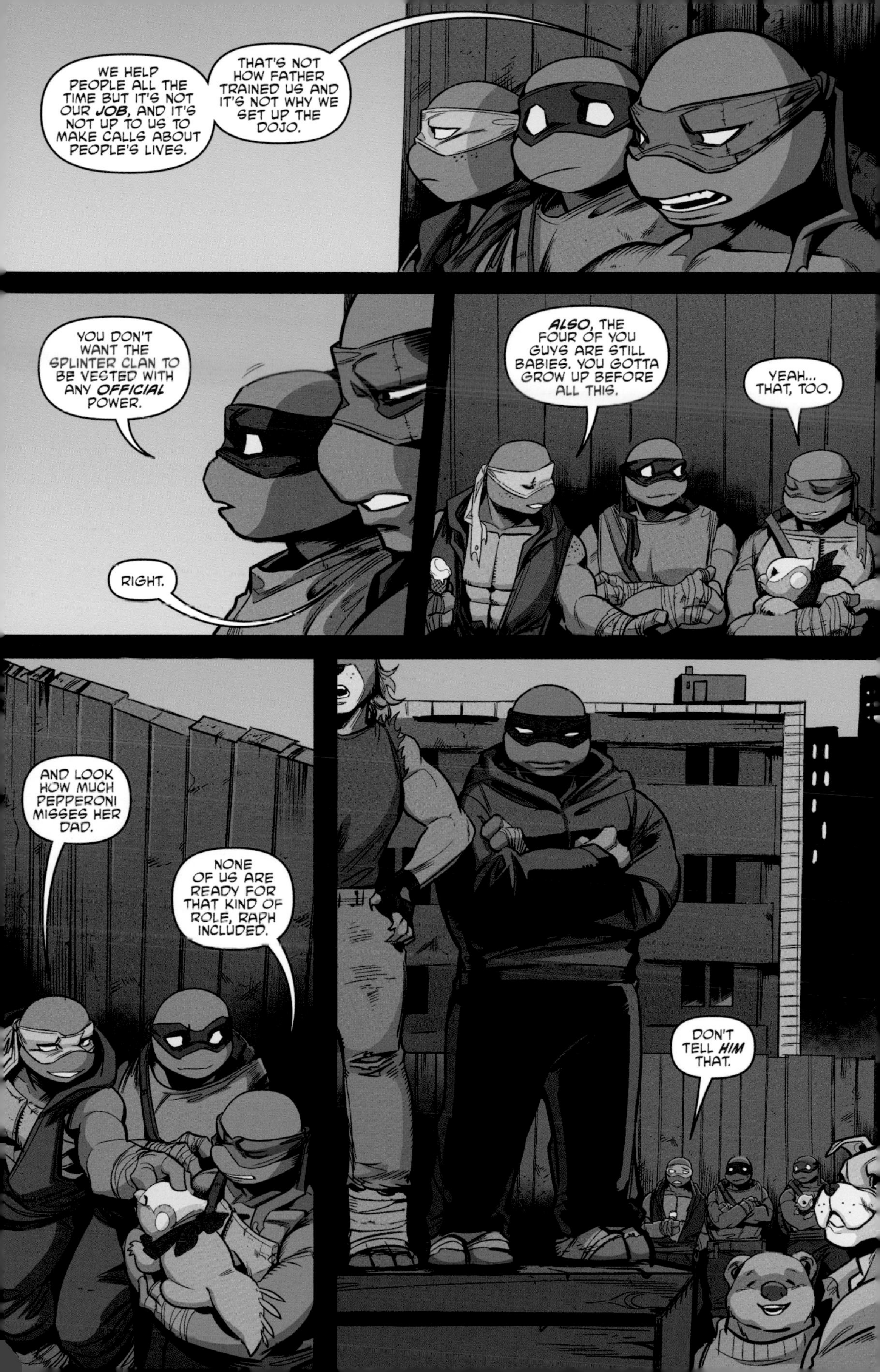
WE HELP PEOPLE ALL THE TIME BUT IT'S NOT OUR *JOB*, AND IT'S NOT UP TO US TO MAKE CALLS ABOUT PEOPLE'S LIVES.
THAT'S NOT HOW FATHER TRAINED US AND IT'S NOT WHY WE SET UP THE DOJO.
YOU DON'T WANT THE SPLINTER CLAN TO BE VESTED WITH ANY *OFFICIAL* POWER.
RIGHT.
ALSO, THE FOUR OF YOU GUYS ARE STILL BABIES. YOU GOTTA GROW UP BEFORE ALL THIS.
YEAH... THAT, TOO.
AND LOOK HOW MUCH PEPPERONI MISSES HER DAD.
NONE OF US ARE READY FOR THAT KIND OF ROLE, RAPH INCLUDED.
DON'T TELL *HIM* THAT.

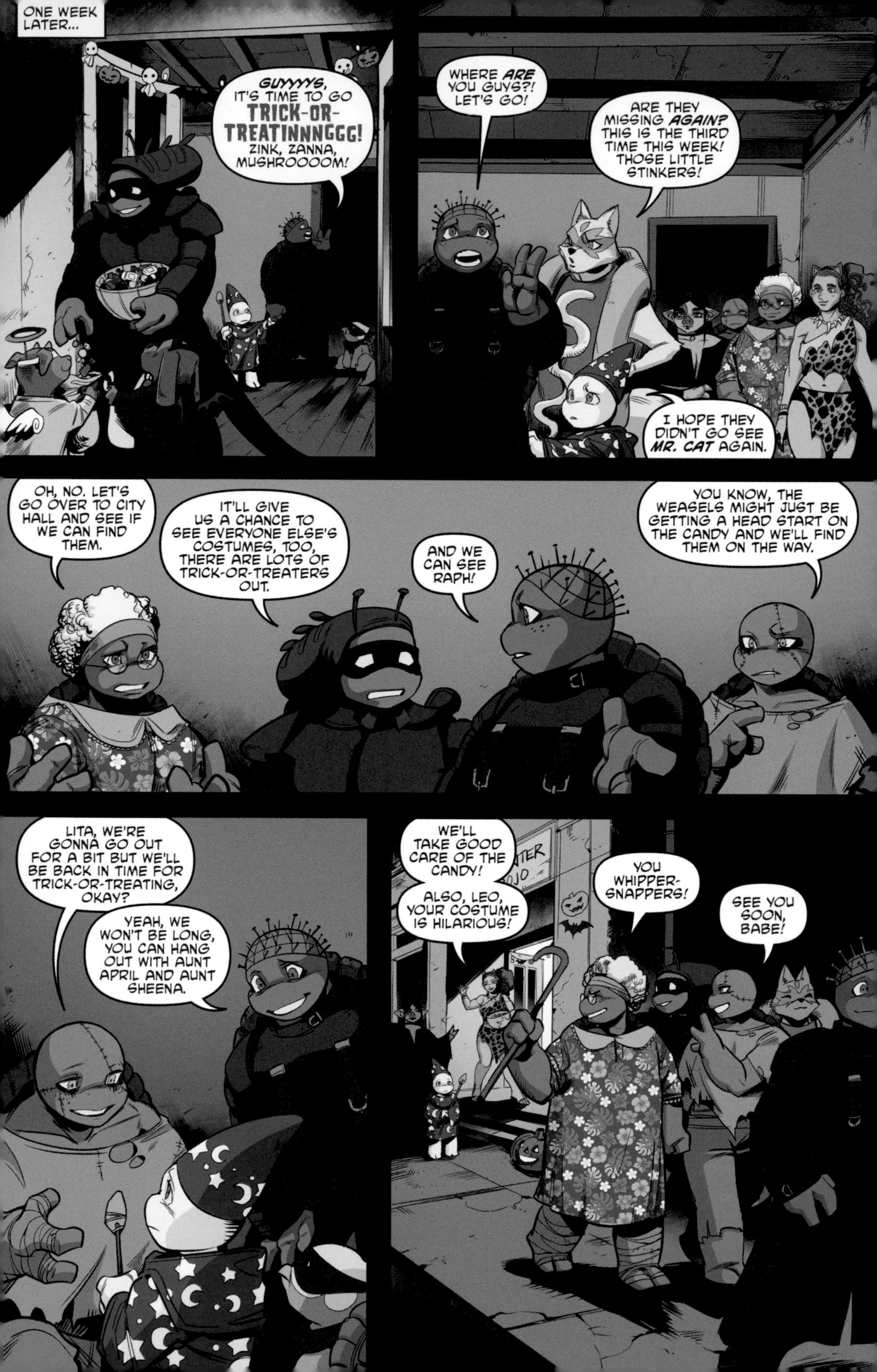
ONE WEEK LATER...
GUYYYYS, IT'S TIME TO GO TRICK-OR-TREATINNNGGG! ZINK, ZANNA, MUSHROOOOM!
WHERE ARE YOU GUYS?! LET'S GO!
ARE THEY MISSING AGAIN? THIS IS THE THIRD TIME THIS WEEK! THOSE LITTLE STINKERS!
I HOPE THEY DIDN'T GO SEE MR. CAT AGAIN.
OH, NO. LET'S GO OVER TO CITY HALL AND SEE IF WE CAN FIND THEM.
IT'LL GIVE US A CHANCE TO SEE EVERYONE ELSE'S COSTUMES, TOO, THERE ARE LOTS OF TRICK-OR-TREATERS OUT.
AND WE CAN SEE RAPH!
YOU KNOW, THE WEASELS MIGHT JUST BE GETTING A HEAD START ON THE CANDY AND WE'LL FIND THEM ON THE WAY.
LITA, WE'RE GONNA GO OUT FOR A BIT BUT WE'LL BE BACK IN TIME FOR TRICK-OR-TREATING, OKAY?
YEAH, WE WON'T BE LONG, YOU CAN HANG OUT WITH AUNT APRIL AND AUNT SHEENA.
WE'LL TAKE GOOD CARE OF THE CANDY!
ALSO, LEO, YOUR COSTUME IS HILARIOUS!
YOU WHIPPER-SNAPPERS!
SEE YOU SOON, BABE!

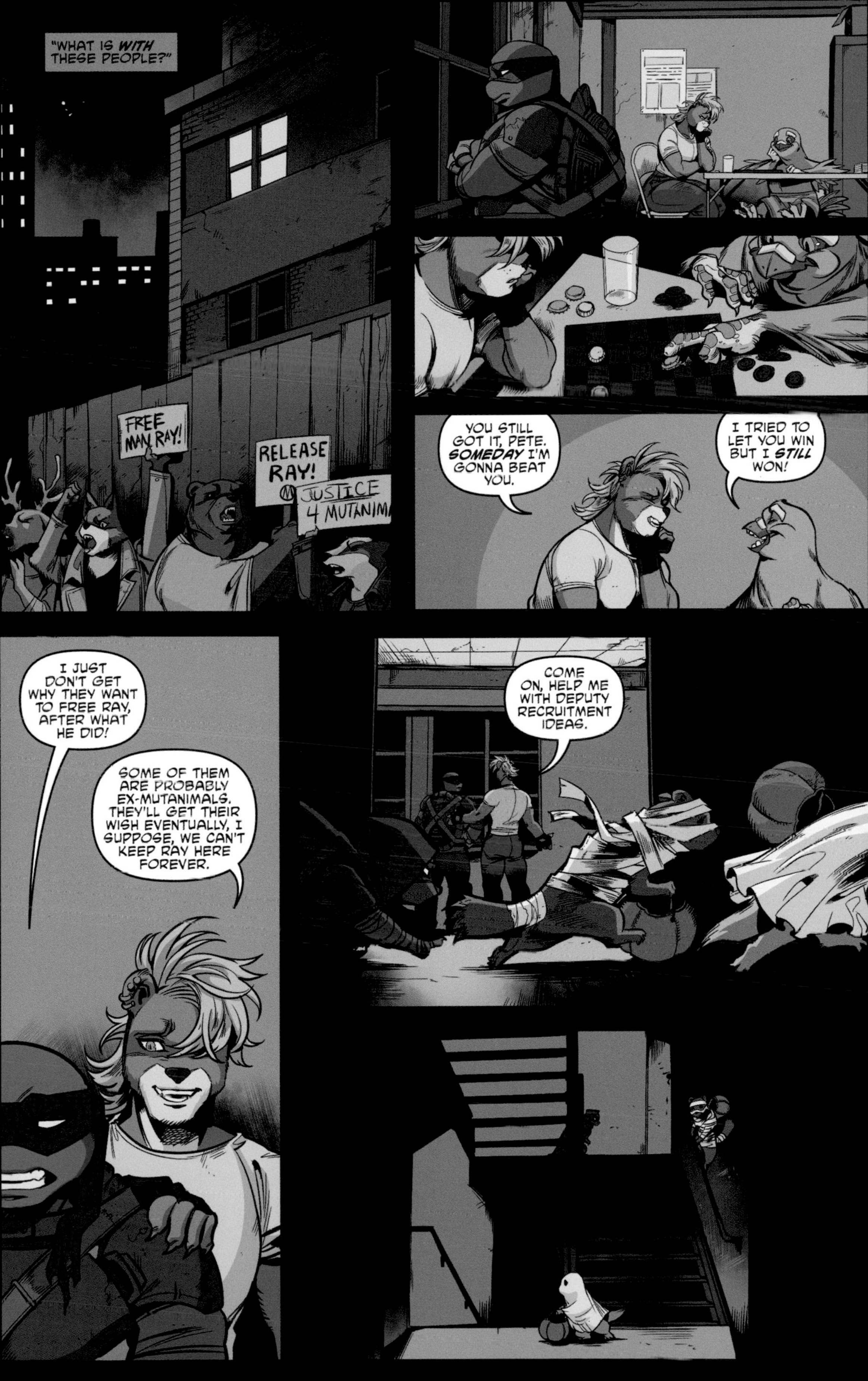
"WHAT IS WITH THESE PEOPLE?"
FREE MAN RAY!
RELEASE RAY!
JUSTICE 4 MUTANIM
YOU STILL GOT IT, PETE. SOMEDAY I'M GONNA BEAT YOU.
I TRIED TO LET YOU WIN BUT I STILL WON!
I JUST DON'T GET WHY THEY WANT TO FREE RAY, AFTER WHAT HE DID!
SOME OF THEM ARE PROBABLY EX-MUTANIMALS. THEY'LL GET THEIR WISH EVENTUALLY, I SUPPOSE, WE CAN'T KEEP RAY HERE FOREVER.
COME ON, HELP ME WITH DEPUTY RECRUITMENT IDEAS.

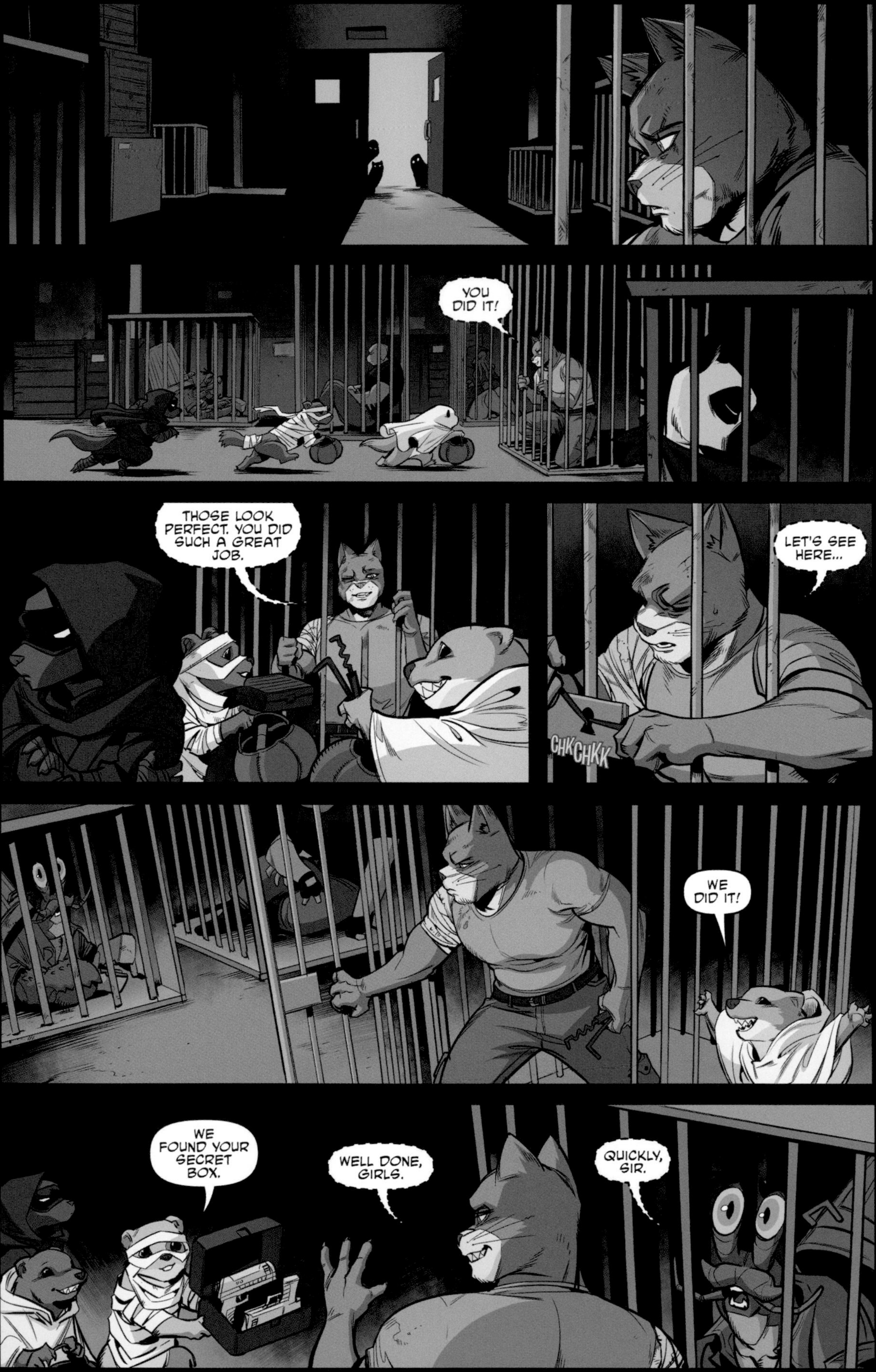
YOU DID IT!
THOSE LOOK PERFECT. YOU DID SUCH A GREAT JOB.
LET'S SEE HERE...
CHKCHKK
WE DID IT!
WE FOUND YOUR SECRET BOX.
WELL DONE, GIRLS.
QUICKLY, SIR.

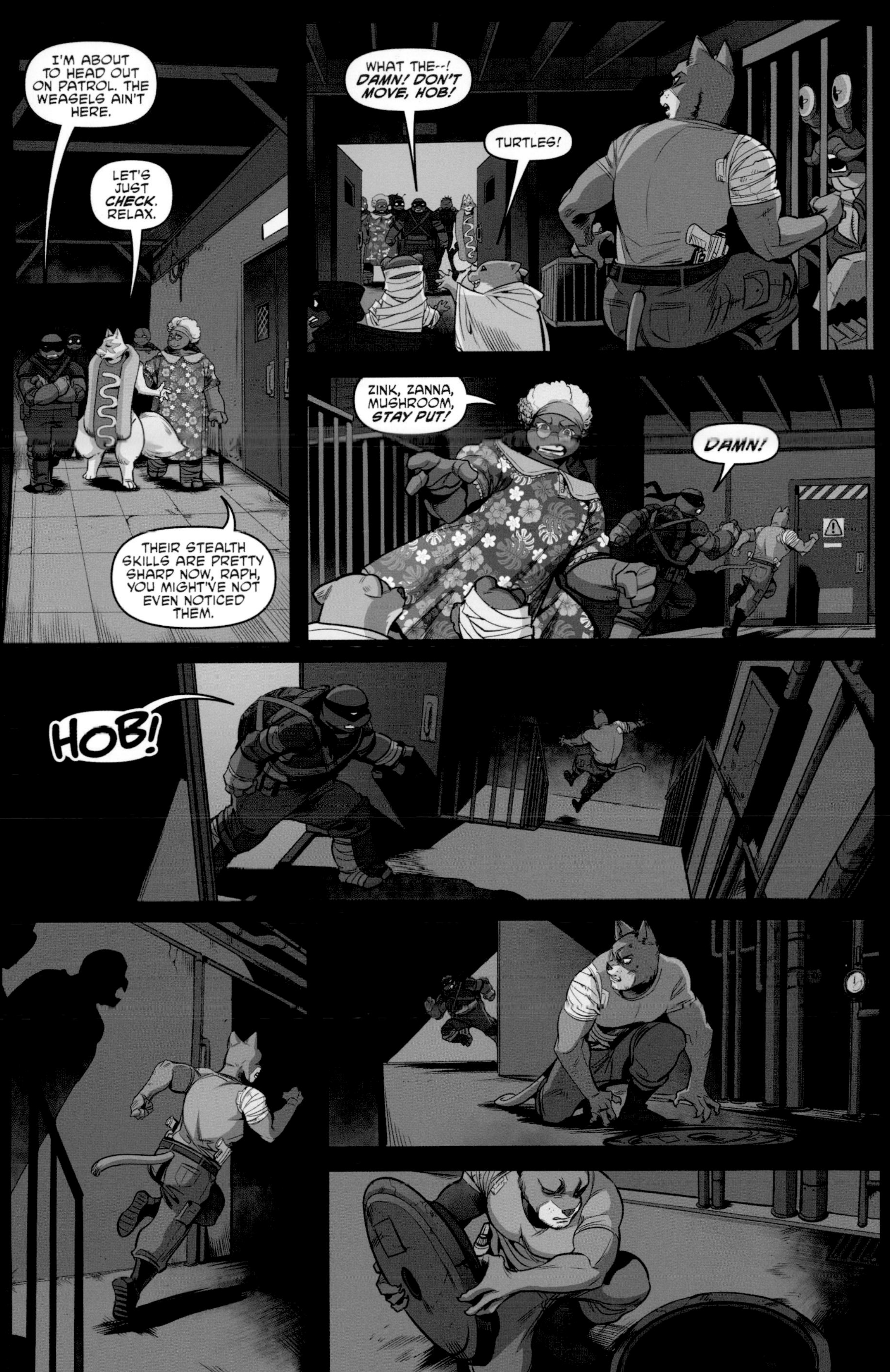

I'M ABOUT TO HEAD OUT ON PATROL. THE WEASELS AIN'T HERE.
LET'S JUST *CHECK*. RELAX.
THEIR STEALTH SKILLS ARE PRETTY SHARP NOW, RAPH, YOU MIGHT'VE NOT EVEN NOTICED THEM.
WHAT THE--! *DAMN! DON'T MOVE, HOB!*
TURTLES!
ZINK, ZANNA, MUSHROOM, *STAY PUT!*
DAMN!
HOB!

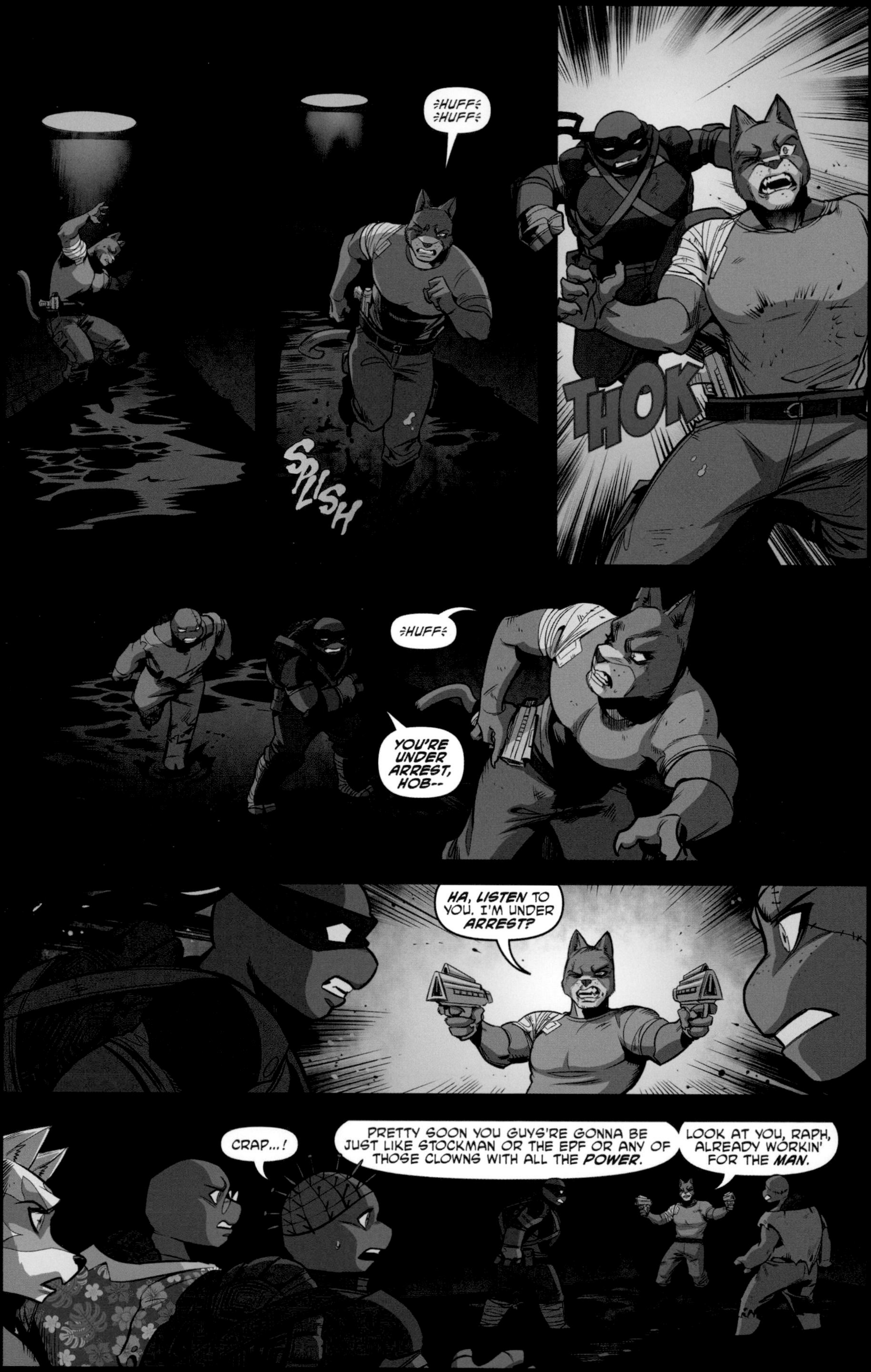

HUFF HUFF
SPLISH
THOK
HUFF
YOU'RE UNDER ARREST, HOB--
HA, LISTEN TO YOU. I'M UNDER ARREST?
CRAP...!
PRETTY SOON YOU GUYS'RE GONNA BE JUST LIKE STOCKMAN OR THE EPF OR ANY OF THOSE CLOWNS WITH ALL THE POWER.
LOOK AT YOU, RAPH, ALREADY WORKIN' FOR THE MAN.

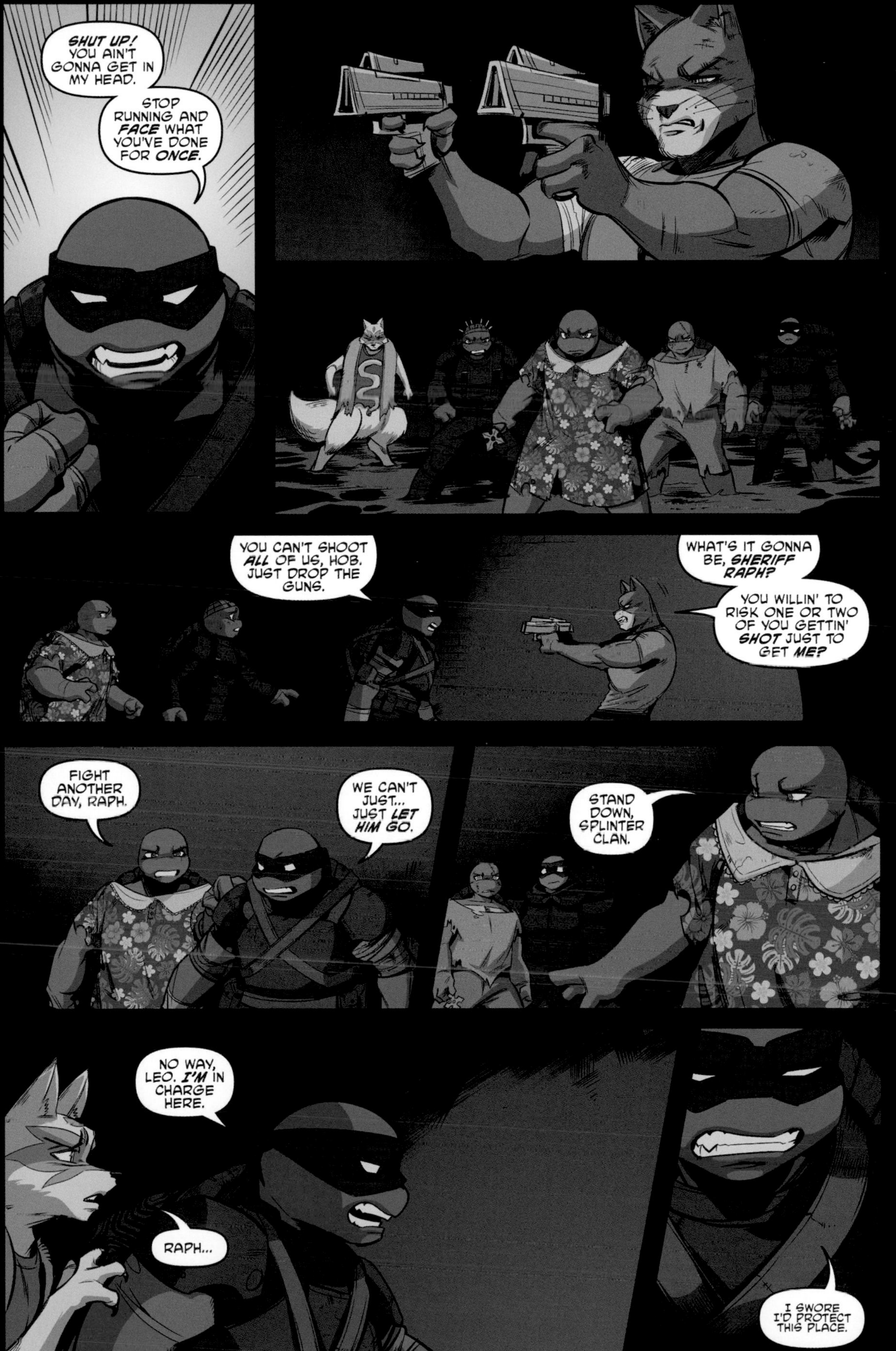

SHUT UP! YOU AIN'T GONNA GET IN MY HEAD.
STOP RUNNING AND FACE WHAT YOU'VE DONE FOR ONCE.
YOU CAN'T SHOOT ALL OF US, HOB. JUST DROP THE GUNS.
WHAT'S IT GONNA BE, SHERIFF RAPH?
YOU WILLIN' TO RISK ONE OR TWO OF YOU GETTIN' SHOT JUST TO GET ME?
FIGHT ANOTHER DAY, RAPH.
WE CAN'T JUST... JUST LET HIM GO.
STAND DOWN, SPLINTER CLAN.
NO WAY, LEO. I'M IN CHARGE HERE.
RAPH...
I SWORE I'D PROTECT THIS PLACE.

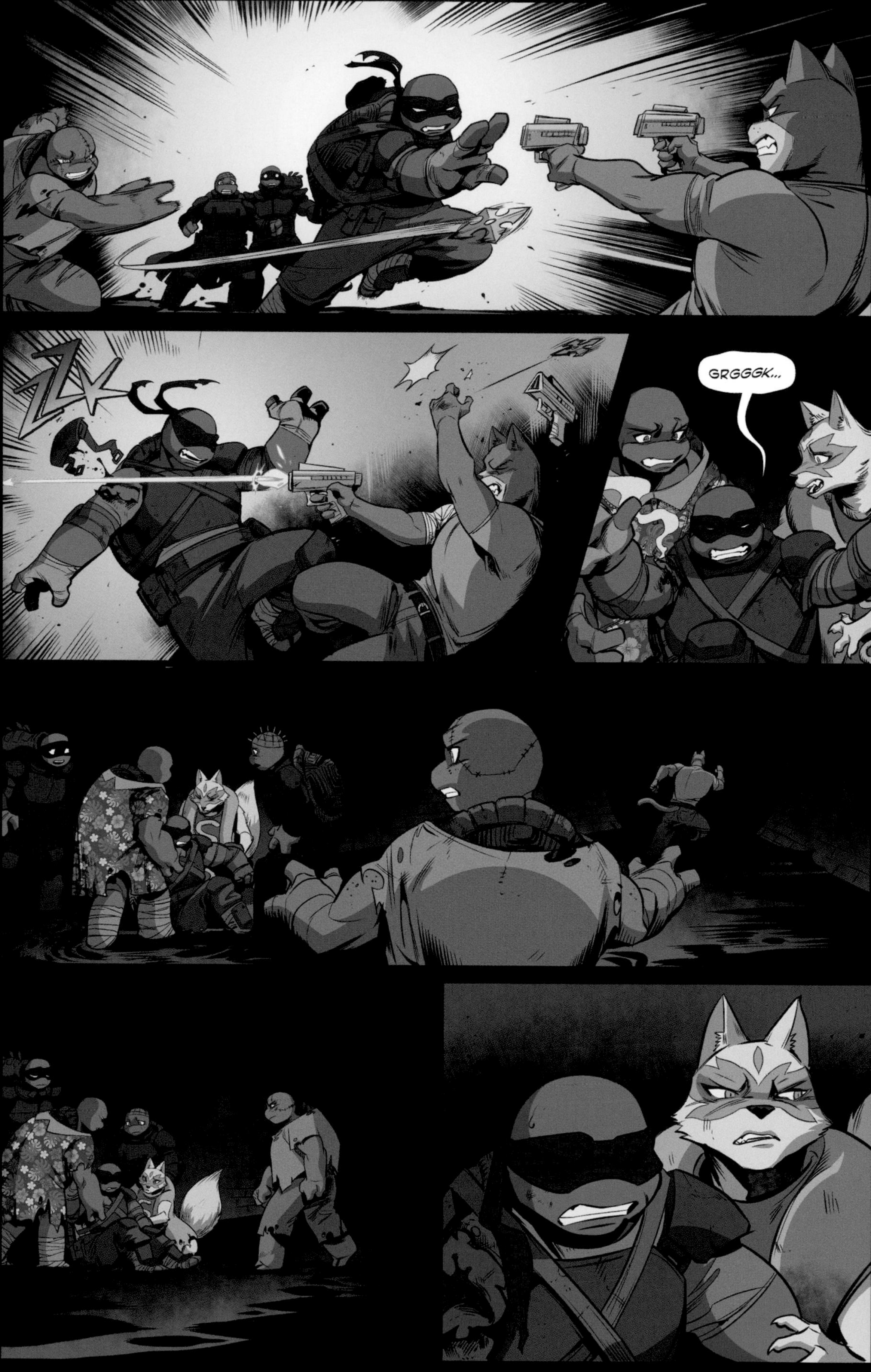
ZZK
GRGGGK...

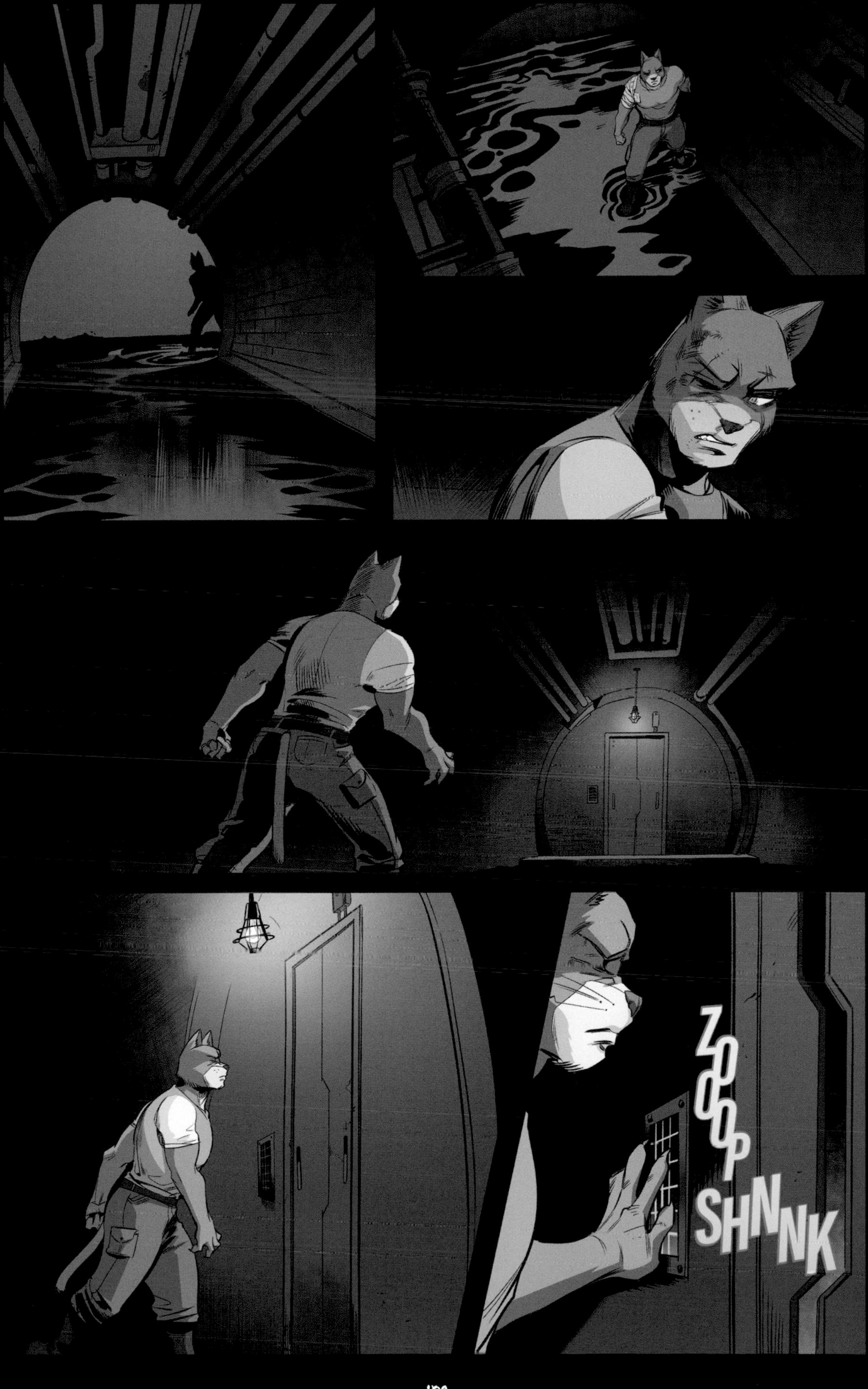
ZOOOP
SHNNK

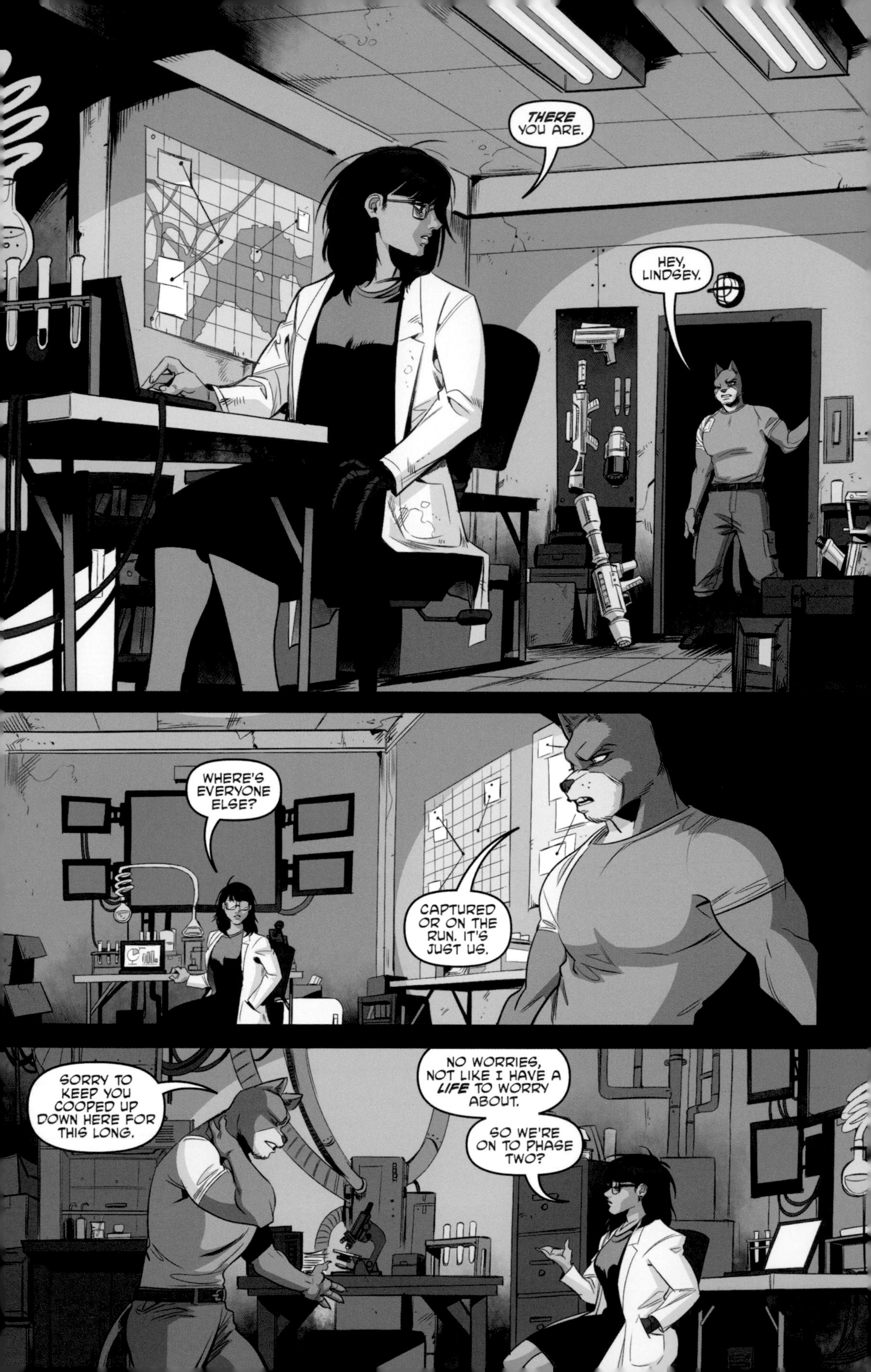

THERE YOU ARE.
HEY, LINDSEY.
WHERE'S EVERYONE ELSE?
CAPTURED OR ON THE RUN. IT'S JUST US.
SORRY TO KEEP YOU COOPED UP DOWN HERE FOR THIS LONG.
NO WORRIES, NOT LIKE I HAVE A *LIFE* TO WORRY ABOUT.
SO WE'RE ON TO PHASE TWO?

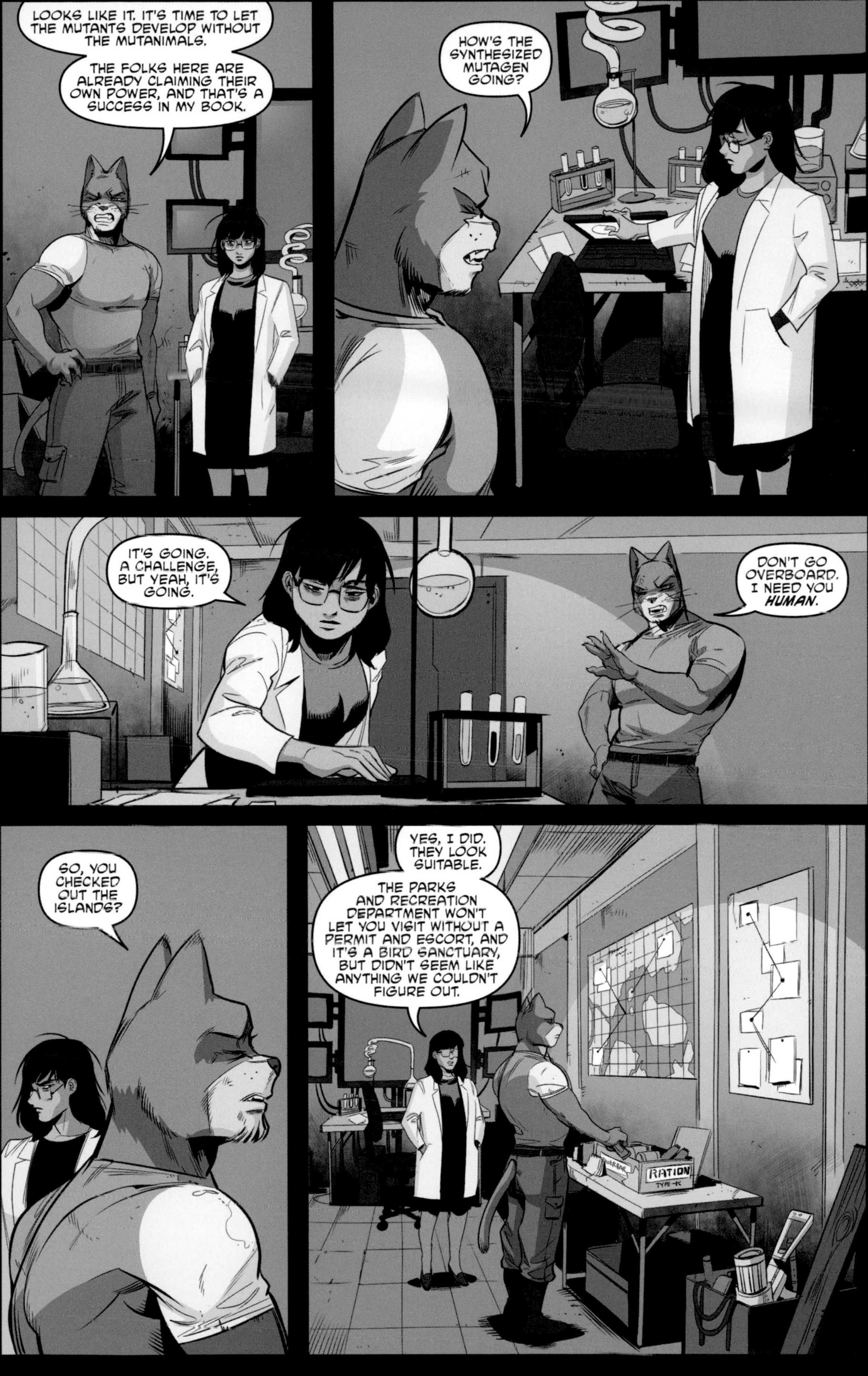
LOOKS LIKE IT. IT'S TIME TO LET THE MUTANTS DEVELOP WITHOUT THE MUTANIMALS.
THE FOLKS HERE ARE ALREADY CLAIMING THEIR OWN POWER, AND THAT'S A SUCCESS IN MY BOOK.
HOW'S THE SYNTHESIZED MUTAGEN GOING?
IT'S GOING. A CHALLENGE, BUT YEAH, IT'S GOING.
DON'T GO OVERBOARD. I NEED YOU *HUMAN*.
SO, YOU CHECKED OUT THE ISLANDS?
YES, I DID. THEY LOOK SUITABLE.
THE PARKS AND RECREATION DEPARTMENT WON'T LET YOU VISIT WITHOUT A PERMIT AND ESCORT, AND IT'S A BIRD SANCTUARY, BUT DIDN'T SEEM LIKE ANYTHING WE COULDN'T FIGURE OUT.
RATION

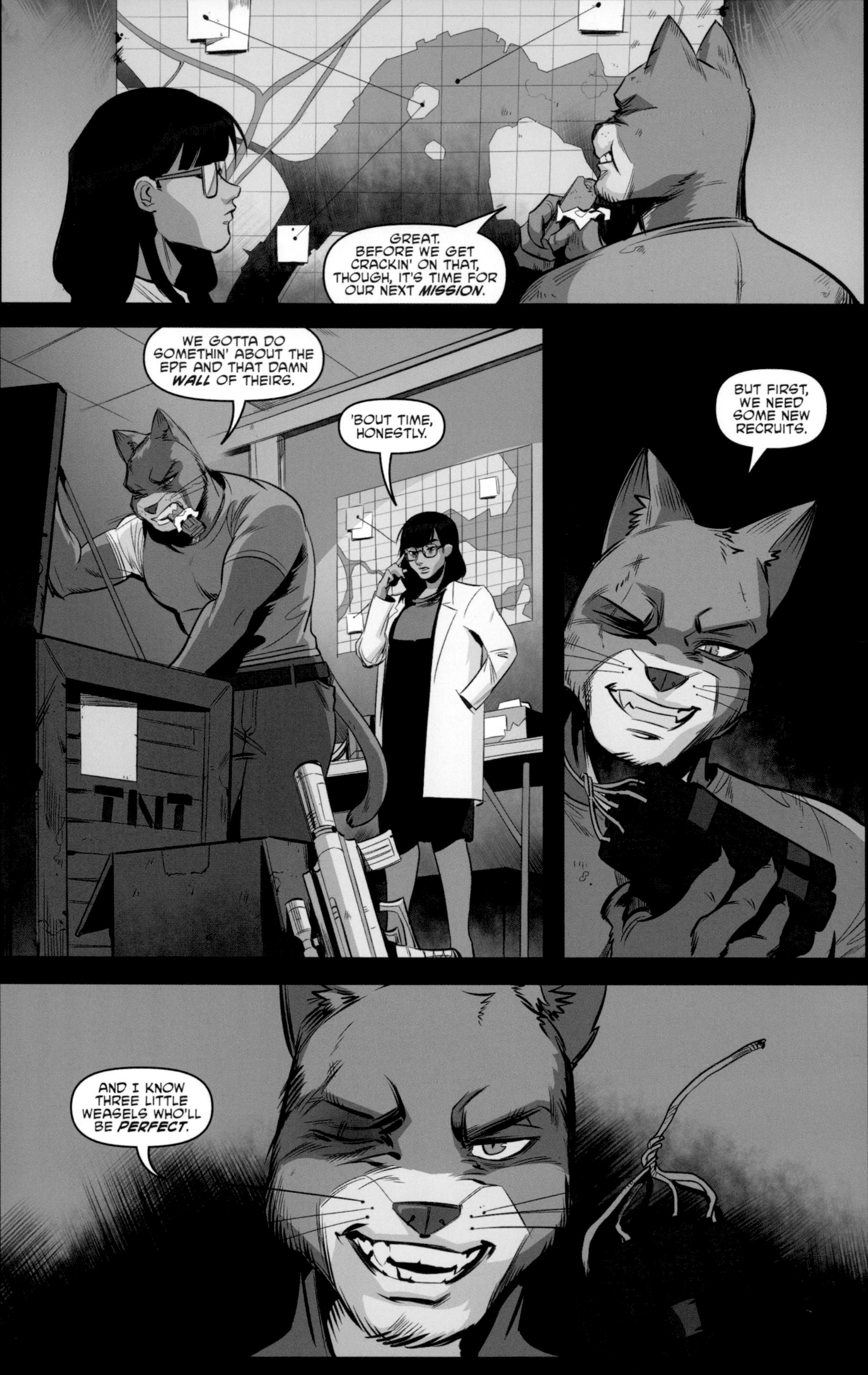
GREAT. BEFORE WE GET CRACKIN' ON THAT, THOUGH, IT'S TIME FOR OUR NEXT MISSION.
WE GOTTA DO SOMETHIN' ABOUT THE EPF AND THAT DAMN WALL OF THEIRS.
'BOUT TIME, HONESTLY.
TNT
BUT FIRST, WE NEED SOME NEW RECRUITS.
AND I KNOW THREE LITTLE WEASELS WHO'LL BE PERFECT.

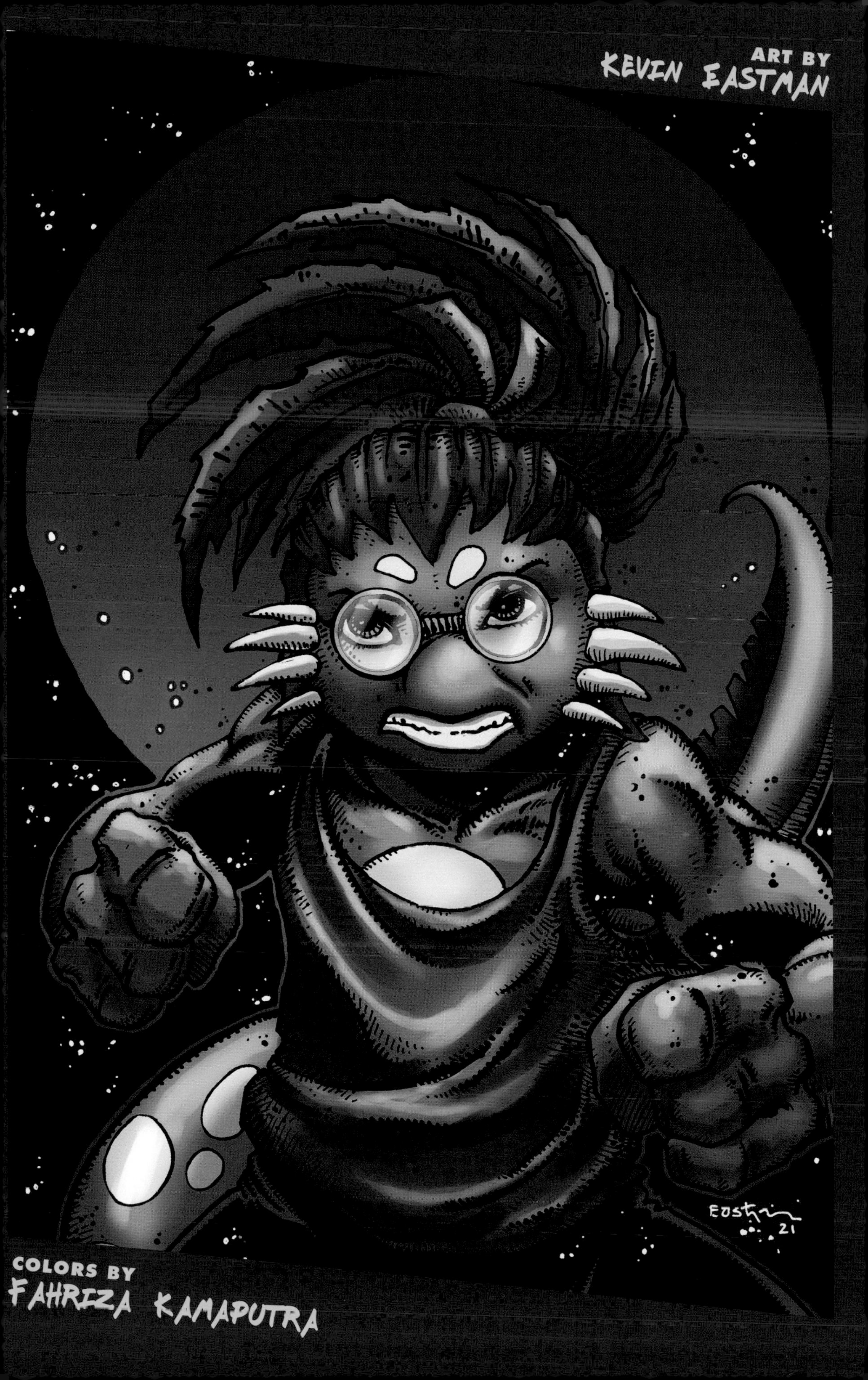

ART BY
KEVIN EASTMAN
Eastman 21
COLORS BY
FAHRIZA KAMAPUTRA

ART BY
JODI NISHIJIMA

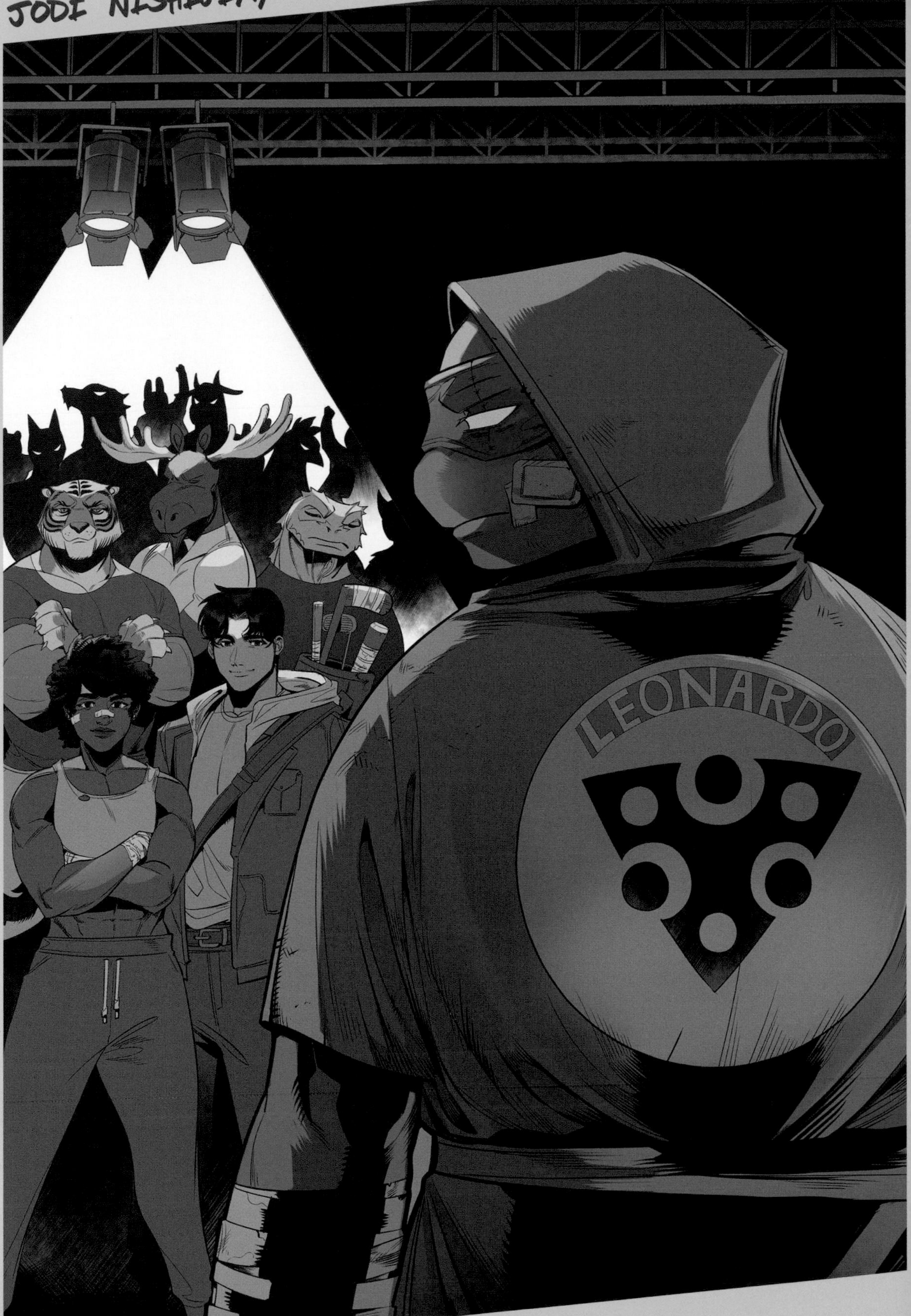

LEONARDO

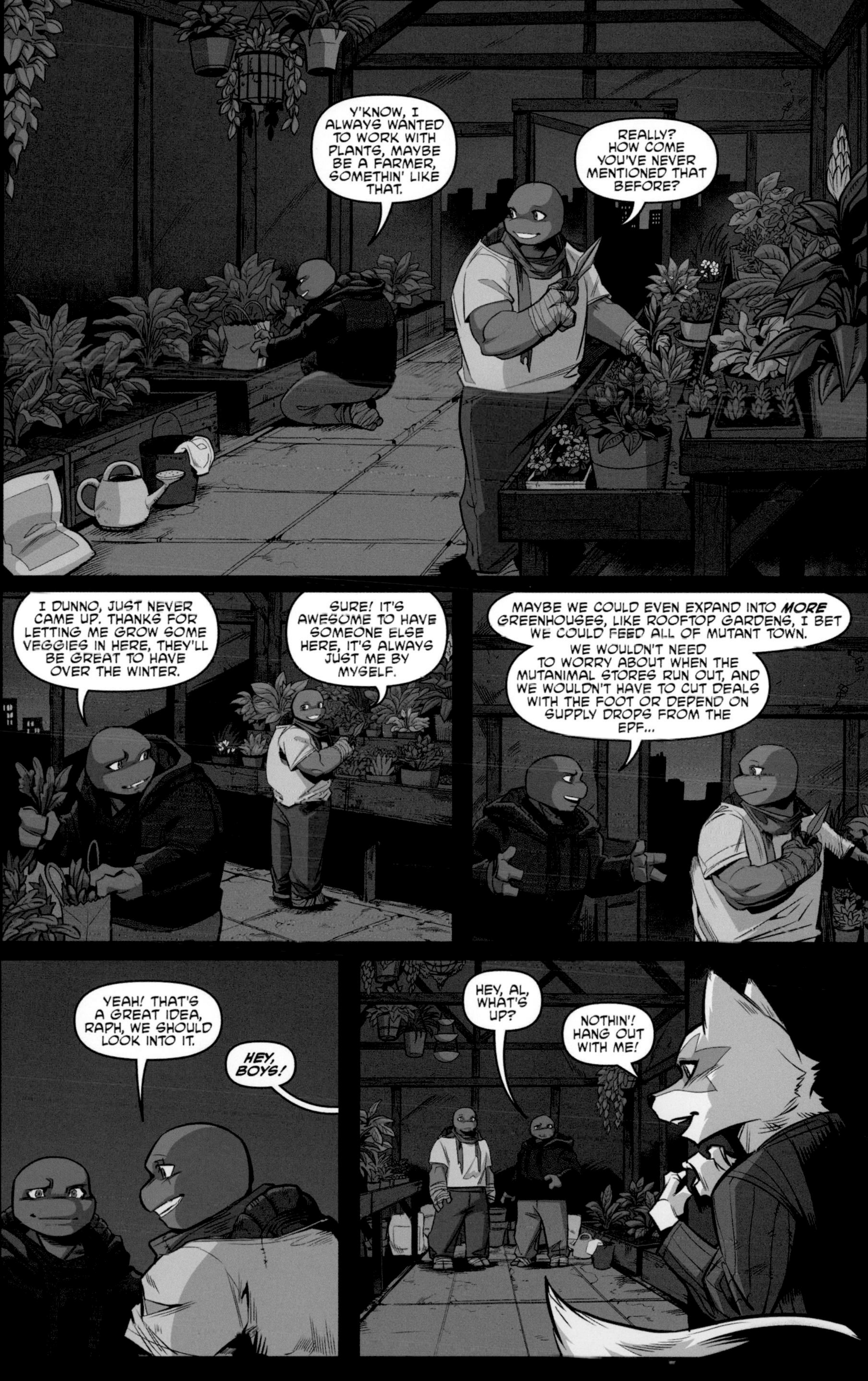

Y'KNOW, I ALWAYS WANTED TO WORK WITH PLANTS, MAYBE BE A FARMER, SOMETHIN' LIKE THAT.
REALLY? HOW COME YOU'VE NEVER MENTIONED THAT BEFORE?
I DUNNO, JUST NEVER CAME UP. THANKS FOR LETTING ME GROW SOME VEGGIES IN HERE, THEY'LL BE GREAT TO HAVE OVER THE WINTER.
SURE! IT'S AWESOME TO HAVE SOMEONE ELSE HERE, IT'S ALWAYS JUST ME BY MYSELF.
MAYBE WE COULD EVEN EXPAND INTO *MORE* GREENHOUSES, LIKE ROOFTOP GARDENS, I BET WE COULD FEED ALL OF MUTANT TOWN.
WE WOULDN'T NEED TO WORRY ABOUT WHEN THE MUTANIMAL STORES RUN OUT, AND WE WOULDN'T HAVE TO CUT DEALS WITH THE FOOT OR DEPEND ON SUPPLY DROPS FROM THE EPF...
YEAH! THAT'S A GREAT IDEA, RAPH, WE SHOULD LOOK INTO IT.
HEY, BOYS!
HEY, AL, WHAT'S UP?
NOTHIN'! HANG OUT WITH ME!

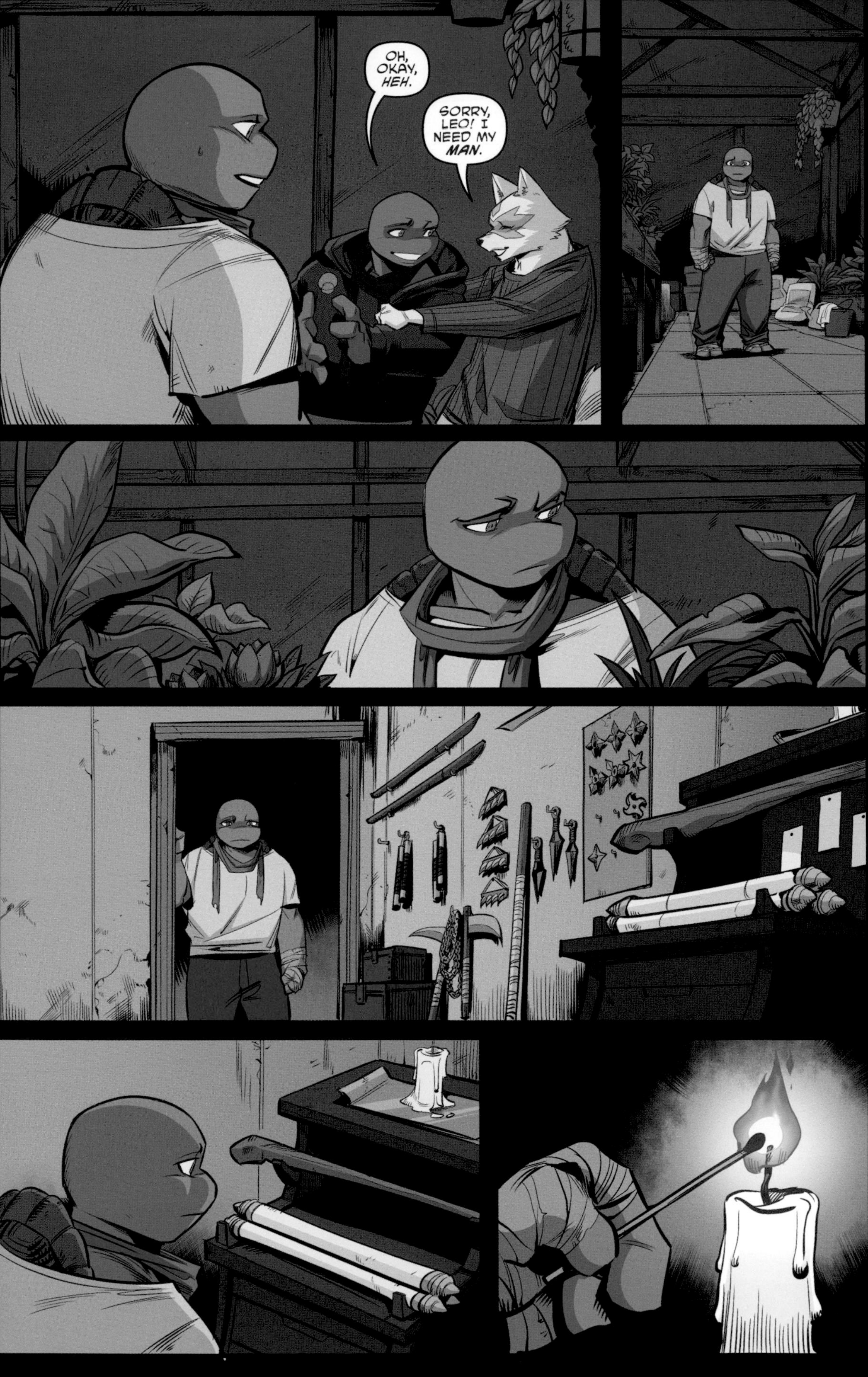
OH, OKAY, HEH.
SORRY, LEO! I NEED MY MAN.

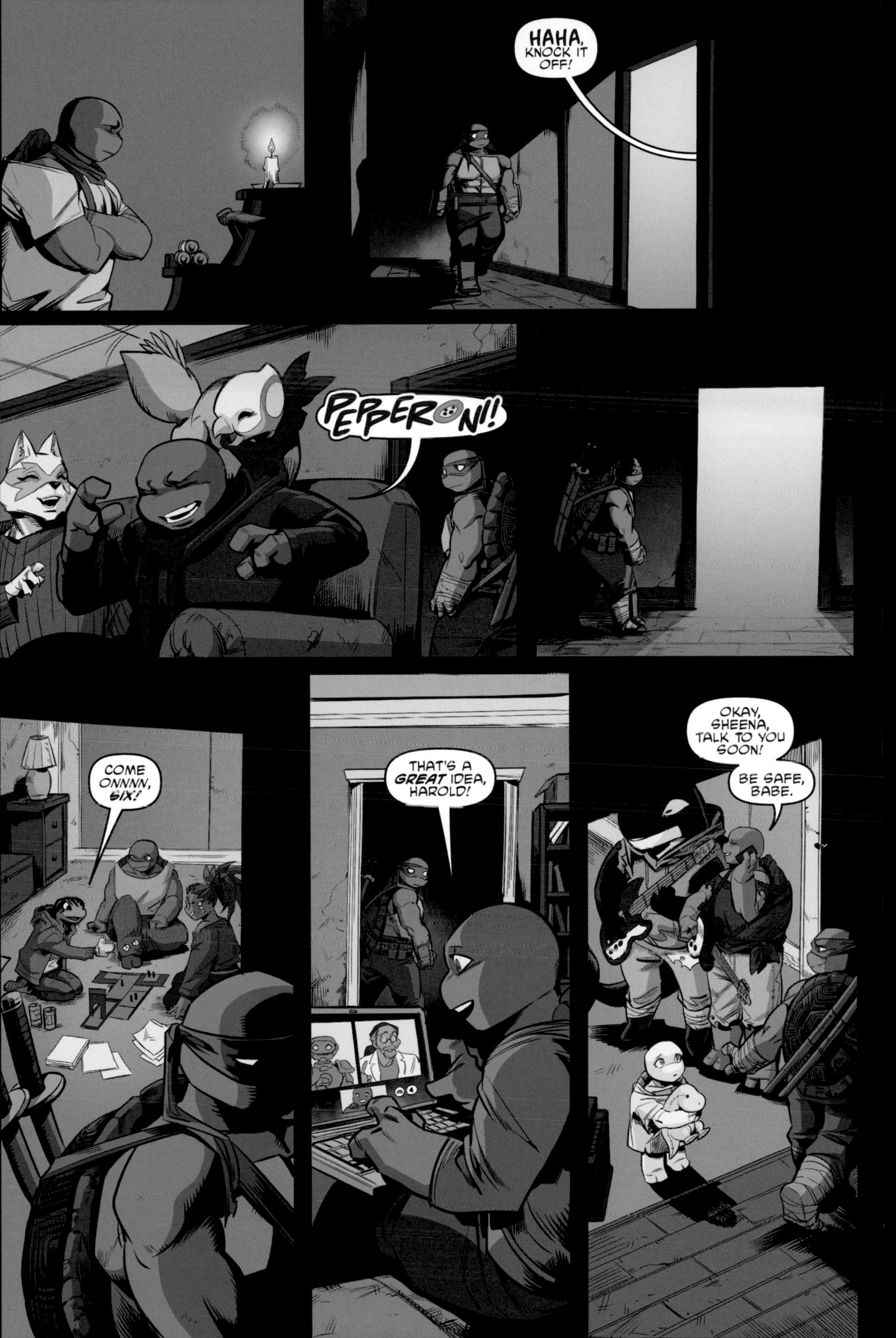
HAHA, KNOCK IT OFF!
PEPPERONI!
COME ONNNN, SIX!
THAT'S A GREAT IDEA, HAROLD!
OKAY, SHEENA, TALK TO YOU SOON!
BE SAFE, BABE.

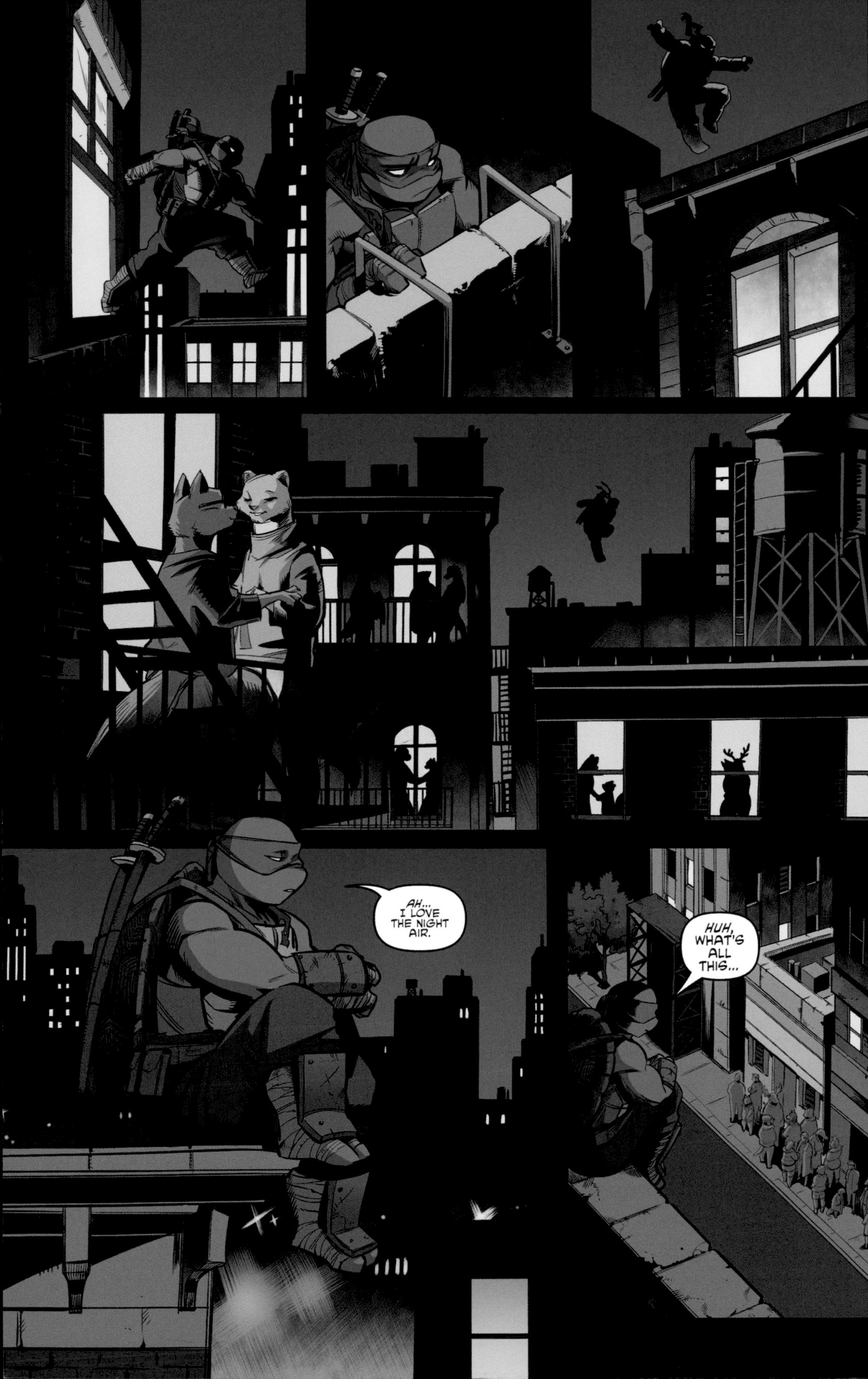
AH... I LOVE THE NIGHT AIR.
HUH, WHAT'S ALL THIS...

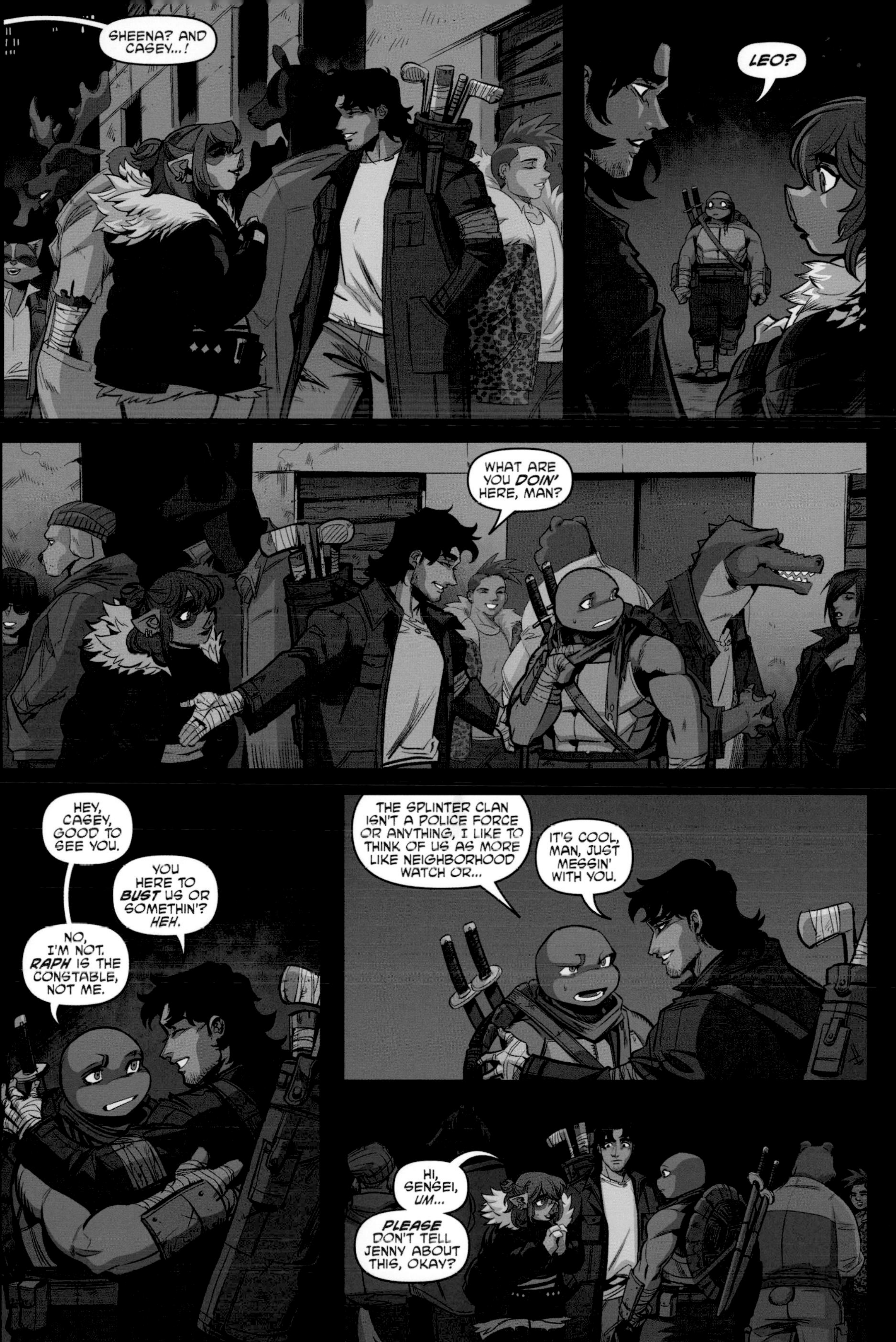
SHEENA? AND CASEY...!
LEO?
WHAT ARE YOU DOIN' HERE, MAN?
HEY, CASEY, GOOD TO SEE YOU.
YOU HERE TO BUST US OR SOMETHIN'? HEH.
NO, I'M NOT. RAPH IS THE CONSTABLE, NOT ME.
THE SPLINTER CLAN ISN'T A POLICE FORCE OR ANYTHING, I LIKE TO THINK OF US AS MORE LIKE NEIGHBORHOOD WATCH OR...
IT'S COOL, MAN, JUST MESSIN' WITH YOU.
HI, SENSEI, UM...
PLEASE DON'T TELL JENNY ABOUT THIS, OKAY?

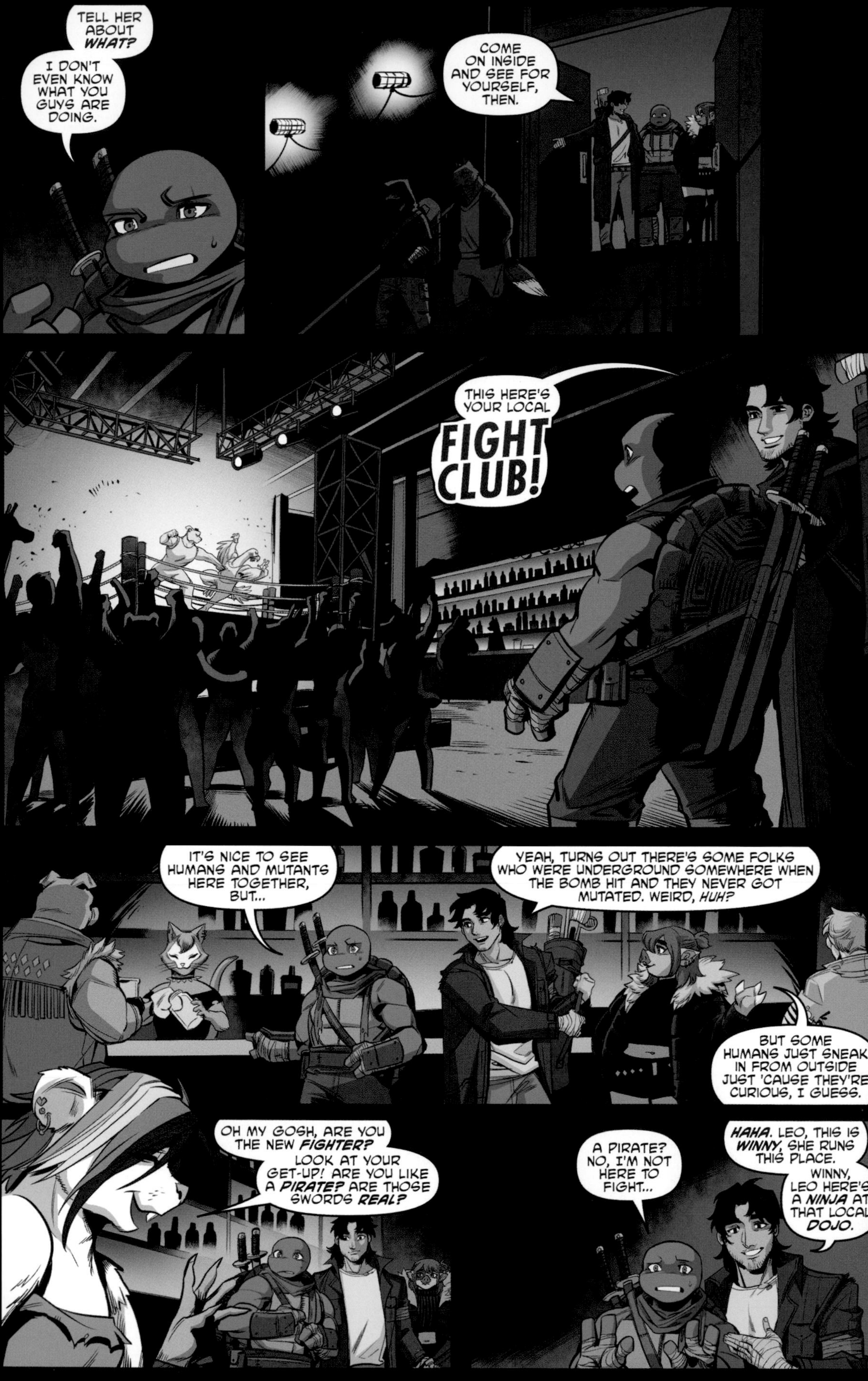

TELL HER ABOUT *WHAT?*
I DON'T EVEN KNOW WHAT YOU GUYS ARE DOING.
COME ON INSIDE AND SEE FOR YOURSELF, THEN.
THIS HERE'S YOUR LOCAL
FIGHT CLUB!
IT'S NICE TO SEE HUMANS AND MUTANTS HERE TOGETHER, BUT...
YEAH, TURNS OUT THERE'S SOME FOLKS WHO WERE UNDERGROUND SOMEWHERE WHEN THE BOMB HIT AND THEY NEVER GOT MUTATED. WEIRD, *HUH?*
BUT SOME HUMANS JUST SNEAK IN FROM OUTSIDE JUST 'CAUSE THEY'RE CURIOUS, I GUESS.
OH MY GOSH, ARE YOU THE NEW *FIGHTER?*
LOOK AT YOUR GET-UP! ARE YOU LIKE A *PIRATE?* ARE THOSE SWORDS *REAL?*
A PIRATE? NO, I'M NOT HERE TO FIGHT...
HAHA. LEO, THIS IS *WINNY,* SHE RUNS THIS PLACE.
WINNY, LEO HERE'S A *NINJA* AT THAT LOCAL *DOJO.*

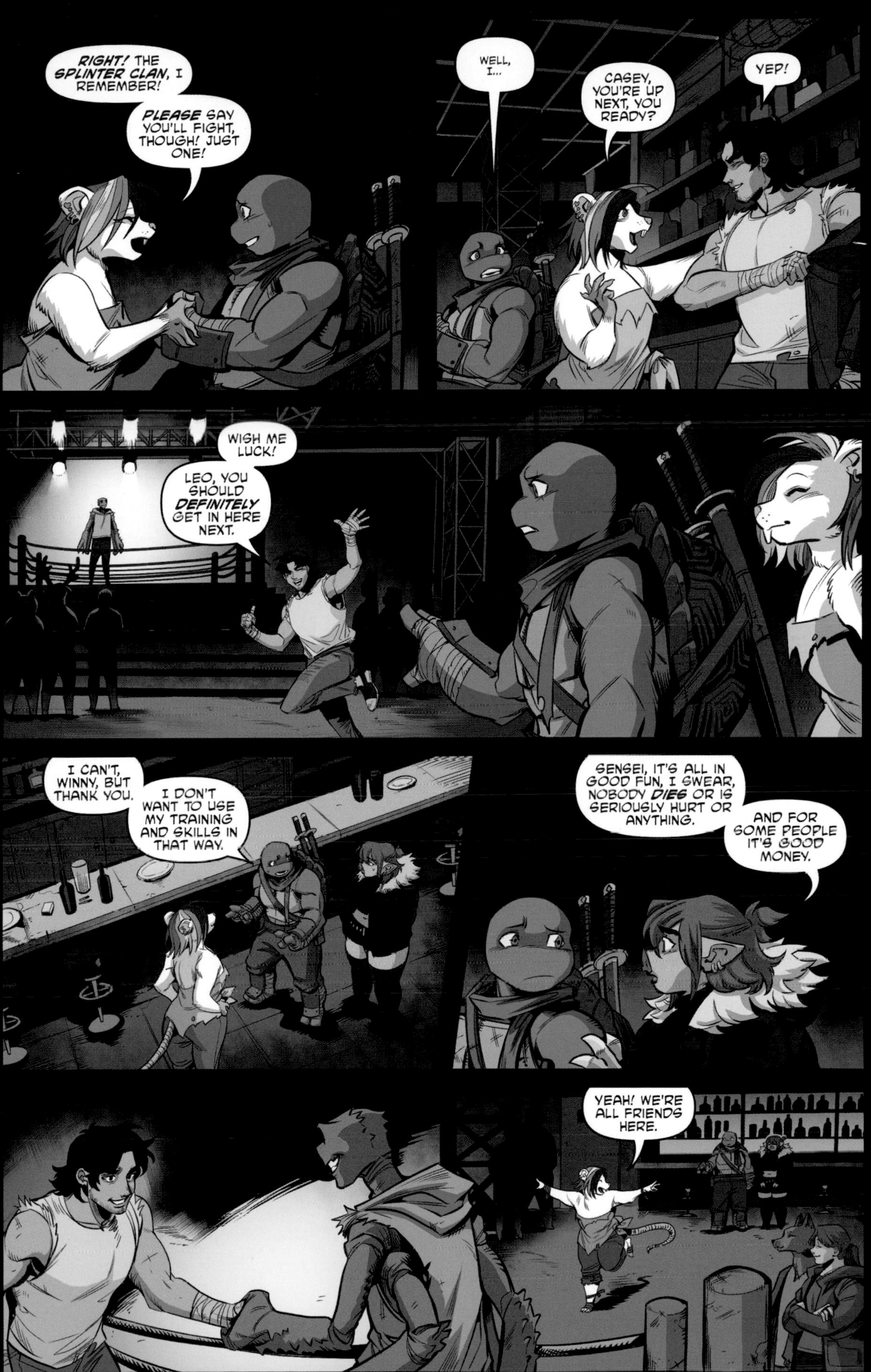
RIGHT! THE SPLINTER CLAN, I REMEMBER!
PLEASE SAY YOU'LL FIGHT, THOUGH! JUST ONE!
WELL, I...
CASEY, YOU'RE UP NEXT, YOU READY?
YEP!
WISH ME LUCK!
LEO, YOU SHOULD DEFINITELY GET IN HERE NEXT.
I CAN'T, WINNY, BUT THANK YOU.
I DON'T WANT TO USE MY TRAINING AND SKILLS IN THAT WAY.
SENSEI, IT'S ALL IN GOOD FUN, I SWEAR, NOBODY DIES OR IS SERIOUSLY HURT OR ANYTHING.
AND FOR SOME PEOPLE IT'S GOOD MONEY.
YEAH! WE'RE ALL FRIENDS HERE.

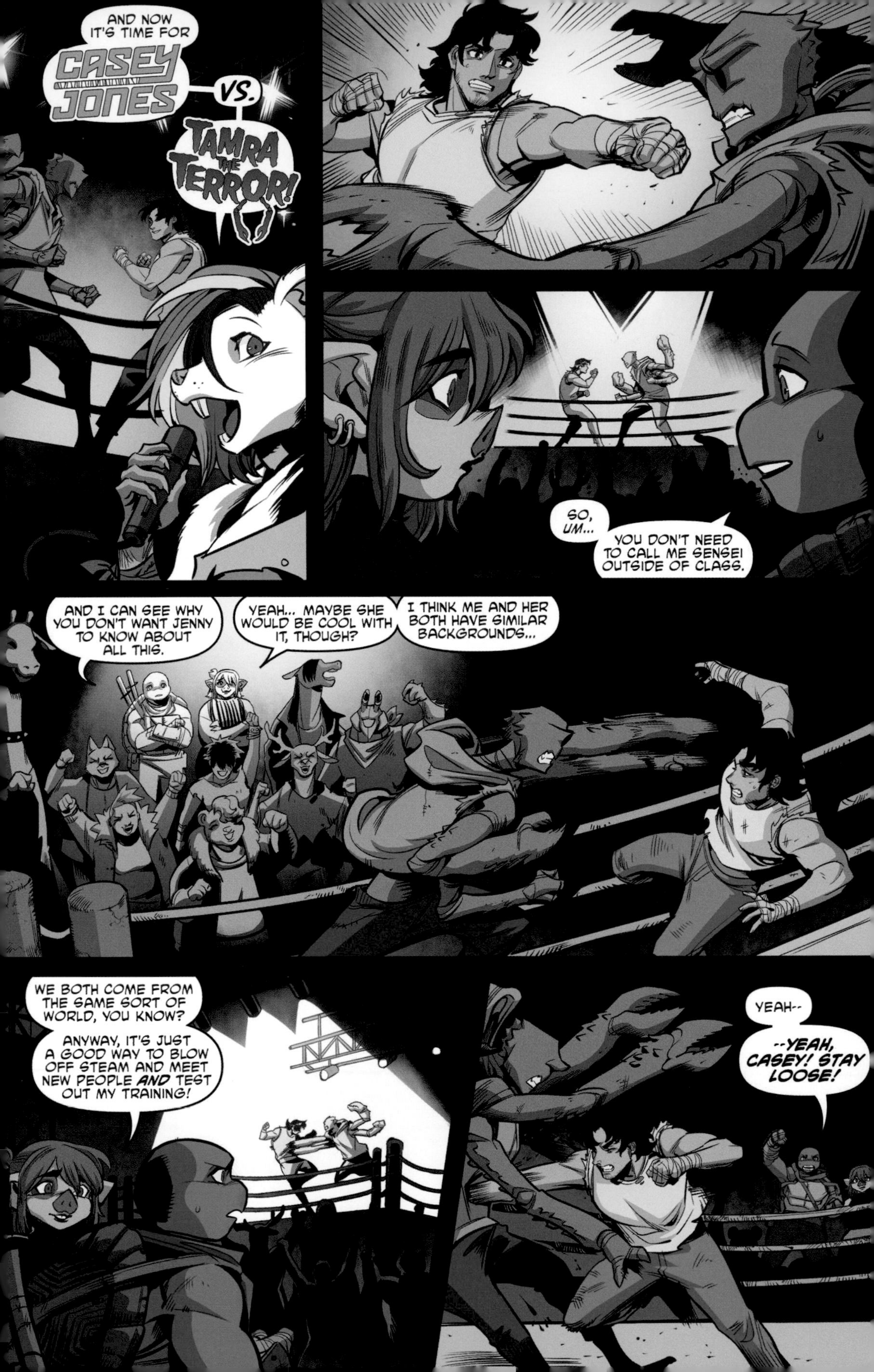

AND NOW IT'S TIME FOR
CASEY JONES
VS.
TAMRA THE TERROR!
SO, UM...
YOU DON'T NEED TO CALL ME SENSEI OUTSIDE OF CLASS.
AND I CAN SEE WHY YOU DON'T WANT JENNY TO KNOW ABOUT ALL THIS.
YEAH... MAYBE SHE WOULD BE COOL WITH IT, THOUGH?
I THINK ME AND HER BOTH HAVE SIMILAR BACKGROUNDS...
WE BOTH COME FROM THE SAME SORT OF WORLD, YOU KNOW?
ANYWAY, IT'S JUST A GOOD WAY TO BLOW OFF STEAM AND MEET NEW PEOPLE AND TEST OUT MY TRAINING!
YEAH--
--YEAH, CASEY! STAY LOOSE!

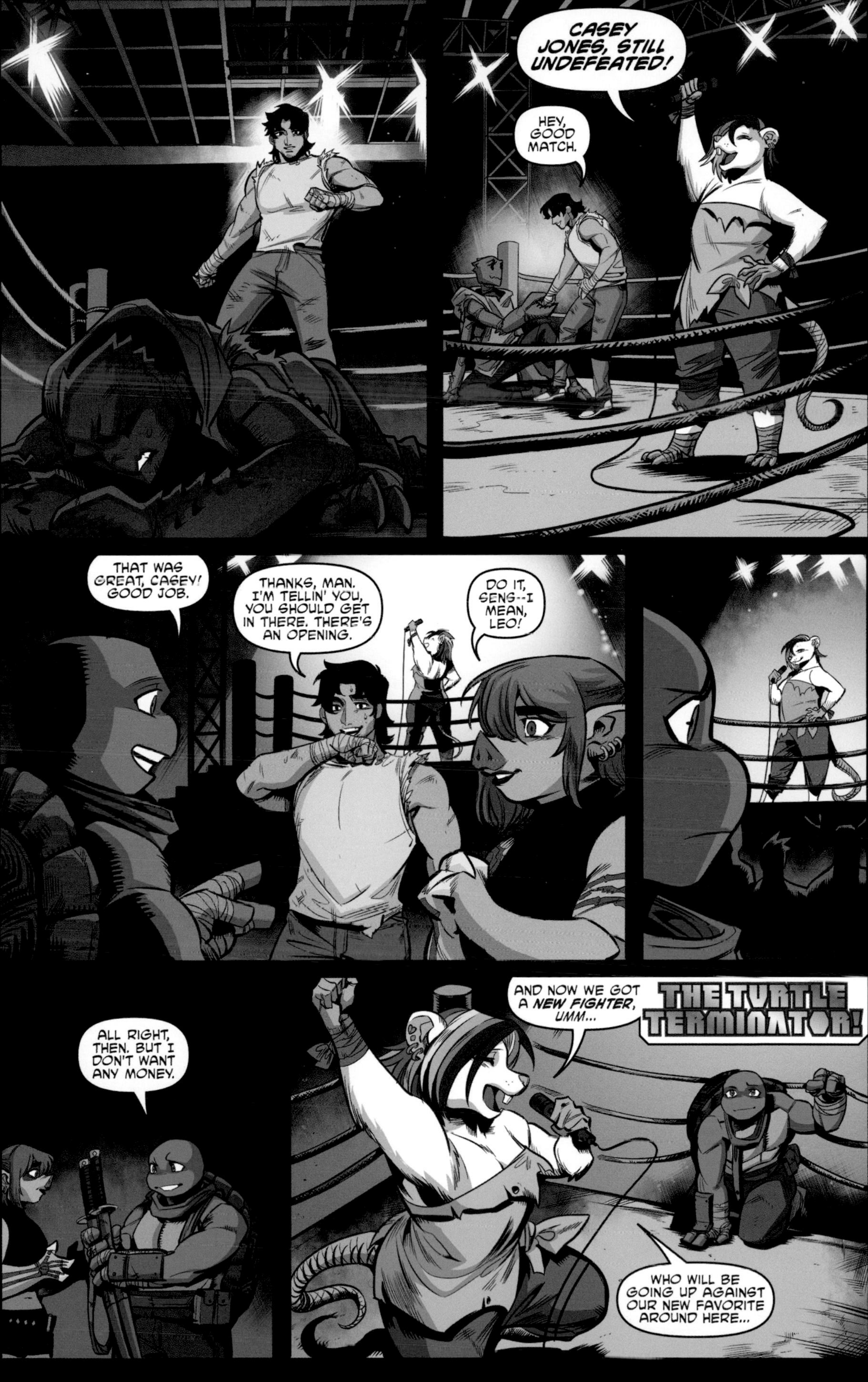
CASEY JONES, STILL UNDEFEATED!
HEY, GOOD MATCH.
THAT WAS GREAT, CASEY! GOOD JOB.
THANKS, MAN. I'M TELLIN' YOU, YOU SHOULD GET IN THERE. THERE'S AN OPENING.
DO IT, SENG--I MEAN, LEO!
ALL RIGHT, THEN. BUT I DON'T WANT ANY MONEY.
AND NOW WE GOT A NEW FIGHTER, UMM...
THE TURTLE TERMINATOR!
WHO WILL BE GOING UP AGAINST OUR NEW FAVORITE AROUND HERE...

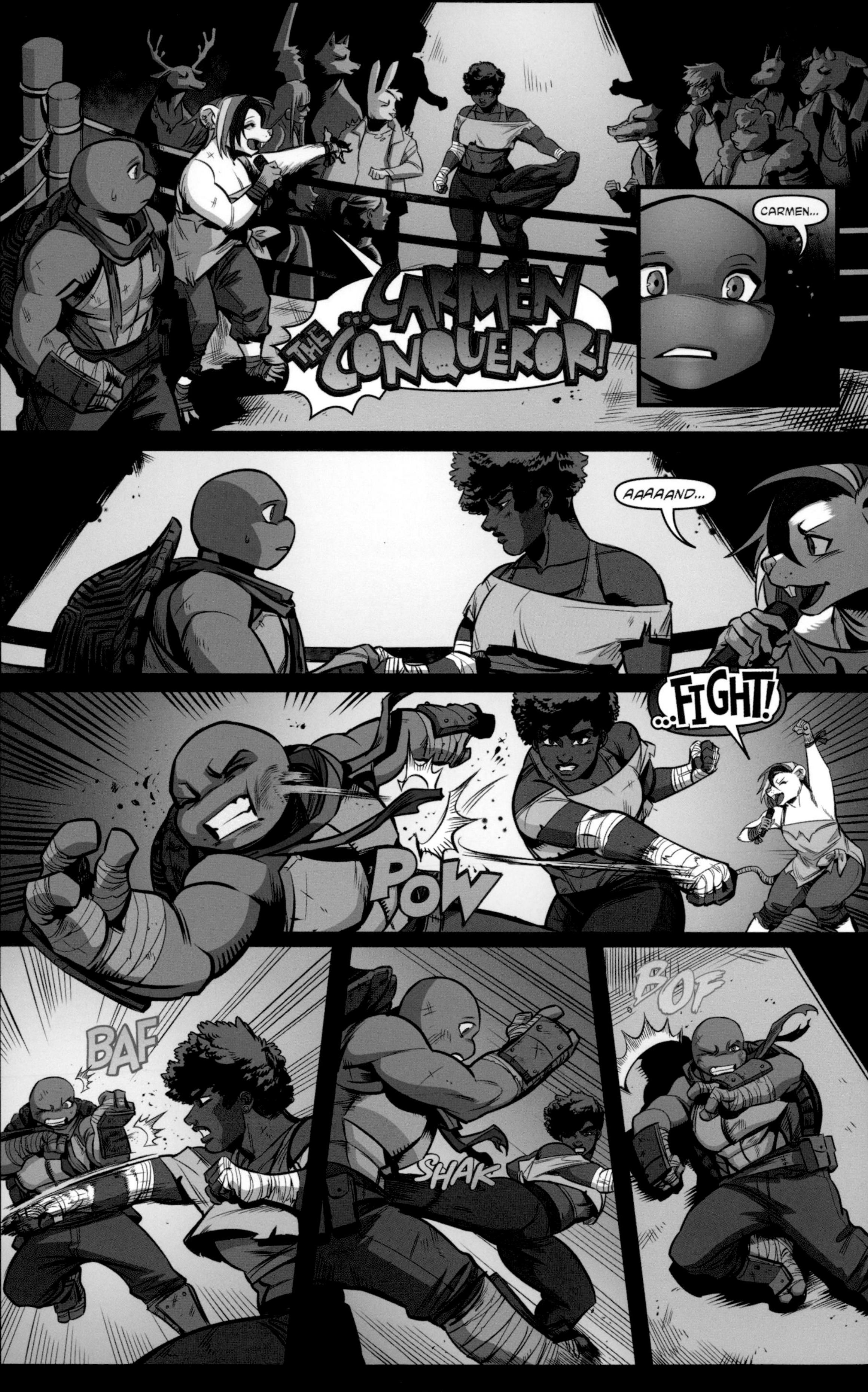
...CARMEN THE CONQUEROR!
CARMEN...
AAAAAND...
...FIGHT!
POW
BAF
SHAK
BOF

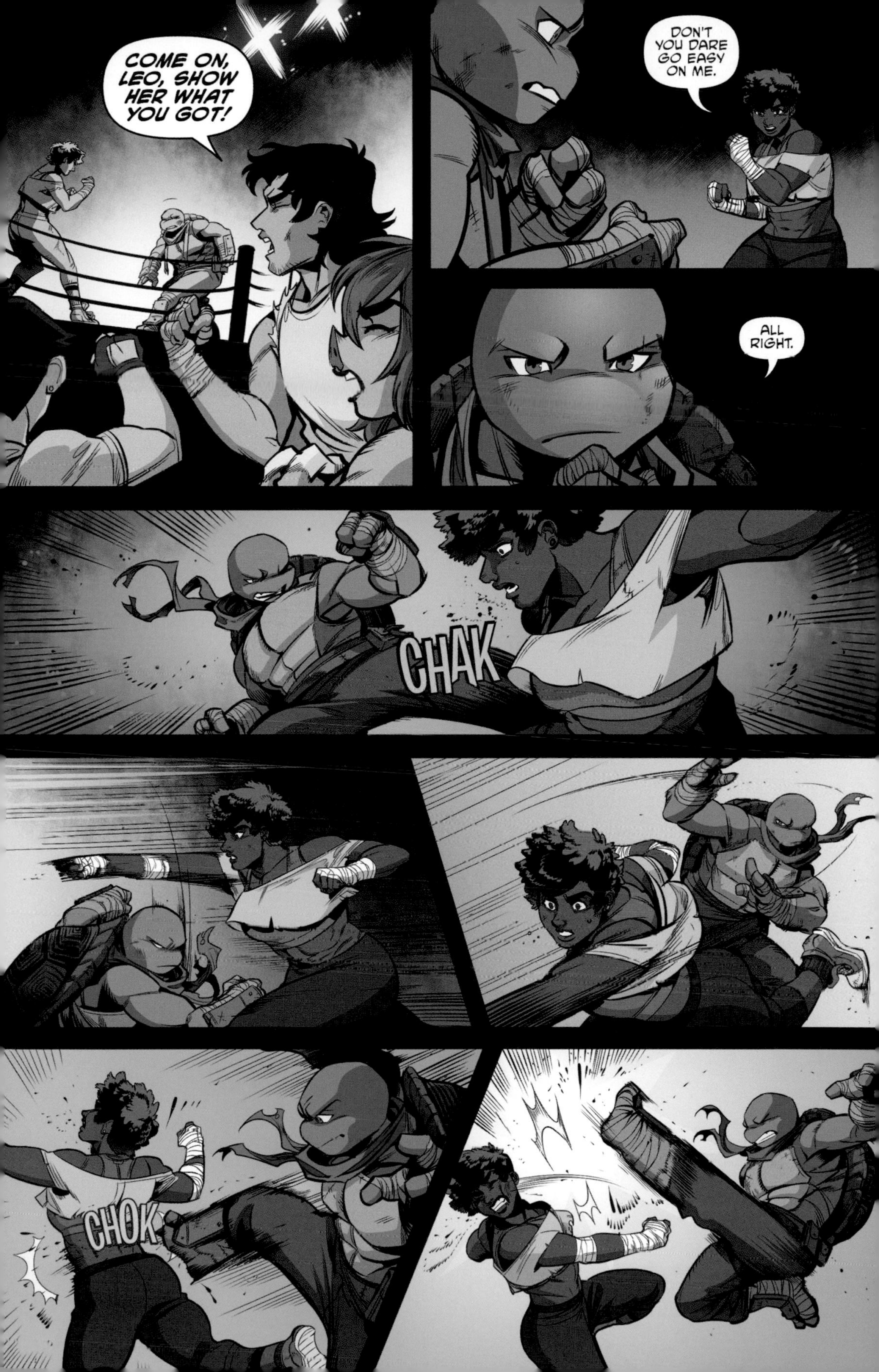
COME ON, LEO, SHOW HER WHAT YOU GOT!
DON'T YOU DARE GO EASY ON ME.
ALL RIGHT.
CHAK
CHOK

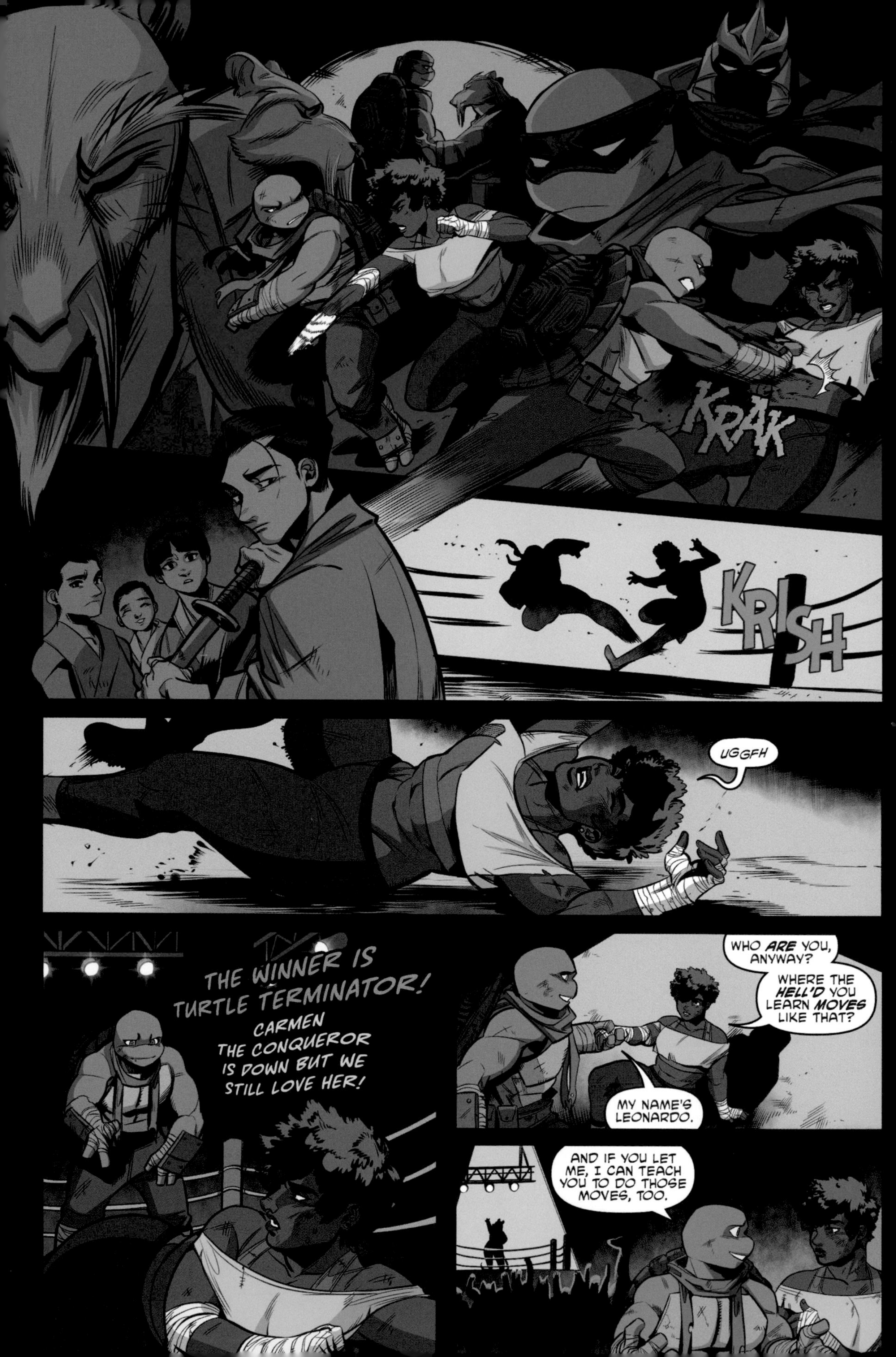
KRAK
KRISH
UGGFH
THE WINNER IS TURTLE TERMINATOR!
CARMEN THE CONQUEROR IS DOWN BUT WE STILL LOVE HER!
WHO ARE YOU, ANYWAY?
WHERE THE HELL'D YOU LEARN MOVES LIKE THAT?
MY NAME'S LEONARDO.
AND IF YOU LET ME, I CAN TEACH YOU TO DO THOSE MOVES, TOO.

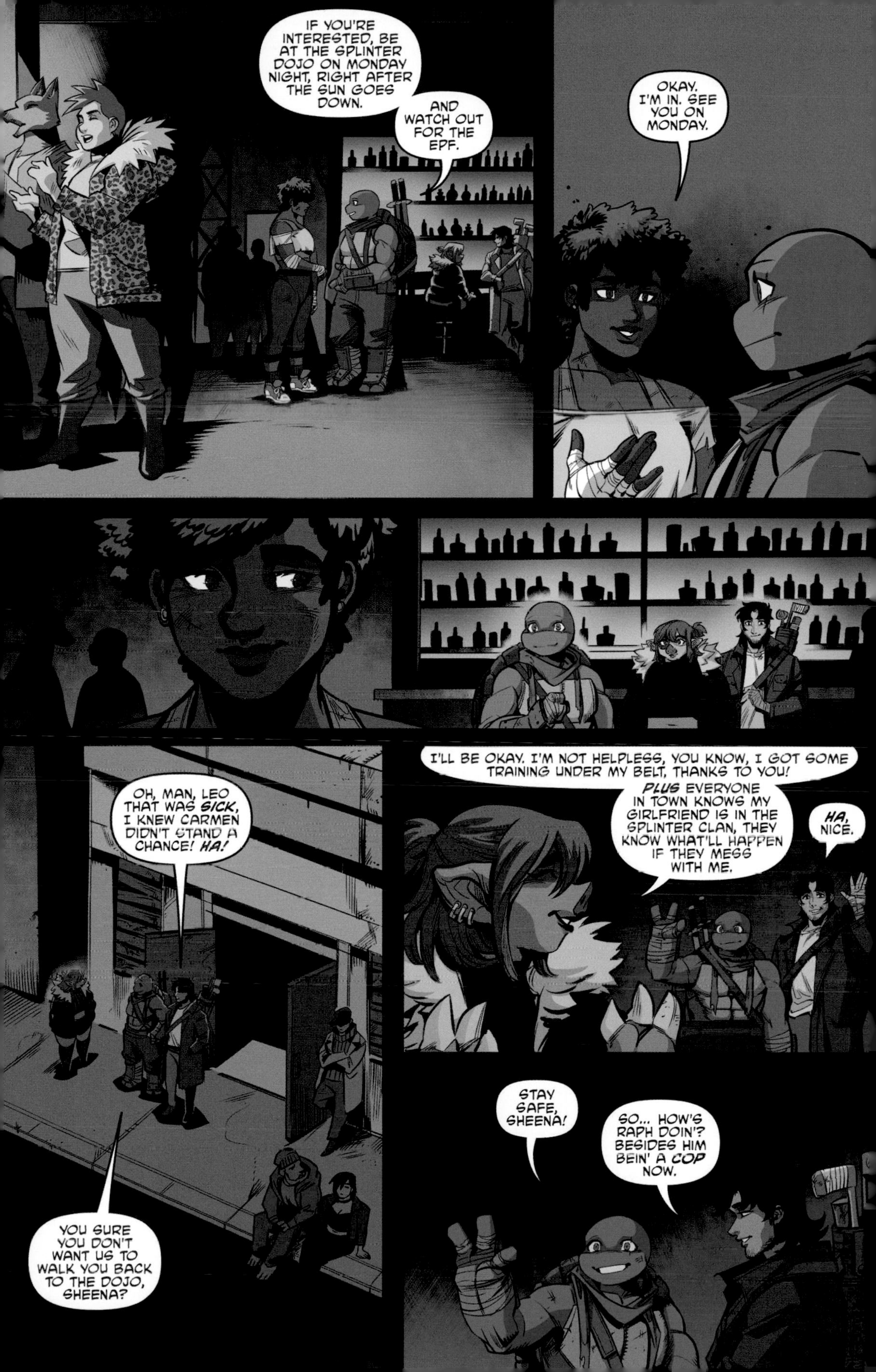
IF YOU'RE INTERESTED, BE AT THE SPLINTER DOJO ON MONDAY NIGHT, RIGHT AFTER THE SUN GOES DOWN.
AND WATCH OUT FOR THE EPF.
OKAY. I'M IN. SEE YOU ON MONDAY.
OH, MAN, LEO THAT WAS SICK, I KNEW CARMEN DIDN'T STAND A CHANCE! HA!
YOU SURE YOU DON'T WANT US TO WALK YOU BACK TO THE DOJO, SHEENA?
I'LL BE OKAY. I'M NOT HELPLESS, YOU KNOW, I GOT SOME TRAINING UNDER MY BELT, THANKS TO YOU!
PLUS EVERYONE IN TOWN KNOWS MY GIRLFRIEND IS IN THE SPLINTER CLAN, THEY KNOW WHAT'LL HAPPEN IF THEY MESS WITH ME.
HA, NICE.
STAY SAFE, SHEENA!
SO... HOW'S RAPH DOIN'? BESIDES HIM BEIN' A COP NOW.

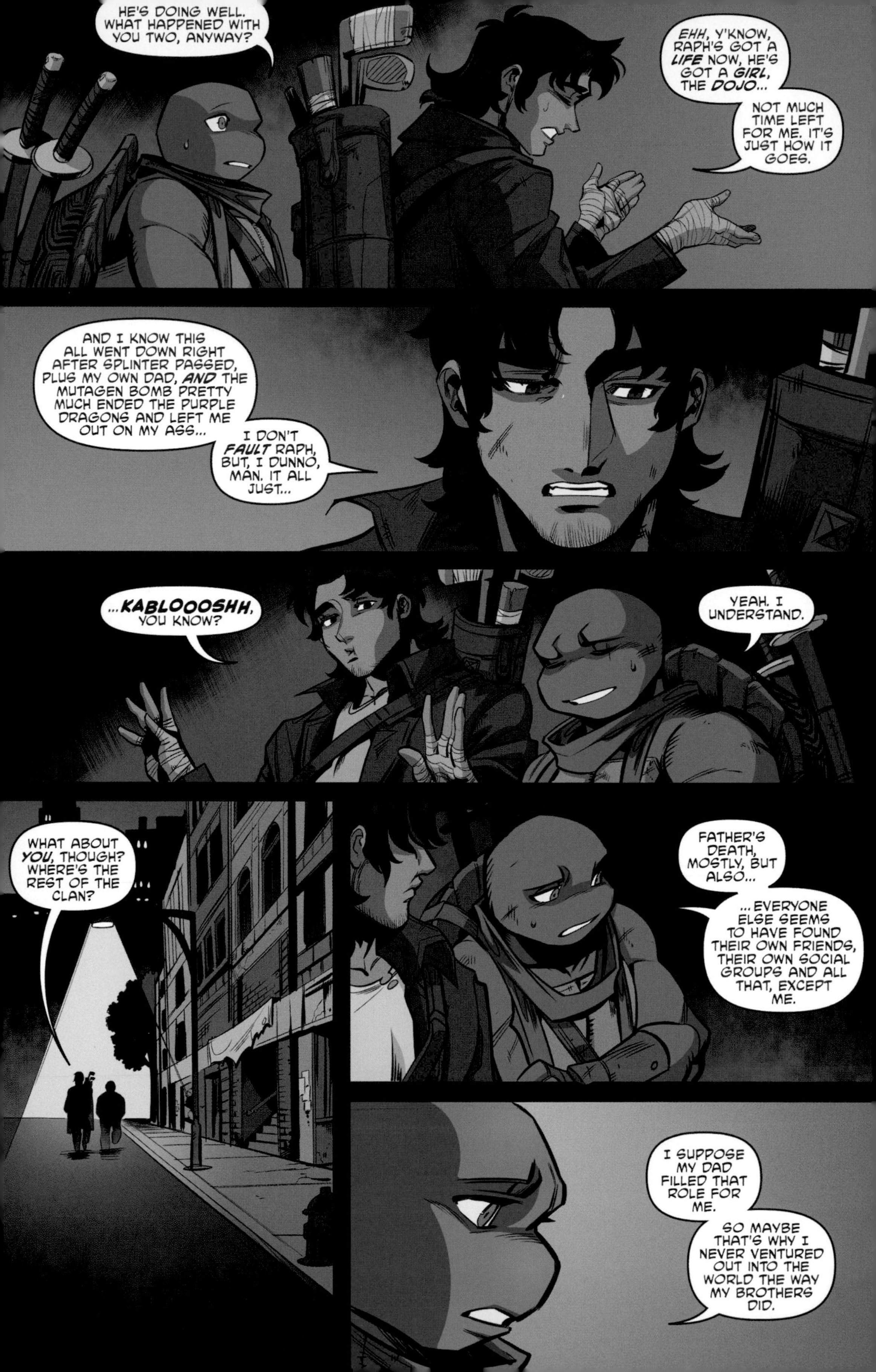

HE'S DOING WELL. WHAT HAPPENED WITH YOU TWO, ANYWAY?
EHH, Y'KNOW, RAPH'S GOT A LIFE NOW, HE'S GOT A GIRL, THE DOJO...
NOT MUCH TIME LEFT FOR ME. IT'S JUST HOW IT GOES.
AND I KNOW THIS ALL WENT DOWN RIGHT AFTER SPLINTER PASSED, PLUS MY OWN DAD, AND THE MUTAGEN BOMB PRETTY MUCH ENDED THE PURPLE DRAGONS AND LEFT ME OUT ON MY ASS...
I DON'T FAULT RAPH, BUT, I DUNNO, MAN. IT ALL JUST...
...KABLOOOSHH, YOU KNOW?
YEAH. I UNDERSTAND.
WHAT ABOUT YOU, THOUGH? WHERE'S THE REST OF THE CLAN?
FATHER'S DEATH, MOSTLY, BUT ALSO...
...EVERYONE ELSE SEEMS TO HAVE FOUND THEIR OWN FRIENDS, THEIR OWN SOCIAL GROUPS AND ALL THAT, EXCEPT ME.
I SUPPOSE MY DAD FILLED THAT ROLE FOR ME.
SO MAYBE THAT'S WHY I NEVER VENTURED OUT INTO THE WORLD THE WAY MY BROTHERS DID.

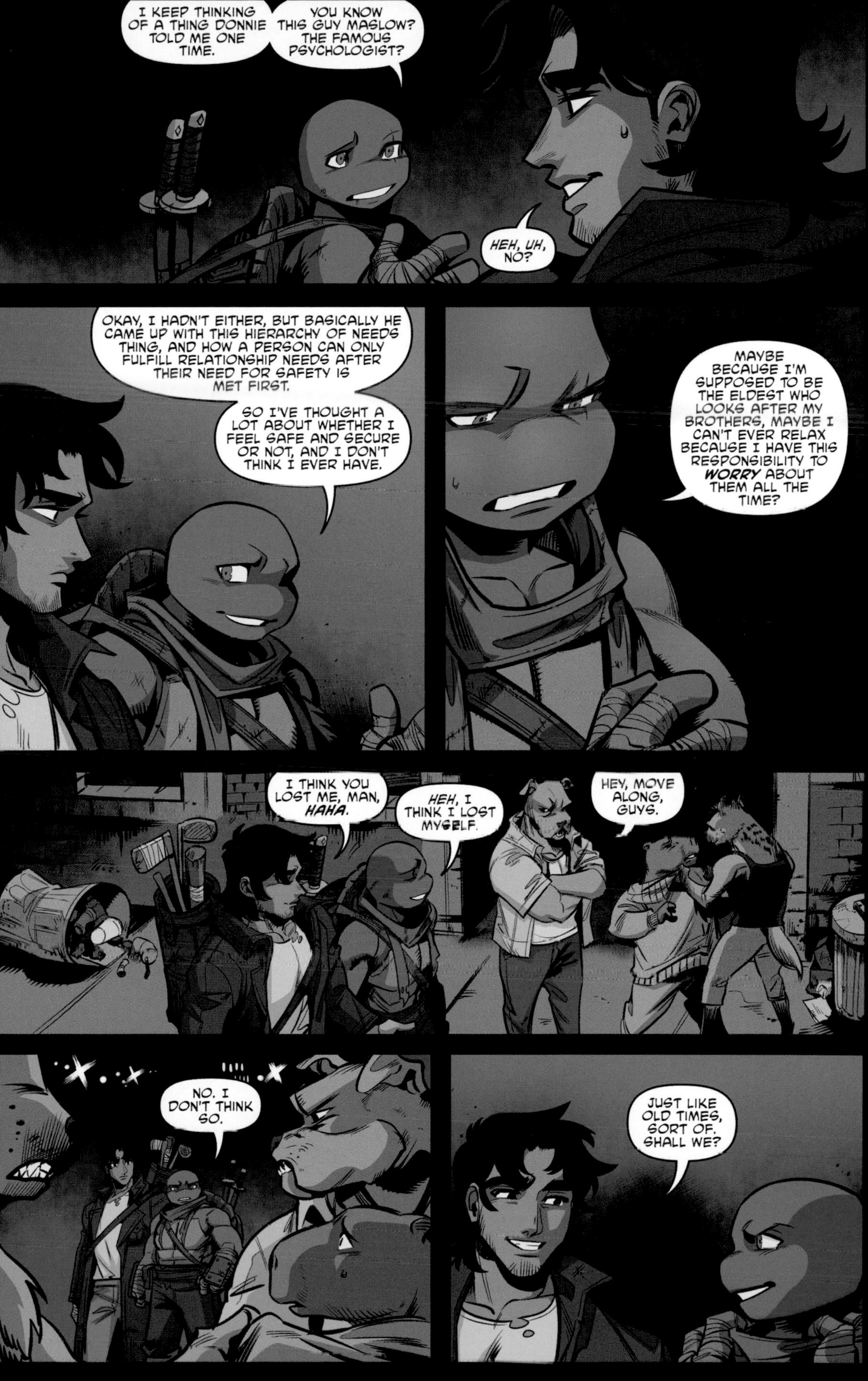
I KEEP THINKING OF A THING DONNIE TOLD ME ONE TIME.
YOU KNOW THIS GUY MASLOW? THE FAMOUS PSYCHOLOGIST?
HEH, UH, NO?
OKAY, I HADN'T EITHER, BUT BASICALLY HE CAME UP WITH THIS HIERARCHY OF NEEDS THING, AND HOW A PERSON CAN ONLY FULFILL RELATIONSHIP NEEDS AFTER THEIR NEED FOR SAFETY IS MET FIRST.
SO I'VE THOUGHT A LOT ABOUT WHETHER I FEEL SAFE AND SECURE OR NOT, AND I DON'T THINK I EVER HAVE.
MAYBE BECAUSE I'M SUPPOSED TO BE THE ELDEST WHO LOOKS AFTER MY BROTHERS, MAYBE I CAN'T EVER RELAX BECAUSE I HAVE THIS RESPONSIBILITY TO WORRY ABOUT THEM ALL THE TIME?
I THINK YOU LOST ME, MAN, HAHA.
HEH, I THINK I LOST MYSELF.
HEY, MOVE ALONG, GUYS.
NO. I DON'T THINK SO.
JUST LIKE OLD TIMES, SORT OF. SHALL WE?

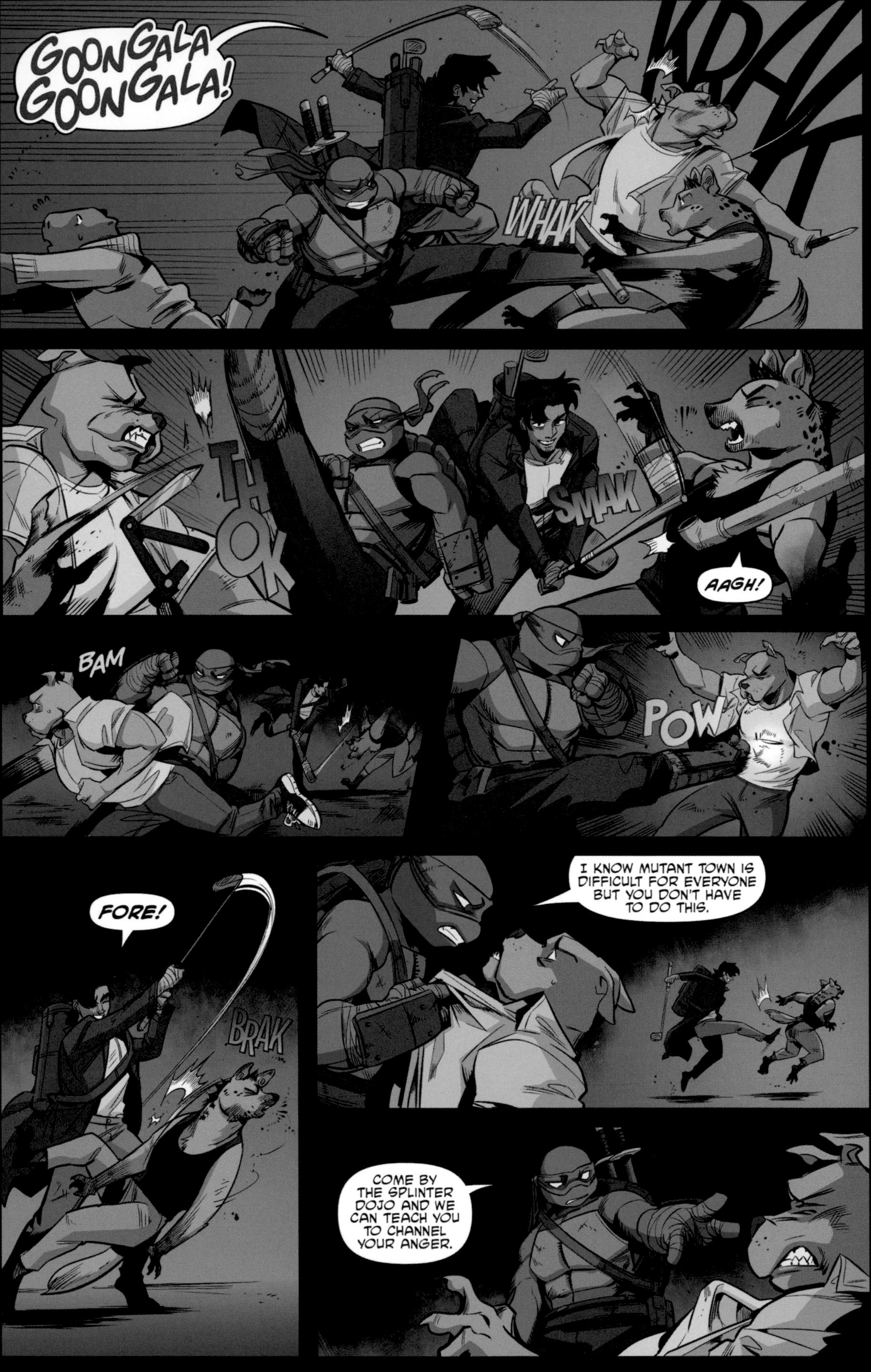
GOONGALA GOONGALA!
KRHK
WHAK
THOK
SMAK
AAGH!
BAM
POW
I KNOW MUTANT TOWN IS DIFFICULT FOR EVERYONE BUT YOU DON'T HAVE TO DO THIS.
FORE!
BRAK
COME BY THE SPLINTER DOJO AND WE CAN TEACH YOU TO CHANNEL YOUR ANGER.

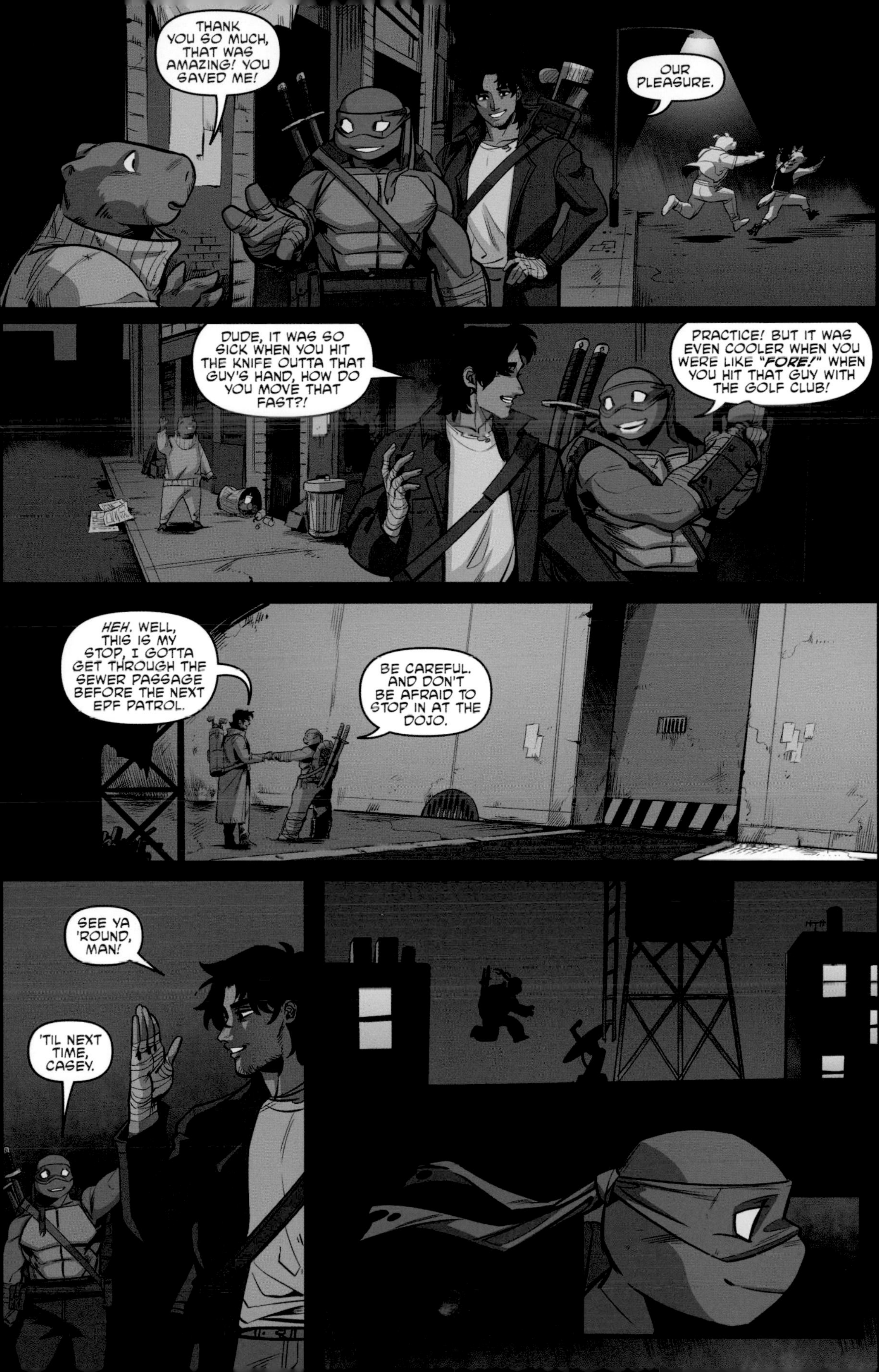
THANK YOU SO MUCH, THAT WAS AMAZING! YOU SAVED ME!
OUR PLEASURE.
DUDE, IT WAS SO SICK WHEN YOU HIT THE KNIFE OUTTA THAT GUY'S HAND, HOW DO YOU MOVE THAT FAST?!
PRACTICE! BUT IT WAS EVEN COOLER WHEN YOU WERE LIKE "FORE!" WHEN YOU HIT THAT GUY WITH THE GOLF CLUB!
HEH. WELL, THIS IS MY STOP, I GOTTA GET THROUGH THE SEWER PASSAGE BEFORE THE NEXT EPF PATROL.
BE CAREFUL. AND DON'T BE AFRAID TO STOP IN AT THE DOJO.
SEE YA 'ROUND, MAN!
'TIL NEXT TIME, CASEY.

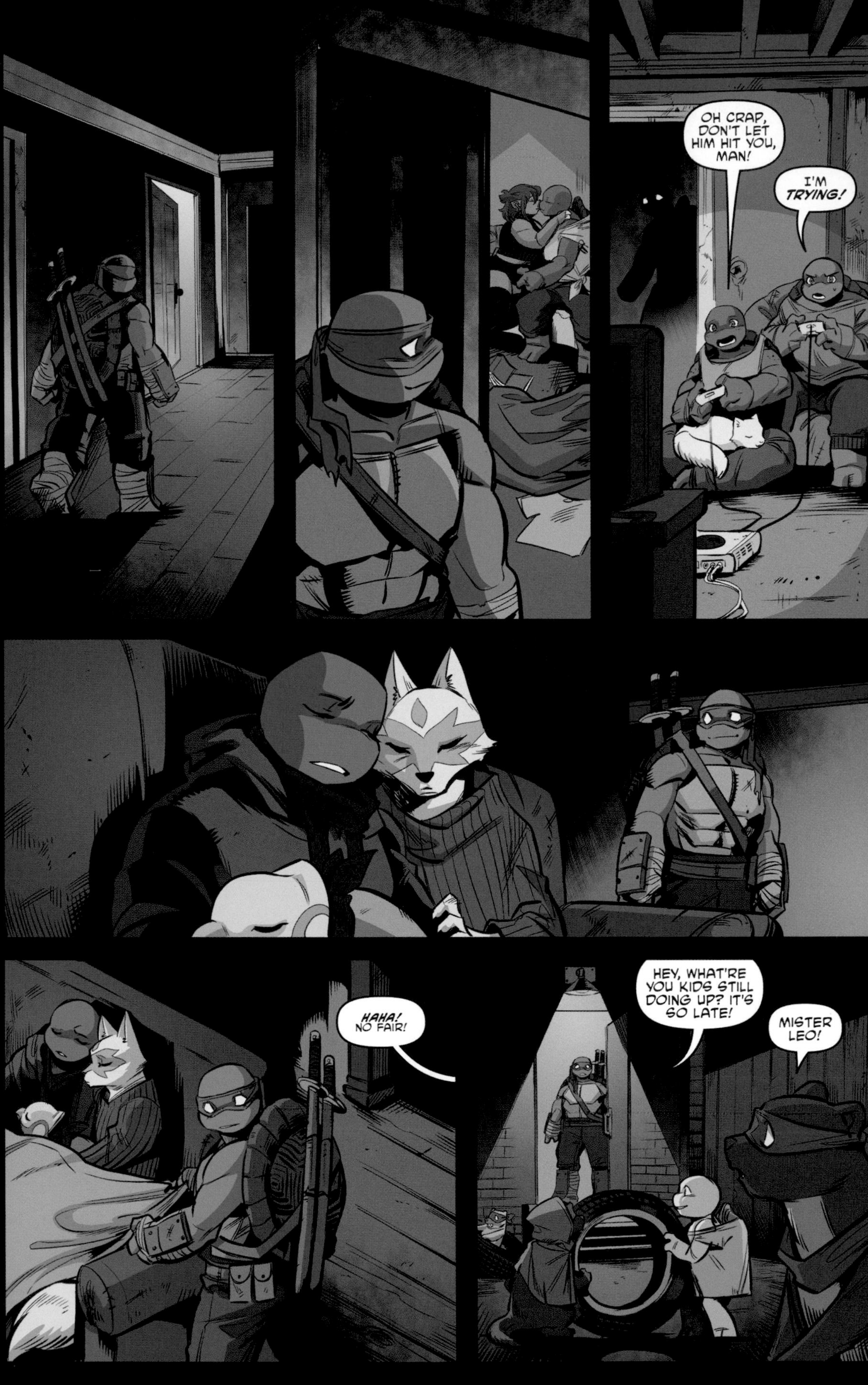
OH CRAP, DON'T LET HIM HIT YOU, MAN!
I'M *TRYING!*
HAHA! NO FAIR!
HEY, WHAT'RE YOU KIDS STILL DOING UP? IT'S SO LATE!
MISTER LEO!

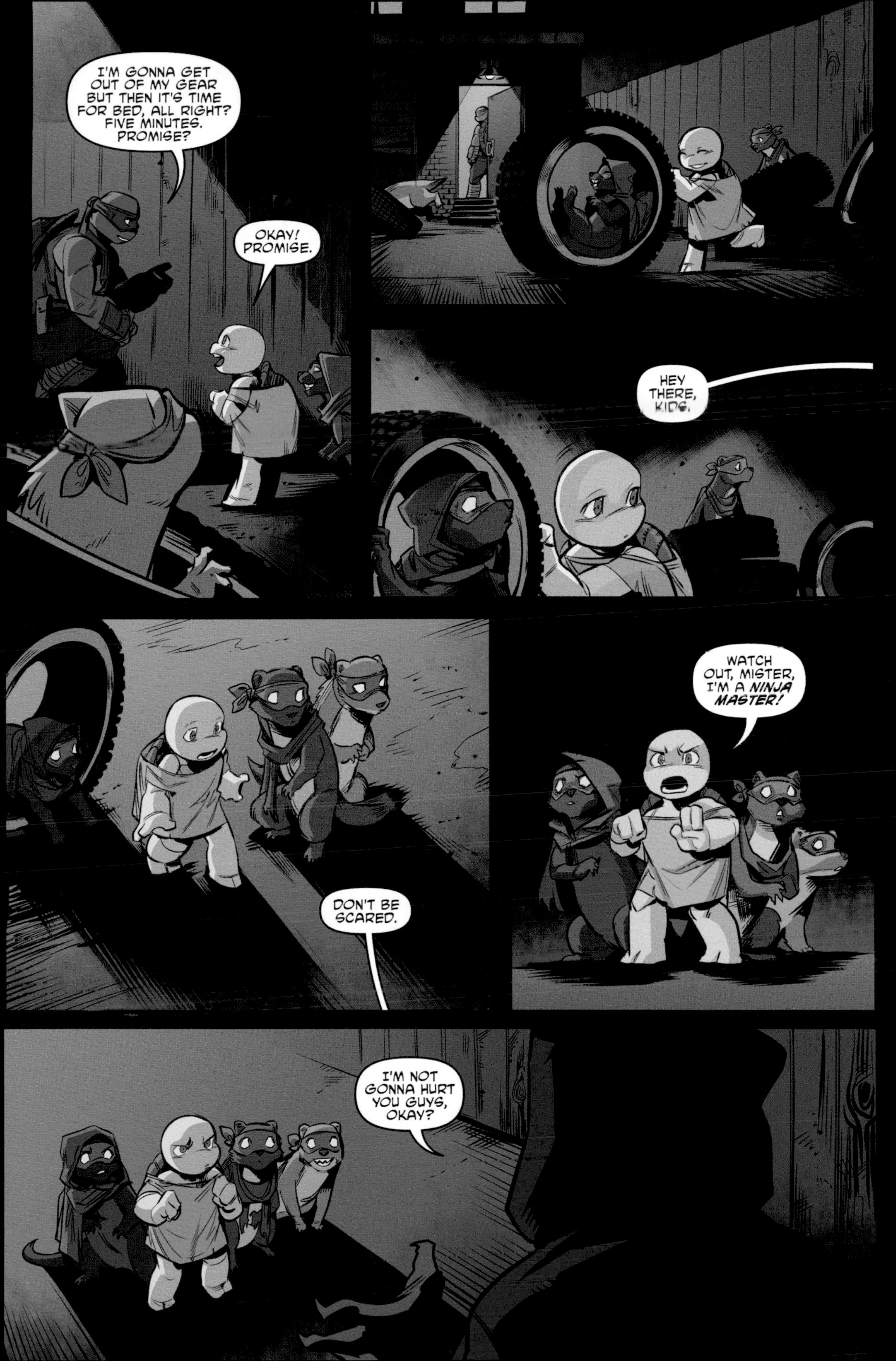
I'M GONNA GET OUT OF MY GEAR BUT THEN IT'S TIME FOR BED, ALL RIGHT? FIVE MINUTES. PROMISE?
OKAY! PROMISE.
HEY THERE, KIDS.
DON'T BE SCARED.
WATCH OUT, MISTER, I'M A *NINJA MASTER!*
I'M NOT GONNA HURT YOU GUYS, OKAY?

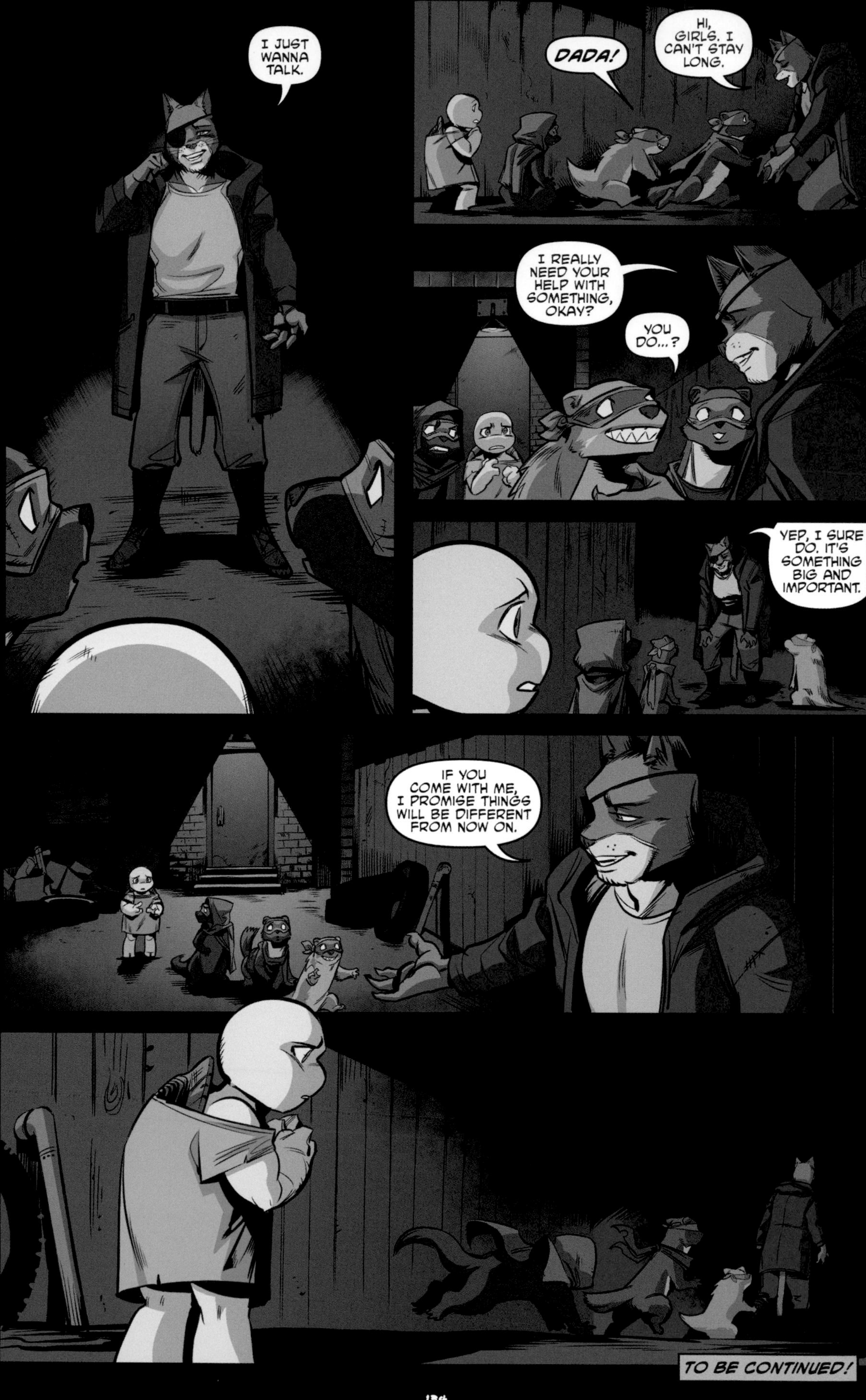
I JUST WANNA TALK.
DADA!
HI, GIRLS. I CAN'T STAY LONG.
I REALLY NEED YOUR HELP WITH SOMETHING, OKAY?
YOU DO...?
YEP, I SURE DO. IT'S SOMETHING BIG AND IMPORTANT.
IF YOU COME WITH ME, I PROMISE THINGS WILL BE DIFFERENT FROM NOW ON.
TO BE CONTINUED!

ART BY
KEVIN EASTMAN

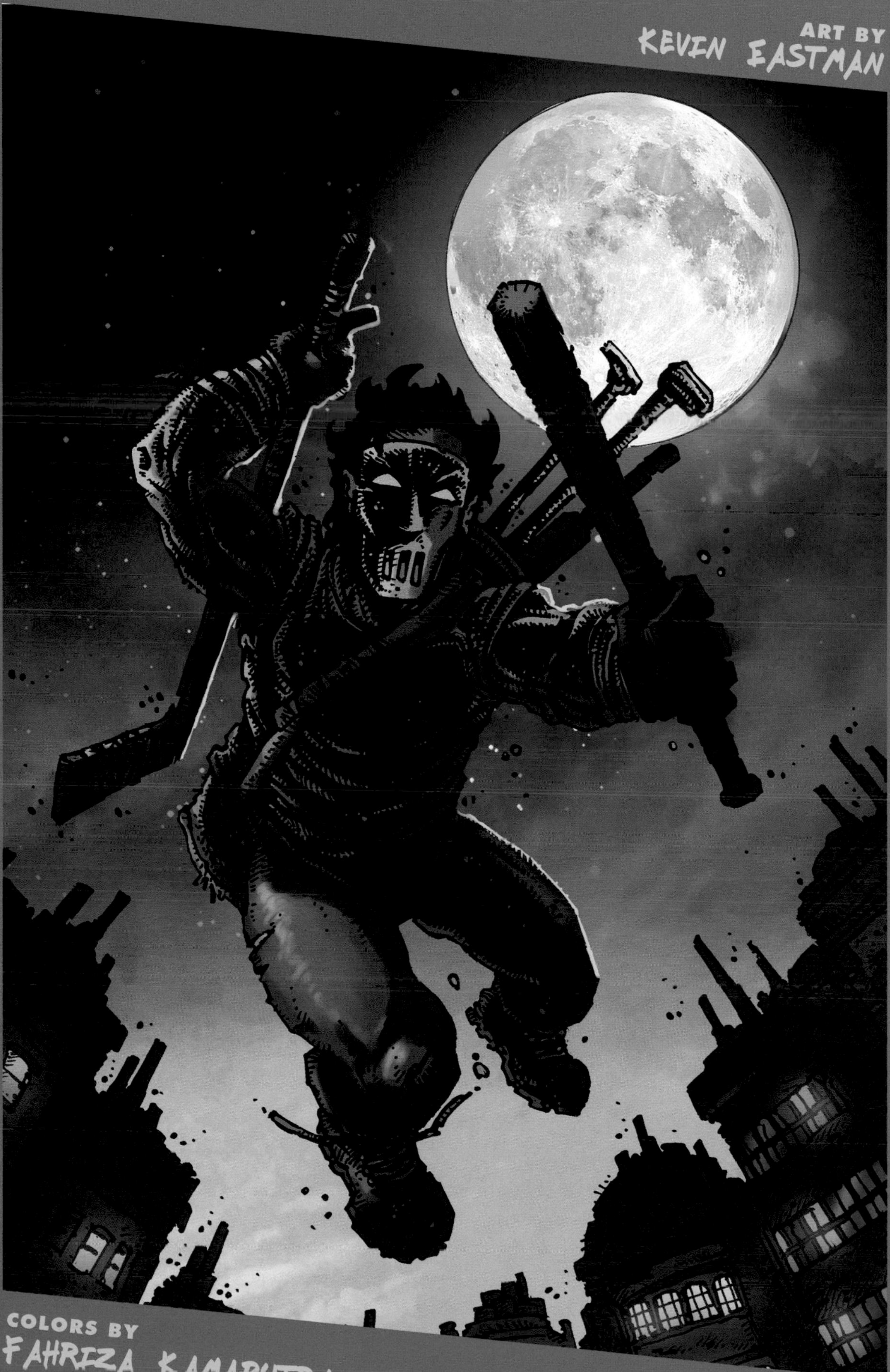

COLORS BY
FAHRIZA KAMAPUTRA

ART BY
KARL JOHNSSON

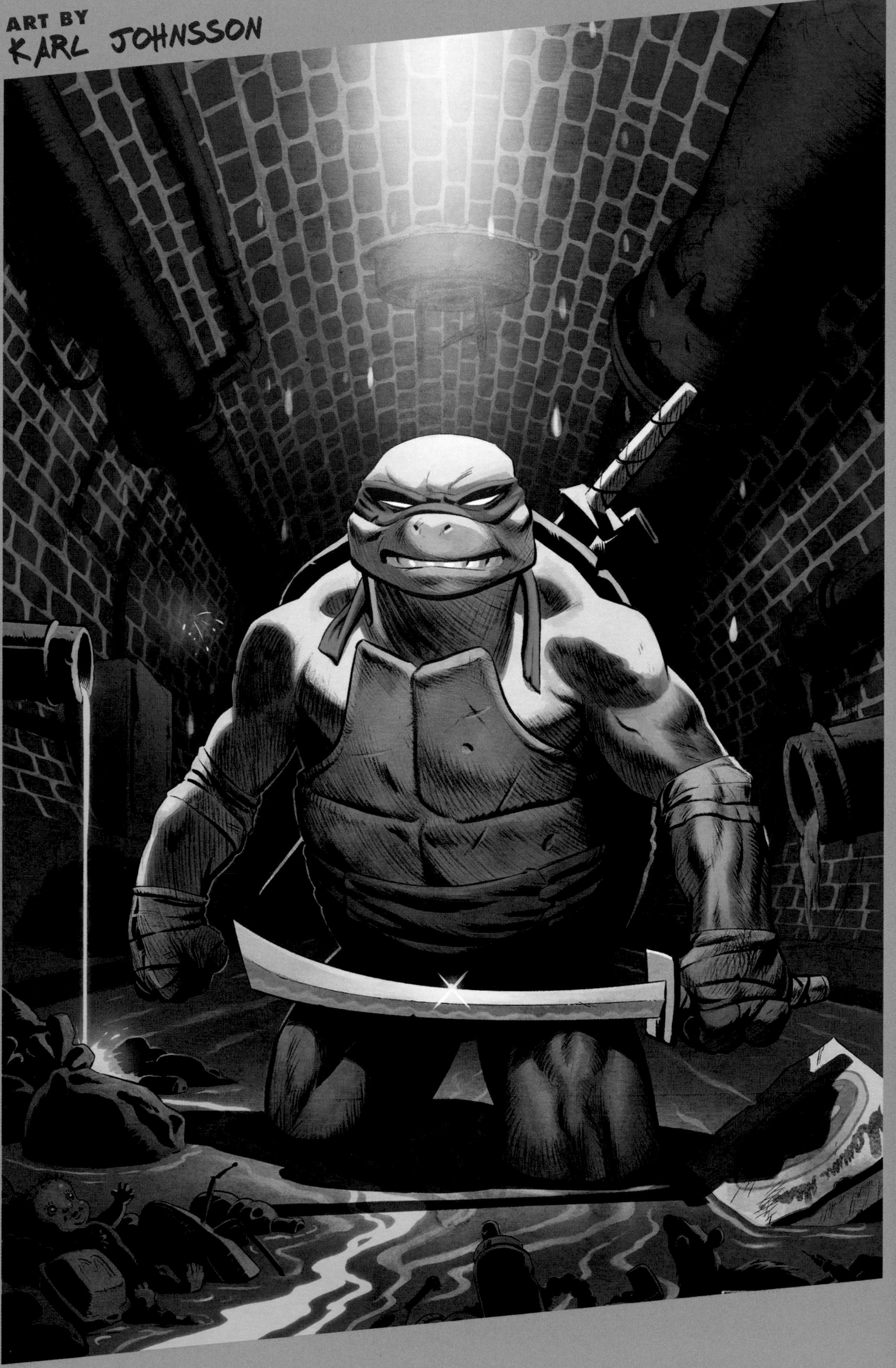

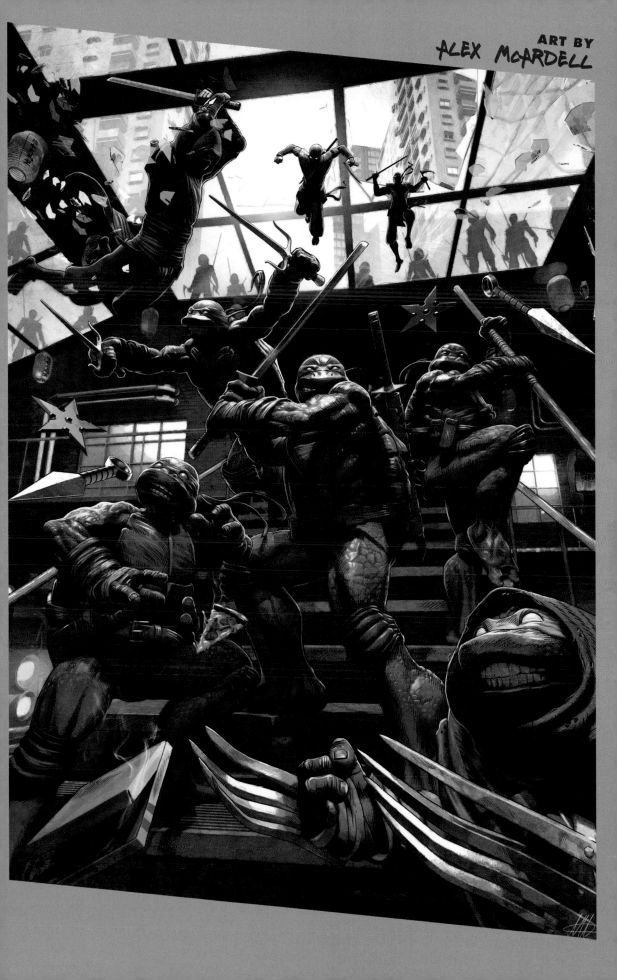

ART BY
ALEX MCARDELL

ART BY
D.J. BRYANT

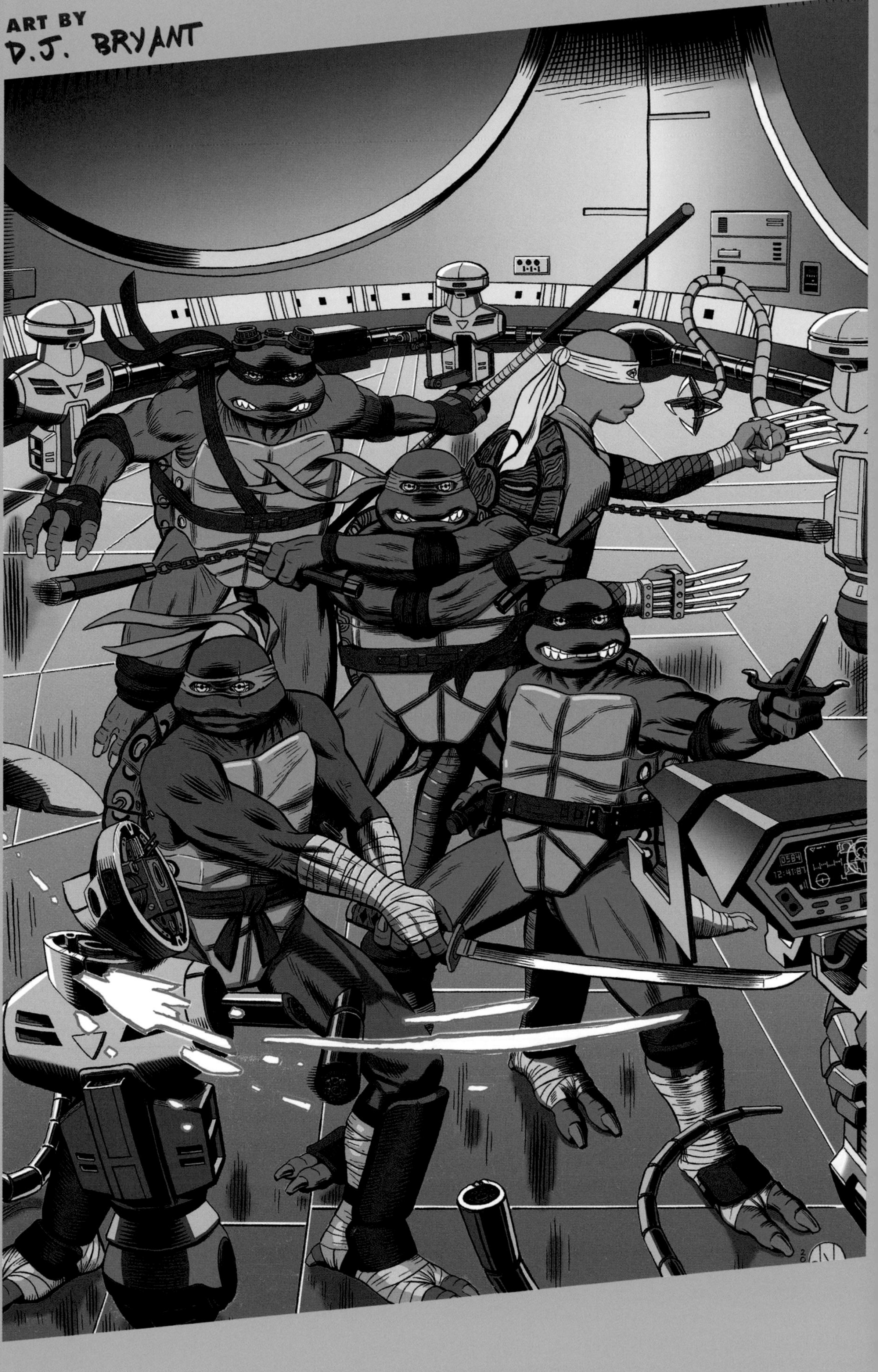

ART BY
PARIS ALLEYNE

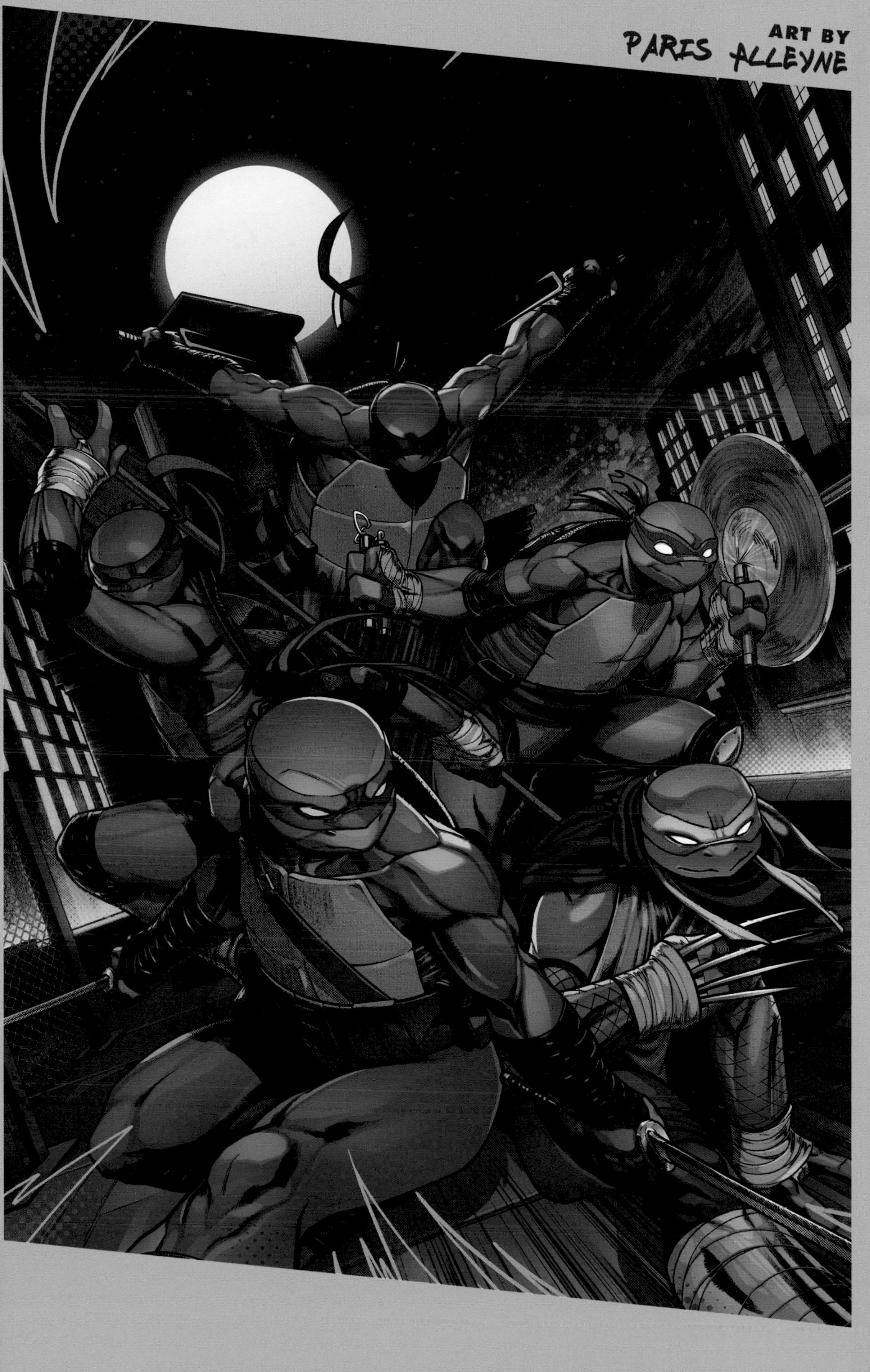

ART BY
SARA PITRE-DUROCHER

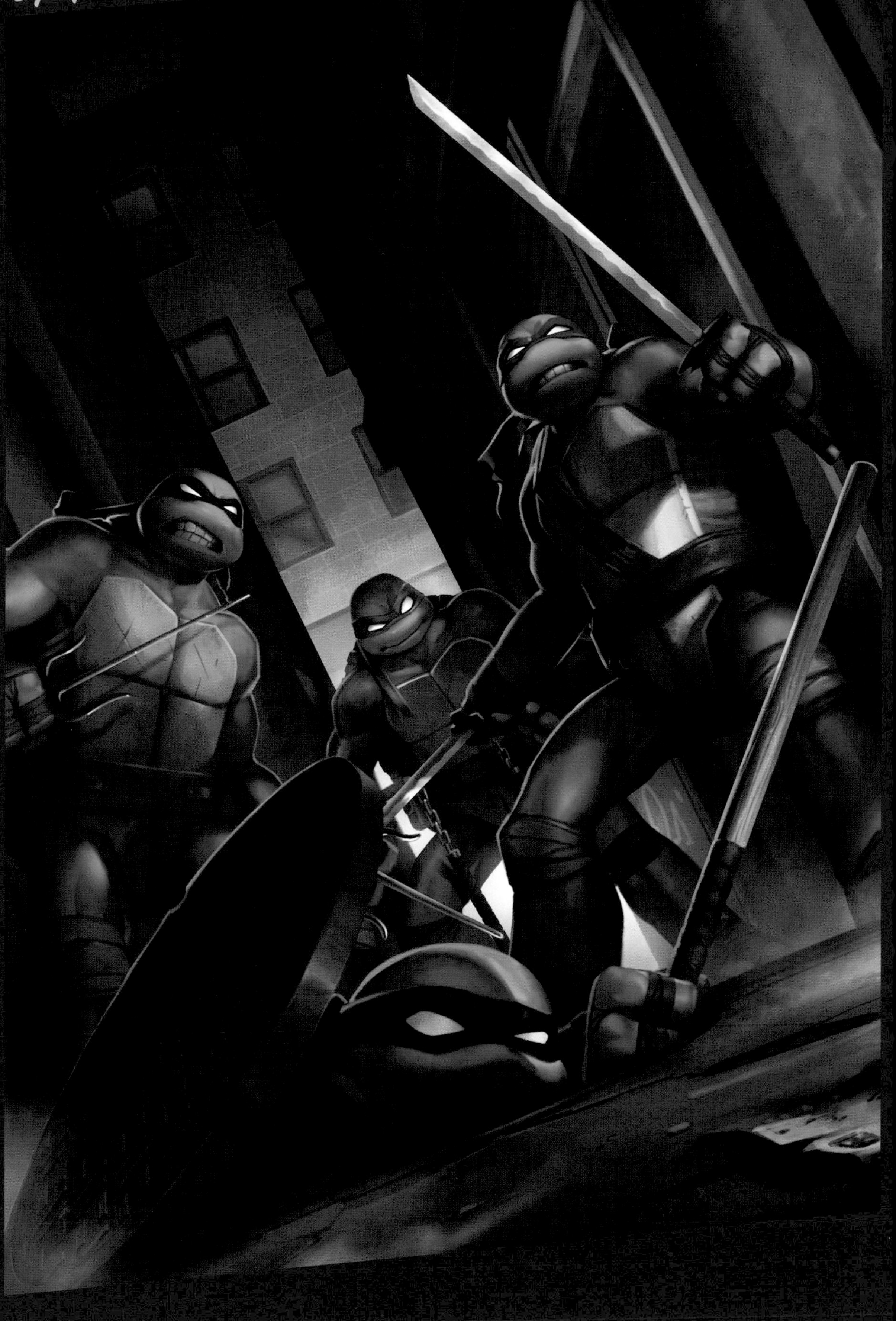

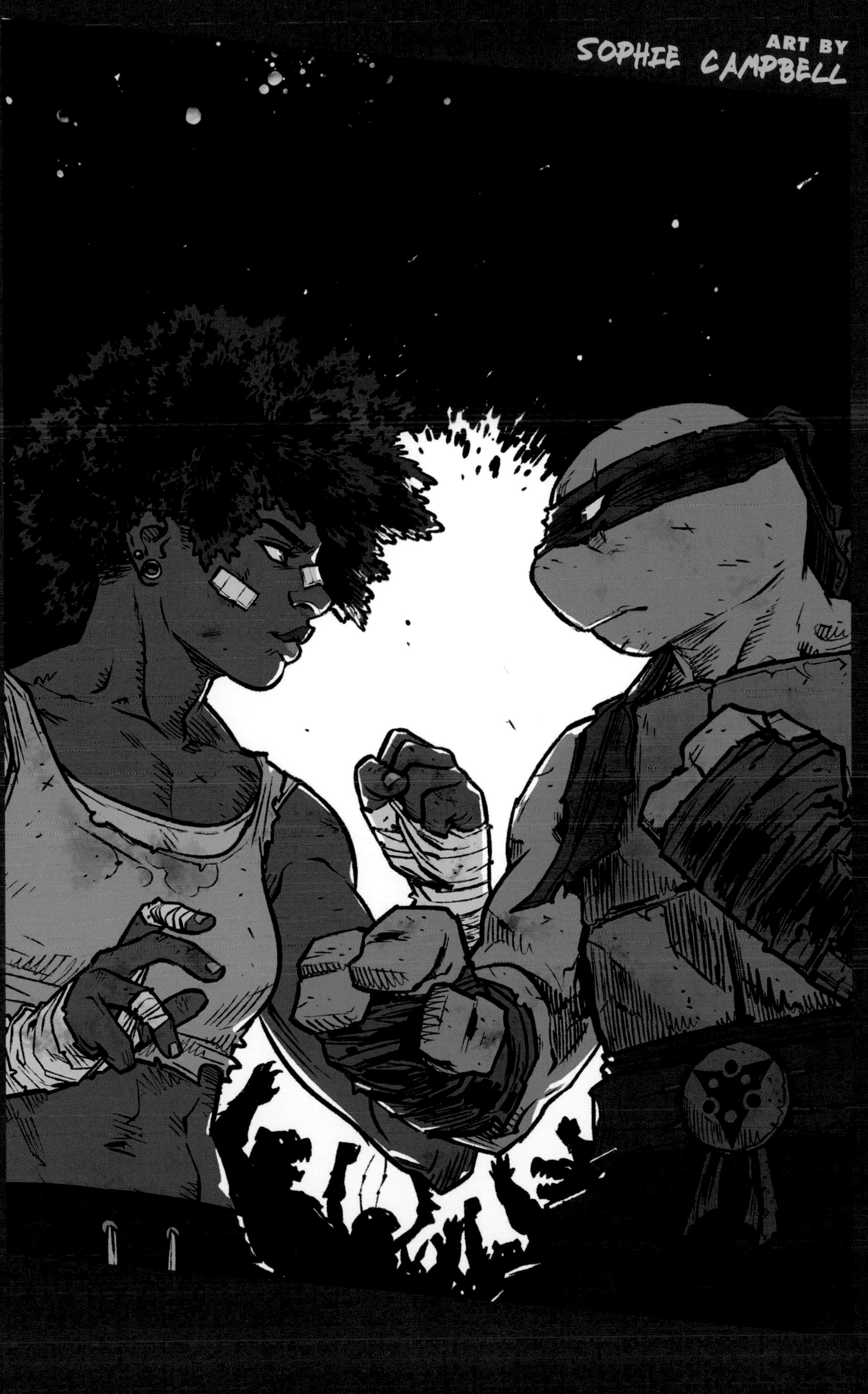
ART BY
SOPHIE CAMPBELL

INKS BY
ART BY
FRANCINE DELGADO MOSTAFA MOUSSA

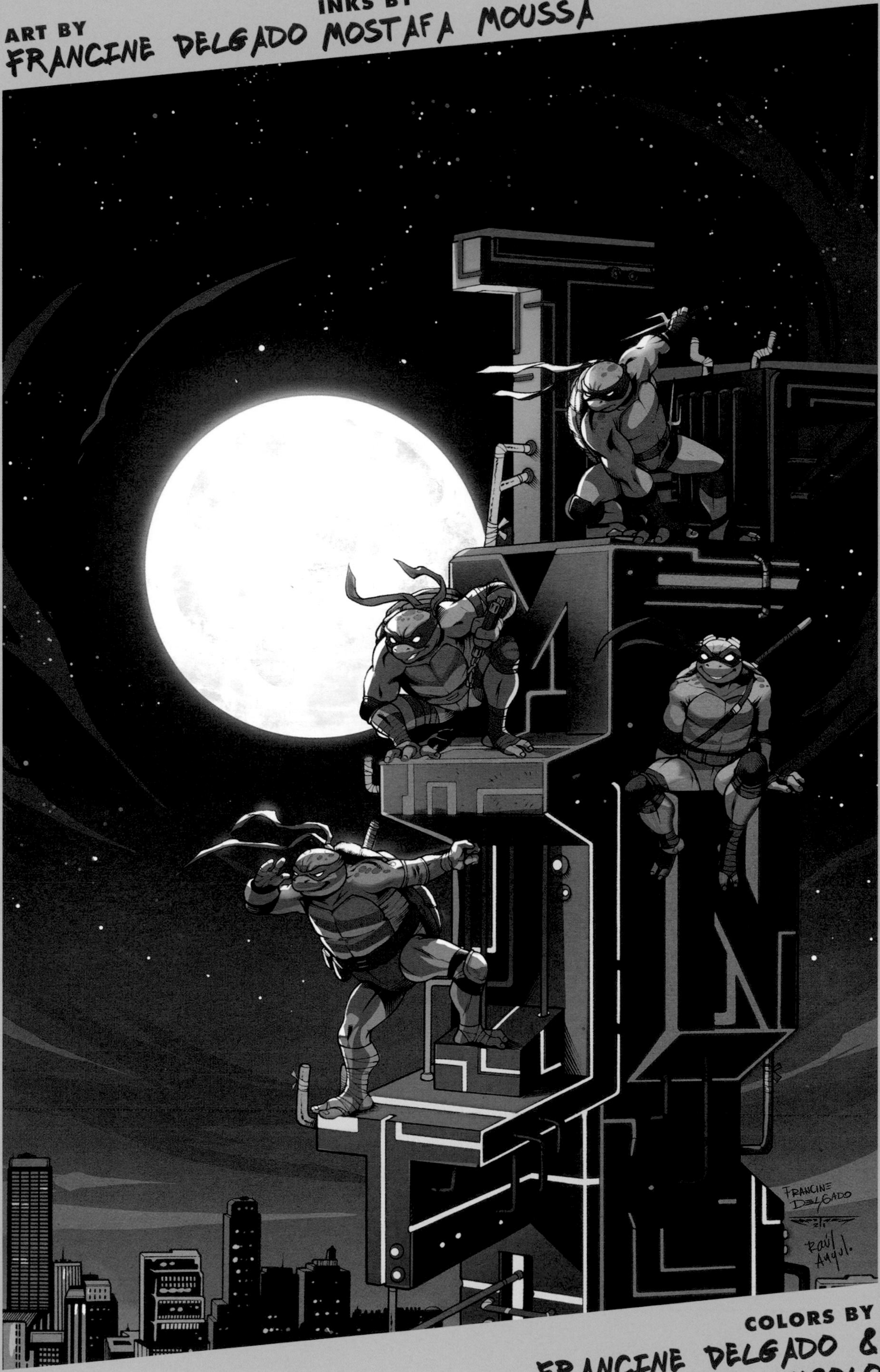
FRANCINE DELGADO

COLORS BY
FRANCINE DELGADO &
RAUL ANGOLO

ART BY
RAYMOND GAY

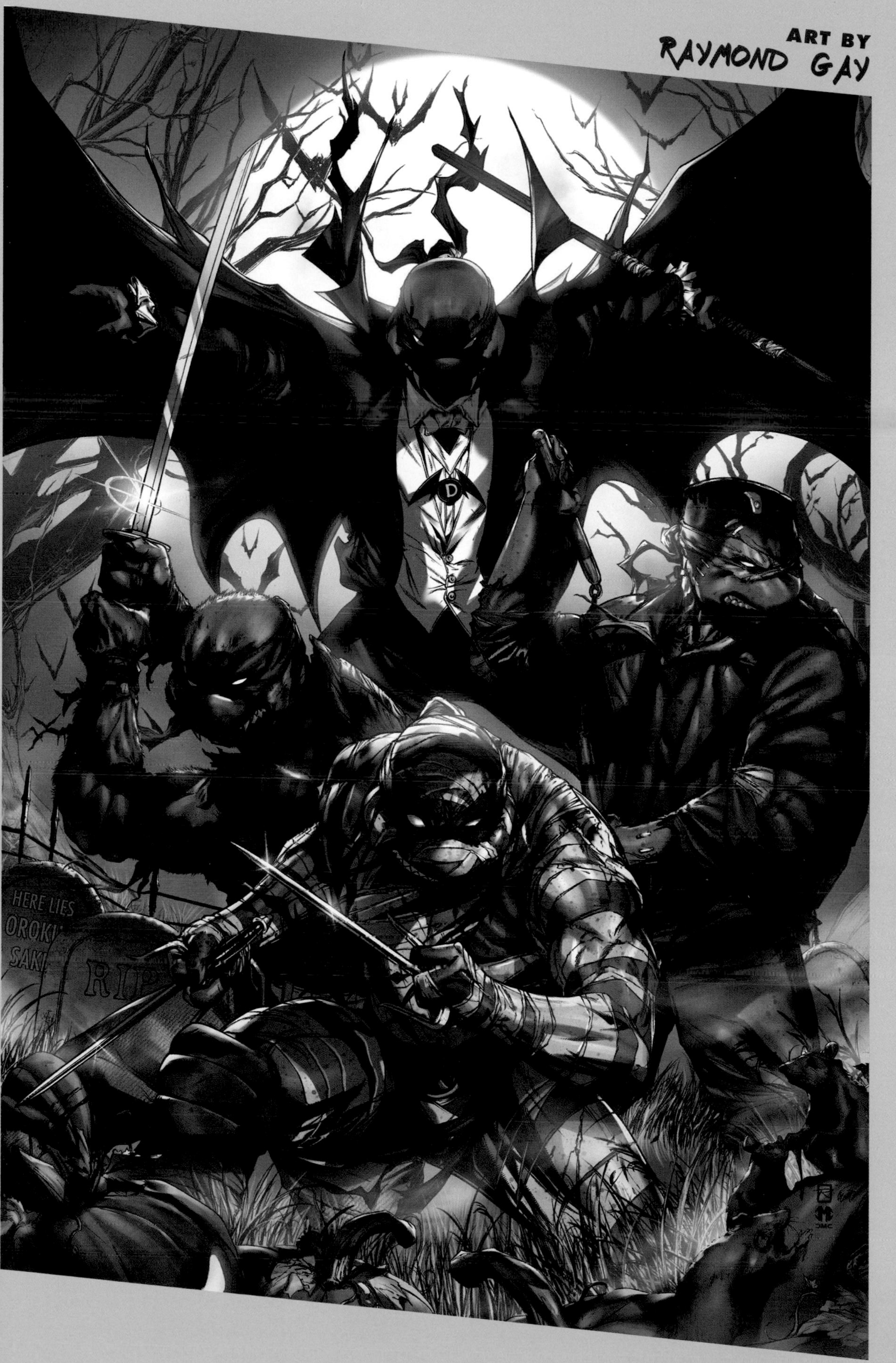
HERE LIES
OROKU
SAKI
RIP

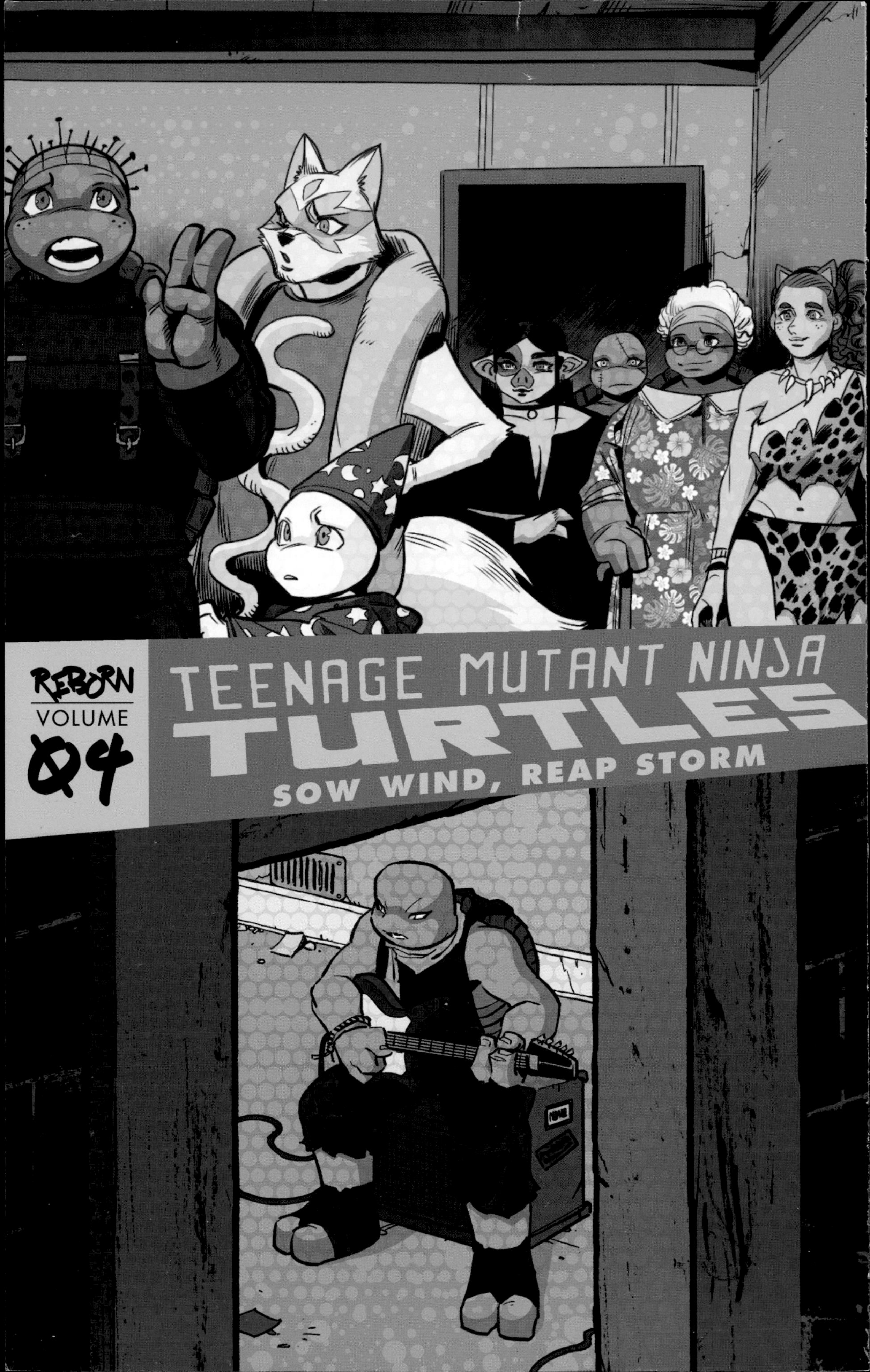
REBORN
VOLUME
04
TEENAGE MUTANT NINJA
TURTLES
SOW WIND, REAP STORM